ADDITIONAL PRAISE FOR
MARKET MAGIC

"Louise Yamada is one of the brightest economic minds around. Her synthesis of common sense with the arcana of the chart room makes this a must-read for anyone who hopes to be a successful investor in the future. You'll be able to do well and to understand how and why it happens!"

—Judy Haberkorn, President–Public &
Operator Services, Bell Atlantic

"Yet another outstanding achievement by Yamada. *Market Magic* is groundbreaking . . . and a must-read."

—Peter S. Watson, Senior Advisor and
Director of International Business and
Economics, Center for Strategic &
International Studies

Market Magic

Market Magic

Riding the Greatest
Bull Market of the Century

To Bill and Kay Odell

Best Wishes!

Louise Yamada

Louise Yamada

John Wiley & Sons, Inc.

New York • Chichester • Weinheim • Brisbane • Singapore • Toronto

A portion of the author's technical studies contained herein have been previously published in licensed reports by the former Smith Barney, now Salomon Smith Barney, and have been available as such to clients of Smith Barney.

It is with the permission of Salomon Smith Barney that these (and a few of Alan Shaw's thoughts in licensed reports) are presented in their present form herein. This book is not intended as an offer or solicitation by Salomon Smith Barney with respect to the purchase or sale of any security.

Author's Note: This book is intended as a thought-provoking exploration of the investment horizon resulting from the author's observation in the hope that readers will continue the question-asking process. There can be no guarantees issued as to future performance in any of the areas discussed; nor is this an offer or solicitation with respect to the purchase or sale of any security. Before making any investment decision, the advice of a qualified investment professional should be obtained to determine suitability of investment choice based on each investor's individual needs, as well as an evaluation of factors not readily apparent to the nonprofessional, which could have a material effect on the quality of any investment.

Supercharts is a registered trademark of Omega Research, Inc.

Library of Congress Cataloging-in-Publication Data:
Yamada, Louise.
    Market magic : riding the greatest bull market of the century / by
Louise Yamada.
        p.   cm.
    Includes index.
    ISBN 0-471-19759-9 (cloth : alk. paper)
    1. Wall Street—History—20th century.   2. Stock exchanges—United
States—History—20th century.   3. Stock exchanges—History—20th
century.   4. Economic history—1945–   I. Title.
HG4572.Y35   1998
332.64′ 273—dc21   97-45104

Printed in the United States of America

10 9 8 7 6 5 4 3

To Kate,
Kathryn Welling,
without whose interest and belief in my research
this book would never have become a reality.

In memory of the two exceptional and inspirational women in my life
who with unflappable affection, humor, dignity, and grace,
strove for intellectual excellence and integrity, aesthetic elegance, and peace;
who will live always in the hearts and aspirations of those who loved them:

Inez D'Amanda Barnell
and Maria D'Antona Melano

Preface

As I completed this preface on the hot, sweltering afternoon of July 16, 1997, only a few steaming blocks away, at the New York Stock Exchange, the Dow Jones Industrial Average just closed above 8000 for the first time ever. This historic day has special meaning for me. In early 1994, with the market seemingly stalled at 3600, many were questioning whether the bull market that commenced in 1982 had any life left. I, on the other hand, due to specific chart configurations at the time, felt strongly that the bull was just beginning to roar; that we were, in fact, experiencing the greatest bull market of our lifetime and the third great bull market of the twentieth century with the potential to extend into the twenty-first century. In September of that year, I became one of the first analysts on Wall Street to officially articulate this and to project the continuing upward drive when (the then) Smith Barney published my special report "Bull Market Extension? There Is Historic Precedent"—predicting that the Dow could achieve 7680 or higher. I supported this prediction with historical records as precedents for continued extension of the bull market and eight months later expounded my projection in a feature interview in *Barron's*. The evidence had been there all along for all to see, but had been almost entirely overlooked.

For 17 years, it has been my pleasure and privilege to work as a technical analyst at the right hand of Alan R. Shaw, chief technical analyst of Salomon Smith Barney and a universally-acknowledged master of his craft. Our chartroom, or "war room" as Alan calls it, is a technological treasure-trove of charts, both electronic and handcrafted, complete with sliding walls replete with floor to ceiling charts that are updated daily by hand. It was from these thousands of charts and myriad statistics that I uncovered the evidence going back to the early 1900s that demonstrated there was abundant precedent for today's equity market to continue to climb. This evidence had been ignored not only because there is so much statistical information that we were literally missing the forest for the trees, but also because many were interpreting expectations for today's stock market based on its behavior in fundamentally unrelated prior market environments. Realizing that we might never see a bull market like this again, I brought my observations to light using the tools of technical analysis and statistical history and even threw open the doors of the chartroom to seek reasons outside, in a quest to understand this great bull. This book will take you on that voyage of discovery with me, seeking and revealing answers to the often confusing and frustrating cross-currents presented by the daily noise of trading and statistics. Long-taken-for-granted intermarket relationships come into question and may need to be revisited; and we will look beyond the daily market chatter to find the larger macrotrends that will shape this market in the future, and create our opportunities for investment.

What will we find? That this bull market is unlike any other. Today's U.S. stock market is a very different two-tier global versus domestic investment arena with propulsive world demographics greatly favoring the global marketers. Today's market is flourishing in a unique era of stable/low inflation, falling interest rates, and a steady business expansion, perhaps fostered by favorable synchronicity with the Long-Wave Economic Cycle and its revolutionary technology. Like money, technology changes everything. Technology itself changes rapidly and remakes the economic landscape from heavy industrial to information-based. The role of the natural resources of the old industrial age will be greatly altered, as water, for instance, rises to rival oil and gold in importance in the new global frontier. The only constant will be change, and the only way to keep abreast of that change is to take nothing for granted and to continually ask relevant, probing questions. We begin that question-asking process in this book. You, the reader, must continue that process after this book's covers are closed. In that way, we will be best equipped to face the challenges and reap the potential investment rewards of the future.

The Structure of This Book

Market Magic is organized to track my 1993 to 1997 question-asking process about the U.S. stock market. It chronicles the insights and ideas I developed as a technical analyst studying and interpreting today's extraordinary bull market, that led me to the conclusion that this is *the* great bull market of our lifetime and the third great bull market of the twentieth century. The evolution of thought is based upon my ongoing question-asking process which I will present throughout this book as the thoughts and realizations developed.

Part One (Chapters 1, 2, and 3) brings the past into the present: employing technical research of this century's prior bull markets, demonstrating that there is historic precedent for the continuation of the current major bull market, and that U.S. equities with a global orientation are the most likely to benefit. Part Two (Chapters 4 through 11) looks behind the charts to identify and explore the extra-market macroforces that will impact the market's future and the most promising areas for future investment. Part Three (Chapters 12 through 14) utilizes a series of probing questions to reassess long-held beliefs and suggests a better way of measuring and understanding current and future market movements. In particular, a new application of physics principles to measure and quantify economic productivity is set forth as a further aid to market analysis. Part Four (Chapter 15) ties up Parts One, Two, and Three, as the basis for identifying and describing future market behavior.

Chapter 1 of Part One states my 1994 premise that there was historic precedent for an extension of the current bull market to achieve and even exceed 7680 in the Dow Jones Industrial Average (DJIA), finding support in low interest rates, changes in the Advance-Decline (A-D) line and in a review of past bull markets from the perspective of record statistics (including a study of 10 percent reversals). Chapter 2 sets forth my 1994 two-tier market thesis, showing how those U.S. equities that have global exposure have been outperforming the stocks of companies whose business focus is primarily domestic (including smaller capitalization stocks), and explaining why this outperformance should continue as the dominant, though not uninterrupted, trend. The identification of structurally underperforming sectors and the role of the dollar in the global marketplace also are explored. In Chapter 3, a review of recent market history allows for specific DJIA predictions for this ongoing bull market.

Chapter 4, which begins Part Two, introduces the topic of demographics, showing how macrochanges in U.S. and world demographics have subtly altered the business and investment landscapes. Chapter 5 shows how those demographic shifts are impacting the stock market. The Kondratieff Long-Wave Economic Cycle is considered in Chapter 6, correlating each cycle with a previous bull market as far back as the 1880s and positing a new Long-Wave/bull market extension into the next century, driven by the technological revolution and the global consumer demographic profile.

A new era of technology is at the heart of what is driving, and will continue to drive, today's economy and bull market. Chapter 7 examines the split between old-tech underperforming industries and new-tech industries, while Chapter 8 shows how the new-tech sectors are experiencing superior relative strength. Technology is changing our economy and markets faster than we have been able to update our measuring tools, and Chapter 9 demonstrates why the ground-shift in the Capital/Consumer ratio understates these emergent realities.

Inflation is an essential consideration in any market valuation analysis but its measurement is becoming increasingly elusive and Chapter 10 discusses why technological advances—and the new raw materials of the new "electron" economy—have made the Commodity Research Bureau/Bridge futures price index (CRB) an inapplicable measure of domestic inflation.

Chapter 10 also points out the direction we should be looking toward as a more appropriate gauge of today's inflation, which is increasingly reflective of global growth; in particular, agriculture and a new pertinent commodity in short supply—water. Chapter 11 links the growing importance of agriculture and its technological advances with the current gravitation in the United States toward de-urbanization to suggest a rising rural growth trend.

Chapter 12, the beginning of Part Three, takes a fresh look at the economic landscape, posing a series of questions that may alter long-held views and lead to a better understanding of today's new economic environment. These questions lead to the examination in Chapters 13 and 14 of specific areas of economic activity impacted by the macroforces identified in Chapters 4 through 8. The unique difficulties of measuring productivity in the largely weightless electron economy of knowledge are outlined in Chapter 13 and new solutions are proposed. Discussed in Chapter 14 is the impact of the new low inflation and low interest rate economic environment, described in Chapter 1, on select aspects of the financial markets.

In Chapter 15, Part Four, the various strands of the previous chapters are woven together to form a likely scenario for the market's future and discuss how one might best track its course through technical analysis.

The investment journey ahead is accompanied by questions, just as my own search for answers in the price charts led to even more questions. By asking the right questions, we can best seek answers for the future. The financial markets and the macroforces that impact them will continue to evolve and change at an accelerating pace. The technical analysis journey recounted in this book can help us not only stay abreast of, but also anticipate, changes yet to come.

LOUISE YAMADA

New York, New York
December 1997

Acknowledgments

I owe a debt of education to Alan R. Shaw, managing director and chief market technician of Salomon Smith Barney, who has been my mentor in technical analysis for my entire equity career. Through his examination and understanding of the markets from an historic perspective, the endless studies and analyses done together over 17 years, I learned how to capture, interpret, compare, and apply the structural, as well as interim shorter term trends in market behavior along with their traditional intermarket functional relationships.

Without a full understanding of history and how markets function in the norm, it is impossible to identify when, how, and to what degree they may function as an exception to the norm, given changing environmental factors. It is with the help of those skills that I was fortunate enough, in 1993–1994, to identify prevailing market trends of the 1980s–1990s and thereafter to project the macrotrends affecting such change that may carry us into and through the twenty-first century. On Wall Street, the saying goes that one is only as good as his or her last call. The next call incumbent on us will be to identify the winding down of this extraordinary secular bull cycle. I can only humbly hope that I may be alert enough and wise enough to identify the warning sings, so as to share them. I thank readers and colleagues for their following and support.

Special thanks must be extended to my son, Yoshi, for his reading of material that is essentially in a foreign language for the uninitiated, giving me feedback, the benefit of his extraordinary English language skills, and further, encouraging me to have enough confidence to follow my own advice. Additionally, I express to him my heartfelt appreciation for enduring the many very difficult, stringent years of our lives and doing so with the gift of understanding, generosity, love, loyalty, support, good humor, and a supreme spirit to survive.

Further appreciation I extend to my friend John for his daily encouragement, loyalty, support, invaluable clarity of thought, and many hours of listening and advising and in bringing his exceptional skills to give professional editing and structuring to this book; to my cousins, Skippy and Frank, for a lifetime of undying support and belief in me through unimaginable mountains and valleys; and to dearest Mark, who has to know that nothing in 30 years of my life would be in order without him.

Thanks, too, to the talents of Lori, Noreen, Sonja, and Rhonda for their support and efforts throughout the original research and writing projects; to Alexa for her intellectual enthusiasm and diligence in helping me quantify the concepts and specific applications of physical science for my productivity hypothesis; to Jon, Frank, and Willy for their technical skills, and to Richard and Julie for introducing my work to John Wiley & Sons, Inc.

Appreciation must also be extended to family and friends who graciously allowed me to go into hibernation until this manuscript was complete.

L. Y.

Contents

Chapter 14 Stock Market Implications and Expectations

206

PART FOUR CONCLUSION

Chapter 15 What Lies Ahead: Other Emerging Forces at Work

227

Notes

241

Index

247

Part One

THE EVOLUTION
OF DISCOVERY

*Technical Underpinnings of
the Greatest Bull Market
of the Twentieth Century*

Chapter

1

U.S. Bull Market Extension? There Is Historic Precedent

In 1994, I identified today's stock market (1982–present) as the great bull market of our lifetime and the third great bull market of this century, basing my conclusion on technical analysis of historical charts and comparisons of the structural similarities and differences in underlying stock market trends. To explore this bull market of the 1980s and 1990s (and beyond), we'll first take a quick look over our shoulders to see how bull markets of the past have behaved from a technical perspective and discover what characteristics they displayed that suggested a continuation of the upward trend. Later, we will tie together these and other trends and the myriad questions they raise, to fashion a new way of looking at the market through technical analysis, with continuing attention to the relevant evolving macroforces.

Let's return to an event that was the genesis of my "evolution of discovery" in grappling with the challenges we all face in attempting to understand and interpret the financial markets and their flow.

Setting the Stage

In 1985, in the early days of my association with Alan R. Shaw, chief technical analyst for the then Smith Barney, he made one of the most profound calls in recent market history, showing once again why he is a legendary technician on Wall Street. That spring, Alan noticed something emerging from the murk of financial statistics that would make a major impact on investment decisions: After years of high and rising interest rates and inflation, a structural bull market might be underway for the bond market.

It was an exciting time in our chartroom, with all the tables piled high with charts and pages of analysis. The technical evidence was compelling. Alan's observations included:

- A major top and a definable break of uptrend in commodity prices (which historically have moved inversely to the bond market as a measure of the presence or absence of inflation in the economy);
- A developing bear market in gold accompanied by a consequent unwinding of inflation psychology;
- A significant break in the uptrend of the Consumer Price Index (CPI) 12-month rate of change, another measure of inflationary pressures; and
- For the first time in 39 years, the yield on the long-term government bond (plotted inversely in Figure 1–1) failed to move to a higher yield, and in fact, established its first structural indication of a shift of trend by reversing at a lower yield in 1984 (Figure 1–1, Points A & B).

Alan published a report titled "Our Technical Bull Case for Bonds" in which he noted interest rates had doubled from 7 percent to 14 percent in the preceding 4 years, suggesting this stretched rubber band could snap back in the next 12 to 18 months to where it started. I remember urging Alan not to delay in putting his report out; it was issued one week before interest rates embarked on their extraordinary swing back to 8 percent. To back up his prediction that the long-term trend for U.S. interest rates in this country could continue to be down for years to come, Alan made a "gentlemen's bet" that we would never see double digit interest rates again in our careers—with the caveat that we might have short careers.

Background of Low Interest Rates

As interest rates continued to drift downward in the years following 1985, I began to wonder whether this environment of declining rates and the emergence of what could be defined as a trend of falling inflation might play out

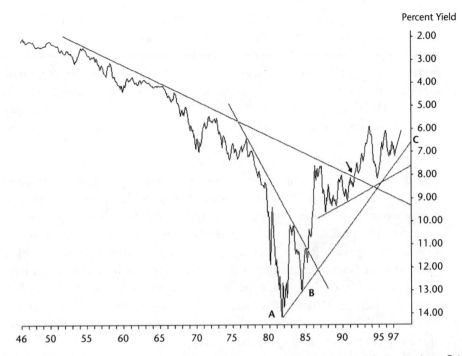

Figure 1-1 Long-Term Government Bond Yield. Chart created with Supercharts® by Omega Research, Inc.

differently than it had in the period from 1966–1981, which was characterized by both rising interest rates and inflation. Perhaps those structural shifts could lead to a different behavioral response in the equity market. (By structural I mean a longer term, or secular, trend that defines the underlying framework of the market, as opposed to shorter term or cyclical trends that take place within the longer term trend.) If so, it might be necessary to adjust our interpretations, expectations, and accustomed responses to seemingly similar market trends which in reality may turn out differently because of a changing underlying structural environment.

Eight years into the bond market trend toward lower interest rates, some intermarket relationships became extremely frustrating to me, particularly the analysis of the 80-plus Standard & Poor's 500 (S&P 500) industry sectors. Their price behavior and relative strength (RS)—their strength or weakness compared to the S&P 500 index performance—progressions were not consistently in line with what our technical expectations might have been, based on the historic pattern of shifting equity market leadership cycles (i.e., from a Capital Goods dominance to a Consumer Goods dominance and vice versa). It also seemed that we were in the throes of the most powerful bull market of our professional lifetime. I began to wonder if this long-term, or secular shift in interest rates might not have some bearing on the decade's extraordinary equity market behavior since 1982. We could not expect the equity market performance in a structural environment of falling to low interest rates and falling to low inflation (1982–present) to respond in the same way as it had in the 1966–1981 period of rising interest rates and rising inflation from which it had emerged. By late 1993, however, I saw that many market watchers were, in fact, trying to interpret this amazing bull market in terms of their expectations based on the 1966–1981 period—a completely different underlying market environment. Accordingly, they concluded the advance had to end soon.

By September 1994, I put forth the results of a year-long thought process that began my "evolution of discovery" based on a rigorous, ongoing question-asking process. First, I reasoned that we could not make statistical comparisons based on an expectation of similar equity market behavior between the two periods; this would be tantamount to comparing apples to oranges. Observations led to question after question, the answers to which revealed some fascinating statistics. My results were published by Smith Barney in September 1994 in a special two-part report titled "Bull Market Extension? There Is Historic Precedent." In these chapters we'll look at the findings of this report and its published evolutionary updates in the context of subsequent market developments.

If one accepts Alan Shaw's thesis that we are in a primary trend of declining interest rates (the technical proof of which was conclusively indicated by the eventual 1991 breakout through the 35-year trend of rising rates, see the arrow on Figure 1–1), then any developing interest rate rise in this new environment would represent a contratrend phenomenon. (A contratrend move is a *temporary* move in the opposite direction from the primary or dominant trend.) Rising rates as a primary trend had been so ingrained in many of our lives that, even in the face of technical evidence of multiyear breakouts to new price highs for bonds, extraordinary targets for bond prices (lower yields), and an absence of inordinate inflation, few seemed comfortable with the concept of an interest rate rise as being only temporary in today's environment. Based on historical data, we can see that the overall duration of interest rate cycles over the 200-year history of the United States (Figure 1–2) has indeed been generous, with cycles of 22 to 37 years marking the six completed trends to date. Note, too, that extended periods of time can be spent in a flat or neutral pattern—a trading range environment within each cycle. We are currently in the seventh shift of long-term rates, and given that we are "only" about 16 years (as of 1997) into this cycle, the historical evidence suggests that we may still see long-term rates work lower or remain stable well into the next millennium.

The long-term government bond yield (Figure 1–1, trendline C) defines the now-established declining interest rate trend. Prior to that date, what we can now call the contratrend rallies in rates were accompanied by equity market declines in 1983–1984, 1987, and 1990. Although the bond

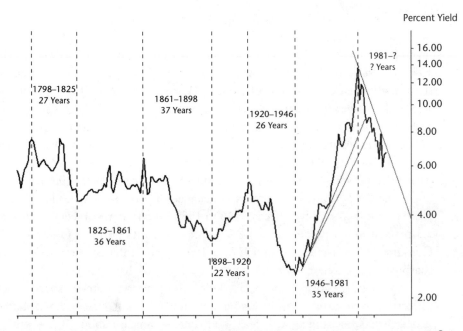

Percent Yield

1981–?
? Years

16.00
14.00
12.00

1798–1825
27 Years

1861–1898
37 Years

10.00

1920–1946
26 Years

8.00

6.00

4.00

1825–1861
36 Years

1898–1920
22 Years

1946–1981
35 Years

2.00

Figure 1–2 200 Years of U.S. Interest Rates. Chart created with Supercharts® by Omega Research, Inc.

market psychology was still skeptical, bonds completed an extraordinary, un-interrupted 2-year advance. The 1994 increases in the Fed funds rate effected a consolidation period for bonds as the market digested those gains. (An ex-tended 5- to 6-year trading range consolidation was not unexpected, given the 6-year consolidation that took place prior to the 1991 breakout.)

We don't really have a comparable period of falling rates or a compara-ble equity background in modern history to study the effect of falling inter-est rates on equity market performance. The last cycle was 1920–1946, which included a period of "unregulated" equity markets that in part may have re-sulted in a severe market decline, followed by deflation, a depression, and World War II—leaving sparse equity market data to study relative to today. It was, however, a period that included the first of three great bull markets in this century. As a result, I have turned instead to a low interest-rate period, 1942–1966, in which the second great bull market of the century took place.

Advance-Decline Line

Using our 70-year chart of the history of the Dow Jones Industrial Average (DJIA) and the New York Stock Exchange cumulative Advance-Decline line (A-D)—a running total of the advancing minus declining issues for each day by which technical analysts measure market strength or potential weakness—

we can see in Figure 1–3 that during the first half (1942–1956) of that great bull market, the cumulative A-D line experienced a 14-year bull cycle of its own (Point 1 on Figure 1–3), having just broken out from a 10-year base in 1945. In 1985, the A-D broke out from another 10-year base, and the indicator has advanced enough to profile only the *second* secular bull trend in progress in the 70-year history of the study (Point 2 on Figure 1–3). This suggests a strong structural similarity of the present cycle to that of the last great bull market of this century. Notice the past completed cycle for the A-D: a 10-year base (1932–1942); a 14-year rise (1942–1956); a 10-year top (1956–1966); a 9-year drop (1966–1975), and then another 10-year base (1975–1985).

The 1942–1966 bull market was made up of two complete leadership cycles: a Capital Goods cycle from 1946 to 1957, when interest rates were low at 2.5 percent to 3.5 percent and the A-D line was in its bull leg; followed by a Consumer Goods cycle from 1957 to 1964, when interest rates rose more sharply to 5.5 percent (on their way to much higher levels) and the A-D line was in a topping process—probably the result of interest rate-sensitive issues reflecting those progressively higher long-term rates. Interest rate-sensitive issues (banks, insurance, utilities, bond funds) comprise about 40 percent of the NYSE listed stocks and historically have been responsible for the cyclical early warning signals of the more serious stock market declines given by this

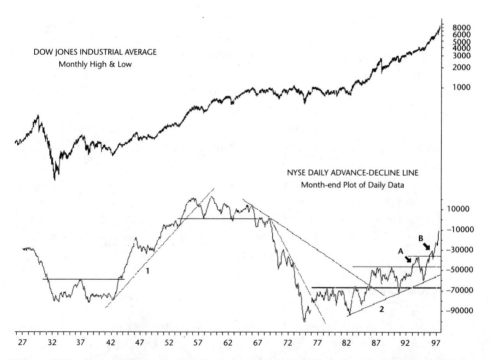

Figure 1–3 Dow Jones Industrial Average and the NYSE Daily Advance-Decline Line. Chart created with Supercharts® by Omega Research, Inc.

cumulative A-D line (in the form of divergences, or nonconfirmations of the equity market's new high levels). As rates rise, these interest rate-sensitive issues respond early and decline. The breadth data then begin to deteriorate, even as the equity market may scale to new highs, to give what is called a negative divergence in the A-D line. A negative divergence is the occurrence of a new high in a primary instrument (in this case the DJIA), accompanied by the failure of a counterpart (in this case the A-D line) to also achieve a new high.

Some interesting record-setting statistics accompanied that 1942–1966 bull market in stocks which are worth exploring and are integral to understanding today's market strength.

Record Bull Market Advances without 10 Percent Reversals

When looking at statistics for record market advances unaccompanied by as much as a 10 percent reversal, I made an interesting discovery (Figure 1–4). (A 10 percent filter study of the DJIA screens out all moves in the index of less than 10 percent.) I noticed that all of the top 10 records (excluding moves prior to 1940) occurred in the 1942–1966 bull market and in the 1982–current bull market—a strong similarity:

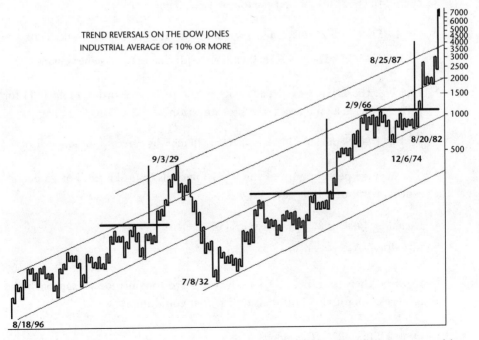

Figure 1–4 Trend Reversals on the Dow Jones Industrial Average of 10 Percent or More. Chart created with Supercharts® by Omega Research, Inc.

Table 1–1
Bull Market Advances without 10 Percent Reversal

Date & Dow Level at Trend Start		Date & Dow Level at Trend End		Percent Gain	Approx. Trend Duration	
08/12/82	776.92	11/29/83	1287.20	65.7	13.5	months
12/04/87	1766.74	7/17/90	2999.75	70.0	31	months
02/13/08	58.62	11/19/09	100.53	71.5	21	months
11/09/03	42.15	12/6/04	73.23	73.7	13	months
06/26/62	535.76	5/14/65	939.62	75.4	35.5	months
05/20/24	88.33	2/11/26	162.31	83.8	20.25	months
07/26/34	85.51	4/6/36	161.99	89.4	20.5	months
09/14/53	255.49	9/23/55	487.45	90.8	24.25	months
07/08/32	41.22	9/4/32	79.93	93.9	2	months
03/31/33	55.40	7/18/33	108.67	96.2	3.5	months
Average of 10 Prior Record Advances				81.1	18.4	months
(EX-1984–87)						
7/24/84	1086.57	8/25/87	2722.46	150.6	37	months
Current Leg						
10/11/90	2365.10	3/20/95	4083.68	73.0	53	months
		8/6/97	8259.31	249.2	82	months

- Based on the 10% filter study which extends back to 1896, 2 of the top 10 record advances for a percent gain without as much as a 10% reversal occurred in that bull market period of 1942–1966.

  9/14/53–9/23/55: +90.8% in 25¼ months (during the Capital Goods leg).

  6/26/62–5/14/65: +75.4% in 35½ months (during the Consumer Goods leg).

- In 1994, the DJIA was already within the top 11 records (Table 1–1) for percent advance (and at a record for duration).

  10/11/90–September 1994: +68.2% in 40 months (a record for longevity).

- The average percent gain of the top 10 periods (out of a total of 75 occurrences) without a 10% reversal was:

  Excluding 1984–1987 (which was up 150%) = +81%

  Including 1984–1987 (top 11 periods) = +87%.

I suggested then that if the DJIA advance were to continue to approach the record averages for this bull market leg, that could imply:

- Dow 4200 = +82% (rounded)
- Dow 4500 = +90% (rounded).

As we know now, both of these levels were not only achieved but also exceeded by a considerable margin.

With the August 6, 1997 DJIA high of 8259.31, the October 11, 1990–present record for longevity expanded to 7 years for a gain of 249.2 percent placing this advance first in the table of records and surpassing the average gain of 87 percent for the top 11 periods (including 1984–1987). The October 1997 decline has set in place a reversal in excess of 10 percent which closes the chapter on this advance.

Record Bull Market Advances Add Fuel

Further evidence fueling the premise that we may be in *the* exceptional bull market of our lifetime becomes apparent if we now look at record bull market advances (Table 1–2) without as much as a 20 percent or more correction (defined as a bear market decline). For purposes of uniformity, technically we define a decline off the high of up to 10 percent as a consolidation; a decline of 10 percent to 20 percent as a correction and a decline of 20 percent or more as a bear market.

- 1946–1956 was up 222%!
- There was no bear market in the entire 10-year period, nor was there a traditional 4-year cycle decline (using a 20% decline as the criterion).
- It was the fourth-largest bull run in history (1921–1929 was the largest, with a 496% advance).

Table 1–2
Bull Market Advances without 20 Percent Reversal

From Date	Level	To Date	Points Level	Percent Gain	Shift Advance	Months of Leader	Advance
08/24/21	63.90	09/03/29	381.17	317.27	496.51%		96
07/08/32	41.22	03/10/37	194.40	153.18	371.62%	L	56
08/12/82	776.92	08/25/87	2722.42	1945.50	250.41%	L	60
10/09/46	161.60	04/06/56	521.05	359.45	222.43%		58
11/09/03	42.15	01/19/06	103.00	60.85	144.37%		36
04/28/42	92.92	05/29/46	212.50	119.58	128.69%		38
12/24/14	53.17	11/21/16	110.15	56.98	107.17%		23
11/15/07	53.00	11/19/09	100.53	47.53	89.68%		24
06/26/62	535.76	02/09/66	995.15	459.39	85.75%		45
12/19/17	65.96	11/03/19	119.62	53.67	81.38%		23

L = Shift of leadership.

Of the top 10 record bull markets, if we again look only at those after 1940:

- All advances occurred in the 1942–1966 period, or in the 1982 to present market trend.

- 1982–1987 was the third-largest of all the records, up 250 percent, again with no 4-year cycle.

At the time, projecting a gain of 225 percent (or roughly equal to the 1946–1956 gain) off the October 1990 low of 2365 pointed to the possibility of:

- Dow 7680 (which was more than surpassed by June 1997).

If I had had the courage at the time to publish a calculated 496 percent advance for the DJIA, it would have been equivalent to 14,095—which we will see is still an achievable possibility as time and further studies evolve.

Capital/Consumer Ratio

One analytical tool that helps identify market leadership cycles is the Capital/Consumer (C/C) ratio. Using S&P's Capital Goods and Consumer Goods indexes, it is possible, by dividing the Capital Goods number by the Consumer Goods number, to determine the dominant outperformance cycle (see Figure 1–5). (When the line is rising it defines a Capital Goods outperformance cycle; when it is falling, a Consumer Goods cycle.) These leadership cycles have, until 1981, lasted from 4 to 7 years on the inside to 8 to 10 years on the outside. The change of stock market focus from one of these leadership cycles to another (a shift of leadership, defined as a shift of relative outperformance between the S&P Capital Goods sectors and the S&P Consumer Goods sectors as the dominant market force in play at a given time) has been accompanied by market declines, either concurrently or within a period of up to 14 months after the statistical turn, or inflection point of the shift of leadership (which allows for the necessary portfolio adjustments).

In 1990, I was curious to see what effect a shift of stock market leadership, as defined by the C/C ratio, had on market behavior. The data showed that the shift of leadership market declines, with one fractional exception, produced setbacks of 20 percent or more (bear markets). However, during the last secular bull market, the leadership shifts of 1946 and 1957 carried the smallest declines of all defined shifts: 23.2 percent in 1946, and 19.4 percent in 1957 (Table 1–3). This period was also an environment of low interest rates and an underlying structurally rising Advance-Decline line.

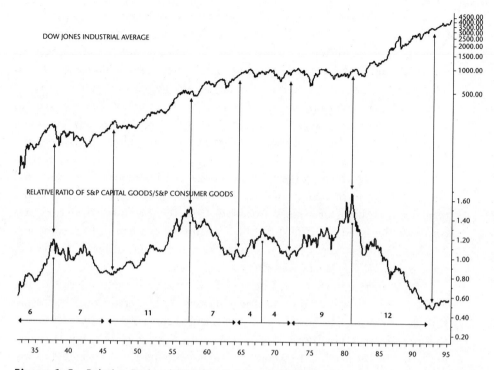

Figure 1-5   Relative Ratio of S&P Capital Goods/S&P Consumer Goods. Chart created with Supercharts® by Omega Research, Inc.

The first leadership leg of our extraordinary bull market experienced a Consumer Goods cycle running from 1981 to 1992—a record breaking 12-year cycle. It looks like this has been followed, in 1992, by a transition process, handing the baton to the fresh leadership of a Capital Goods cycle. It is interesting that while transitions from Capital to Consumer have been swift, sharp, and dramatic, transitions from Consumer to Capital, have been long,

Table 1-3
Shifts of Capital/Consumer Leadership

Dates of Market High	DJIA Level	Dates of Market Low	DJIA Level	Percent Reaction
03/10/37	194.40	3/31/38	98.45	−49.1
* 05/29/46	212.50	5/17/47	163.21	−23.2
04/06/56	521.05	10/22/57	419.79	−19.4
* 02/09/66	995.15	10/7/66	744.32	−25.2
12/03/68	985.21	5/26/70	631.16	−35.9
* 01/11/73	1051.70	12/6/74	577.60	−45.1
04/27/81	1024.05	8/12/62	776.92	−24.1

Note: All shift to consumer except those with an *, which are shift to capital.

laborious, multiyear affairs. (We will revisit this indicator in Chapter 9 and Chapter 15 in light of further observations and changing macroforces.)

In 1994, there was a difference in the relationship between the C/C ratio shift and a general market decline: The time elapsed from the C/C ratio 1992 inflection point to the expected accompanying market decline exceeded 14 months—the record time elapsed, at least as measured by the major indices like the DJIA (which only declined 9.6 percent during this period). However, the secondary market measurements, defined by individual stocks (specifically the more domestically-oriented sectors and the smaller capitalization tier), experienced bear markets with declines of 20 percent, 30 percent, and 40 percent, from their highs of early 1994, which places them *within* the historical time frame (for a market decline) from inflection to correction. Accordingly, I argued that the shift of leadership decline had in fact, come and gone, as if with a "stealth" bear market, in a somewhat different fashion in this instance. Time has proven this to be the case.

That difference may well be explained by the character of this equity market cycle (as will be discussed in Chapter 2). The traditional leadership shift decline proved to be behind us, represented this time not by inclusion of the more internationally-oriented DJIA and other globally-exposed issues, but rather by the declines in secondary and more domestically-oriented issues.

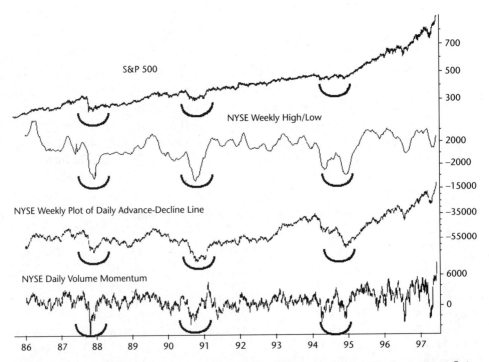

Figure 1–6 Bear Market Oversold Extremes. Chart created with Supercharts® by Omega Research, Inc.

By all technical measurements, 1994 did experience a bear market environment. Figure 1–6 shows the 1994 oversold extremes (very low readings) achieved in the technical indicators (of new highs versus new lows, breadth or A-D, and the up-down volume momentum relationship) which reflect extreme readings similar to those of prior equity bear market experiences of 1987 and 1990.

Discount Rate Study: "Three Steps and Stumble"

One of the most closely watched harbingers of market movement is Federal Reserve Board action, or inaction, on interest rates. Another interesting bull market observation came from my discount rate study years ago: "Looking at the 'Three Steps and Stumble' rule and the 'Real' Dow." The "Three Steps and Stumble" rule, originally formulated by the late Edson Gould, is frequently cited as a caution flag for market behavior. Concentrating on the discount rate part of the theory, the assumption is that if the Federal Reserve raises the discount rate three times consecutively the equity market will stumble. I looked at this assumption over time, and I found that the relationship is really dependent on the underlying trend of the equity market. For example, when the underlying market is strongly entrenched in a bull trend, three discount rate hikes have not always effected a bear market. In fact, as the discount rate history (Figure 1–7) and Table 1–4 show, it has often taken many more than three discount rate increases to reverse a strong bull market uptrend. If, on the other hand, the market is already in a technically vulnerable state, three consecutive discount rate rises have, in fact, acted as a negative catalyst within the already precarious equity market environment. One can note that following September 1994, there were two further discount rate hikes, a third in November 1994 and a fourth in February 1995, yet the major averages remain buoyant into 1997. Bear in mind the premise that we are in a long-term trend for declining interest rates and the 1994–1995 rise should represent yet another contratrend move; and that, there is an absence of domestic inflation from a technical perspective. Other considerations:

- From 1946 to 1953 the discount rate rose five times with no bear market following the sequence of rises.
- Between 1955 and 1956 the rate rose six times before a decline began (a seventh rise took place into the decline of 1957). At that point, the leadership shift from Capital to Consumer Goods was occurring. This could, in part, have contributed to the decline of 1956–1957 (for a drop of 19.4 percent—the smallest of leadership shift declines).

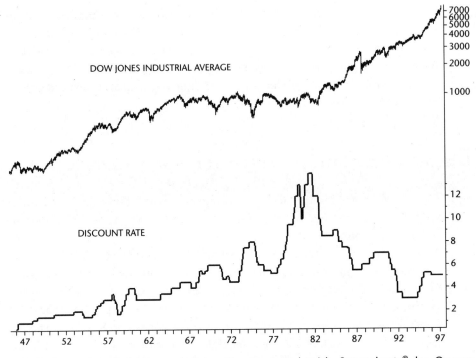

Figure 1–7 Historical Discount Rate. Chart created with Supercharts® by Omega Research, Inc.

Table 1–4
Market Response to Discount Rate Hikes

Dates	Number of Discount Rate Hikes	Market Response
1946–53	5	No Bear Market
1955–57	7	–19.4% Decline –Shift of Leadership
1958–59	5	No Bear Market
1963–66	3	–Bear Market –Shift of Leadership –End 1942–66 Secular Bull Market
1967–68	3	–Bear Market
1973–74	7	–Bear Market –Shift of Leadership
1977–80	14	No Bear Market
1980–81	4	–Bear Market –Shift of Leadership
Late 1987–89	3	No Bear Market
1994–95	4	No Bear Market in Major Indices

- Between 1958 and 1959 the discount rate rose five times before a 17.4 percent correction occurred in 1960. Rates then fell as the equity market moved higher, prior to the 1961–1962 bear market (which was not a result of rising rates).

- Between 1963 and 1966 the discount rate rose three times and *did* result in a bear market (also accompanied by a leadership shift, this time from Consumer to Capital Goods). The important point here is that this also marked the completion of the 1942–1966 secular bull trend.

Notice that all the above examples are encompassed by the extraordinary secular bull market period of 1942–1966 and, in spite of a number of discount rate increases, the equity market continued in its bull leg until the leadership shift of 1956–1957. That decline, as we have noted, was just shy of a defined bear market. Thereafter, equities extended further for a second major leg up (led by a Consumer Goods leadership cycle) that lasted until 1966. At that point, the third discount rate rise did impact the equity market, which by then was (not surprisingly) technically extended and tired. The A-D line was signaling structural negative divergences and, in the progression of its own secular trend, completing the 10-year topping process (1956–1966). It was also the point at which the low interest rate environment, which I believe helped fuel the 1942–1966 bull market, came to an end. Interest rates began to define a more visible uptrend (on the way to record high levels). At that point in 1966, a full-fledged bear market decline did indeed ensue, especially noticeable in "real" terms (the DJIA adjusted for inflation by the CPI) (Figure 1–8) and in the trend of the A-D line (Figure 1–3).

The citings between 1967 and 1974 in Table 1–4 do not correspond to the secular bull cycle of our discussion (nor to a similar underlying equity market structure in terms of low interest rates and inflation) so, not surprisingly, did result in bear markets (and also in leadership shifts). Additionally, from 1977–1980 there were 14 discount rate hikes. As can be seen on the chart (Figure 1–7), the market was in a neutral/sideways trend, but the thirteenth rate rise in early 1980 did precipitate a sharp 16 percent market decline, but not a defined bear market (20 percent or more). The discount rate fell into 1980, then rose once again in four steps, which undoubtedly helped to effect the 1981–1982 bear market and another leadership shift (from Capital to Consumer Goods) just prior to the takeoff of the next secular bull market.

Now, if we look at the next set of data that are encompassed by the secular bull market from 1982 to the present:

From late 1987 to mid-1989 there were three discount rate increases with no bear market resulting from this sequence of rises. The discount rate was flat for a year before the 1990 bear market,

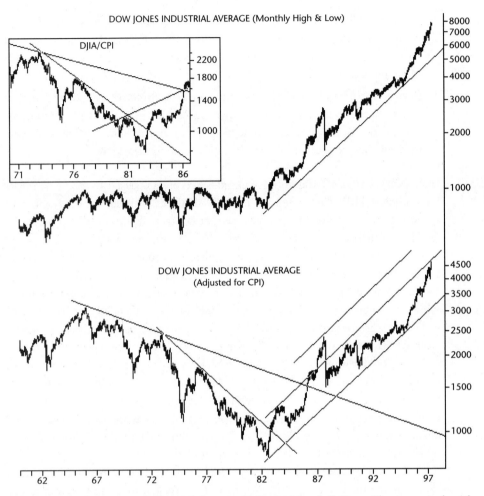

DOW JONES INDUSTRIAL AVERAGE (Monthly High & Low)

DJIA/CPI

DOW JONES INDUSTRIAL AVERAGE
(Adjusted for CPI)

Figure 1-8 Dow Jones Industrial Average Adjusted for Inflation. Chart created with Supercharts® by Omega Research, Inc.

which was short-lived and no doubt partially impacted by the brief Desert Shield/Storm Middle East conflict. Thereafter, interest rates declined sharply into 1991–1992.

Again, the forces of a secular bull market appear to have overridden some traditionally accepted cyclical patterns and theories. So, in addressing the 1994 discount rate rises, I asked: Is the market vulnerable now (or would it be vulnerable) to a third discount rate hike, or will the underlying bull trend remain strong enough to ignore further discount rate rises for the time being? Given the assumption that we remain in the bull market cycle, I suggested that perhaps the latter would prevail. With the benefit of hindsight it is clear that it did, in terms of the major equity indices.

By the spring of 1995, the 1994 "stealth" bear market, which excluded the major indices, was behind us. Interest rates, which had risen to just over 8 percent, had begun to fall again, in line with the contratrend thesis of a structural secular trend for lower rates. Just as 1987–1991 witnessed a trading range for interest rates, so might interest rates enter a stable trading range somewhere between approximately 6 percent to 7 percent (just as they fluctuated between 8 percent to 9 percent or so from 1985–1991 prior to breaking the 35-year trend of rising interest rates in 1991). The expected trading range has, as of October 1997, lasted 5-plus years (Figure 1–1). The 200-year history of interest rates also suggests a period of neutral rates within most cycles. The 8 percent level now represents support and is also the intersect point for both the 1981–1985 uptrend and for the 1987–1991 uptrend line. If one were to ask, "What would it take to change your mind about the long-term trend of interest rates?" the answer would be, "A violation of the 8 percent level." If interest rates exceeded 8 percent, breaking both uptrend lines and support, we would need to go back to the drawing board and rethink the interest rate picture.

When the DJIA broke through 4000, the 50-unit point-and-figure chart (Figure 1–9) of the DJIA confirmed the estimated targets of 4200 and 4500 I calculated earlier from the DJIA 10 percent reversal studies and the average gains in the top 10 and top 11 records. By April 1995, Dow 4250 was achieved and as of August 6, 1997 the Dow achieved 8259.31.

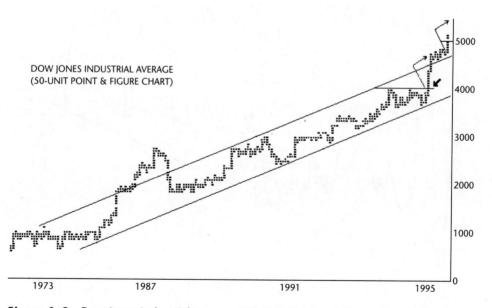

Figure 1–9   Dow Jones Industrial Average (50-Unit Point and Figure Chart). Chart created with Supercharts® by Omega Research, Inc.

Consumer Price Index and Inflation

Featured daily in the press are worries about rising inflation, whether it be creeping or soaring, and no doubt keeping some bullishness at bay. As far back as 1985, there was an emerging shift of trend not only in the Consumer Price Index (CPI), mentioned earlier, but also in the DJIA adjusted for inflation (DJIA/CPI—see Figure 1–8 insert). A technical pattern called an inverse head and shoulders formed from 1980–1985. (An inverse head and shoulders is a technical configuration that resembles a head and two shoulders upside down; it represents the potential for a powerful advance.) Within that context, the 1974–1982 downtrend had been breached, suggesting the long trend of inflation from the 1967 peak was slowing and might even be reversing. Looking at these longer term studies from a technical perspective,

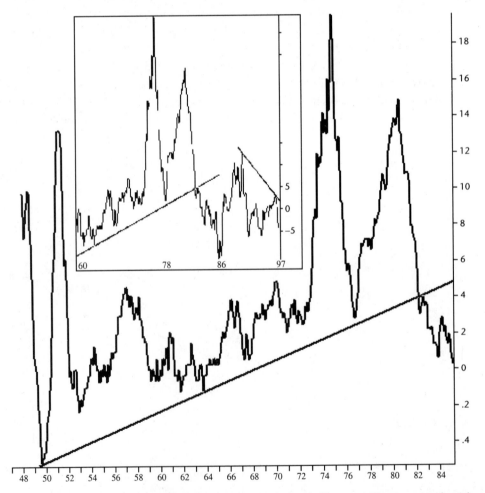

Figure 1–10 Producer Price Index, 12-Month Rate of Change. Chart created with Supercharts® by Omega Research, Inc.

inflation has not been—and does not yet appear to be—a major factor. In fact, the progression evident at that point in 1994 was on the verge of completing (or breaking out to the upside from) a year-long consolidation (a trading range between two levels). Looking at the Dow in real terms (or adjusted for the CPI, Figure 1–8), we can see that the second downtrend off the 1967 peak was broken in 1986 and the established long-term uptrend off the 1982 low is still intact.

Since 1982, inflation has not been an overriding negative factor within the framework of the current secular bull market trend, having remained relatively low (with the exception of a brief rise in 1987–1990). Not only has the DJIA/CPI advance reached the head-and-shoulder projection, or target (calculated at 2200) that developed in the early 1980s, but also has exceeded the 1967 peak to achieve a record level on an inflation-adjusted basis. Years after the 1982 reversal point, in fact, inflation remains tame, similar to the low/stable inflation environment in force during the post-war years of the 1952–1966 period in the last major bull market, and during the 1921–1929 first great bull market of the twentieth century.

Additionally, if one had viewed a chart of the Producer Price Index (PPI—an economic measure of inflationary trends) in 1985 (Figure 1–10) one would have been able to project another argument for the abatement of inflation: A 32-year uptrend had been broken. The technical interpretation

Figure 1–11 London Gold Price. Chart created with Supercharts® by Omega Research, Inc.

again points to a major structural shift in the forces of inflation. Gold, another harbinger of inflation, broke two uptrends by 1990 and continues weak (see Figure 1–11). There do not appear to be any inflationary pressures from gold to date. Further consideration will be given to gold, the CPI, and PPI in Chapter 13.

Summary

Our review of relevant market history has established the historical precedents for further extension of the 1982–present bull market. Technical corroboration is furnished by the similarities between today's bull market and its predecessor in 1942–1966, including: a shared background of low interest rates and low/stable inflation; an analogous Advance-Decline line trend pattern; the experience of numerous record market advances without any 10 percent reversals; as well as record bull market advances without bear market interruptions. Further support is found in a similar pattern of changes in the C/C ratio accompanied by smaller than expected declines. In addition, these two bull markets have shown comparable strength in weathering discount rate rises. The technical evidence suggests this bull market is poised to continue. Given the important foundation of stable/low inflation (new aspects of which will be discussed further in Chapter 10 and Chapter 15), what must be kept in mind is that the current bull market is occurring in a unique and rapidly changing environment; to fully understand it we must look toward the technically manifested behavior of the macroforces that will be shaping the market in the future. The next chapter examines the first of those forces: the remarkable division of the U.S. equity market into two separate tiers determined by the geographical focus of a company's business activities.

Chapter

The Two-Tier Market Thesis

A new development taking place within the 1982–present bull market has been the evolution of the market into a newly separated two-tier environment—a dominant tier of U.S. globally-exposed stocks (the new growth stocks) versus a lower tier of U.S. domestically-exposed stocks that face relative structural underperformance. This development is a major key to understanding the future of today's bull market. This chapter explains that the globally-exposed tier has outperformed the domestically-exposed stocks (including the small-cap tier), and why it should continue to do so, notwithstanding cyclical interruptions. Specific sectors that should continue to underperform over the long term are identified and the expectation of outperformance by the DJIA is fully explored. How the globally-exposed stocks will fare in the face of the rapidly changing world demographics is discussed in Chapter 4.

Global versus Domestic: Globally-Exposed U.S. Equities

Keeping in mind all the bullish measures from the preceding chapter and the parallels between the current bull market and that of 1942–1966 the question may be asked: What is going to take the market higher over time and for how long? The theory I postulated in 1994 was that:

> We may be entering a very different two-tier market structure, not heretofore experienced, composed of globally-exposed U.S. equities (the new growth stocks) versus domestically-exposed U.S. equities. In light of such a new market perspective, the dynamics of many long-held intermarket relationships may need to be revisited, and a different way of perceiving them may be required.

Let's go back a step to see how I came to this conclusion. The technical evidence summarized in Chapter 1 would indicate that we have been passing through the earlier stages of a Capital Goods cycle, with the turn of the C/C ratio out of the 12-year Consumer Goods cycle (1981–1992). But this time something was different.

In 1981, the chart patterns of the then emerging Consumer Goods leadership were impressive in that prices were breaking out through the individual stocks' entire price histories, as can be seen in the Beverages, Foods, and Household Products sectors (Figure 2–1, Points A). (Breaking out describes a stock moving through price (or RS) levels which had been resistant to advancement for a period of time; such a breakout implies continued appreciation.) Ultimately, their advances resulted in the longest leadership cycle (12 years) in our 69-year statistical history, as well as in the greatest distance traveled (i.e., up over 1,400 percent for the Foods group alone). The Capital Goods cycle of 1946–1957, then a record, has now become the second-longest cycle in both respects (refer to Figure 1–5). From the beginning of the current relative Capital Goods cycle (December 1992), many of the Capital

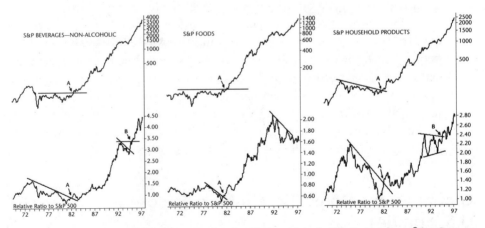

Figure 2–1   Selected S&P Consumer Goods. Chart created with Supercharts® by Omega Research, Inc. The price line is shown as the top line on all sector charts throughout the book.

Figure 2–2 Selected S&P Capital Goods Sectors. Chart created with Supercharts® by Omega Research, Inc.

Goods stocks (accompanied by a few Consumer cyclical and even fewer Financial issues) were similarly breaking out, or had broken out, through multiyear consolidations in sectors like Chemicals, Electrical Equipment, Machinery-Diversified, and Manufacturing-Diversified (Figure 2–2).

In a rotational fashion, many stocks in these groups already witnessed impressive price advances and had entered (or already completed) consolidation or corrective trends in 1994, presumably to re-emerge later in a continuing rotation. Others were just beginning to emerge, and were still in their initial advancing phase.

What has been different since 1992, however, is that simultaneously many Consumer Staples names also have been *extending* their gains in strong technical fashion. By 1995, even within the relative Capital/Consumer cycle identification, for more than a year there had been other frustrating crosscurrents within the Consumer Staples group analysis. Unlike certain periods in the past (when inflation was rising), and a group's strength could carry even the more speculative names into an advancing phase, this has not necessarily been the case over recent years. In some cases, it has been just the opposite, where only one or two names outperformed in the emerging groups. Similarly frustrating is that the emergence of the new Capital cycle has not led to the usual capitulation of all those prior leadership groups in the waning Consumer cycle. It became apparent that one or two groups did *not* conform to the apparent structural decline in the Consumer Goods areas. Instead, many (but not all) Consumer Goods areas reversed their negative relative strength bias and continued to rise (Figure 2–1, Points B).

In assessing this frustrating U.S. sector performance, the emerging unifying thread among these overachieving stocks seemed to be the degree to which the company was globally-exposed in its business. Examining the component charts, under the surface there appeared to be an even larger theme of market leadership transcending the traditional notion of pure Capital/Consumer or pure small capitalization/large capitalization dominance—and that was the emergence of a two-tier market theme that could be defined as one of *globally-exposed U.S. equities (the new growth) versus domestically-exposed U.S. equities.* Yet those former traditional measures of Capital/Consumer, large cap/small cap themes may co-exist as subtrends to the macroconcept of global versus domestic and now may need to be separately analyzed as a Capital/Consumer Goods subtrend to the global U.S. equity universe and similarly, as a Capital/Consumer subtrend to the domestic universe—rather than as the major trends of the broad market as we have done historically.

Domestically-Exposed U.S. Equities: Small Cap

Let's digress a moment to study the small-capitalization stock performance to understand some further technical evidence supporting the global/

domestic equity thesis. There continues to be extensive discourse over the impending outperformance of mid-cap and small-cap equity issues that "must," as conventional wisdom tells us, come to the fore because they "always have," generally in a burst of speculative excess. The technical perspective indicates a very different picture from these expectations of outperformance, at least at this point in time.

Historically, the Value Line Index has functioned as an unweighted proxy for smaller equities. In its short history (since the 1960s), the Value Line Index has experienced cycles of relative outperformance versus the capitalization-weighted S&P 500. Comparing the two indices provides a barometer of small versus big stock performance. (While some may argue this is not the best of measurements, nevertheless we have found many small stock managers can relate their own performance over time to the broad up and down sweeps the Value Line/S&P ratio has traced back to 1961.)

In 1992, the smaller cap issues were performing well. At the time it appeared as though a reversal in the long-term Value Line trend of outperformance of small versus large capitalization stocks might be at hand (Figure 2–3), reversing a multiyear trend based on the historical 5- to 8-year cycles of outperformance and underperformance. At the time, we set forth some conceptual technical arguments for such a scenario.

The 1992 Value Line relative performance trend appeared to be establishing a consolidation (Figure 2–3, arrow A), as in the previous cycles of 1964 and 1974. Because the long-term relative strength line had been turning up, having just experienced an 8-year cycle of underperformance, the time appeared "ripe" for the next cycle of outperformance to begin. The relative strength (RS) of the Value Line composite *could have been* on the verge of completing a 2-year double bottom. So, we informally used the Value Line chart as a back-door entry into the argument for the elusive shift of leadership from the 11-year-old Consumer cycle into a new Capital Goods cycle. One can see on Figure 2–4, for at least the last 30 years, the outperformance periods for the smaller stocks also have accompanied a Capital Goods reign (as measured by the C/C ratio, however small the sample); concomitantly, the underperformance years for Value Line paralleled the years of Consumer Goods dominance. (Recall that when the C/C ratio line is rising it represents a Capital Goods cycle; when falling, a Consumer Goods cycle.) This allowed us to construct a logical scenario for the long-overdue shift in leadership: If small stocks outperform in Capital Goods cycles, and small stocks now look poised to enter a sustainable better relative trend, then the next cycle of Capital Goods leadership should not be far off. At the time, this was the only evidence we had of the potential for small stocks to outperform. Underlying data for the new S&P 400 Mid Cap had not yet been devised (nor had the sector frustrations of 1993–1994 yet developed). By February 1993, the small cap evidence hadn't progressed much. The small-cap RS was still in nothing more than a trading range with no definitive overriding trend.

Figure 2–3 Value Line Relative to S&P 500. Chart created with Supercharts® by Omega Research, Inc.

Further complicating the small stock evidence, the NASDAQ, always considered a small stock index, was becoming less so because many of its major component names could qualify for inclusion in the NYSE based on their heavy capitalization weight. Over 10 percent of the NASDAQ's weight is in the first five names on the list, 21 percent in the first 25 (Tables 2–1 and 2–2). In 1996, the NASDAQ was up 15 percent; but taken apart, the bigger capitalization NASDAQ 100, however, was up 40 percent, while the balance of NASDAQ was barely up 3 percent. Care must be taken in lumping together the performance of the NASDAQ index as an expectation for "small" stocks, simply because it is capitalization-weighted, like the S&P 500. This barometer has also been making new highs due more to the strength of the heavier-weighted components than the influence of its small cap components.

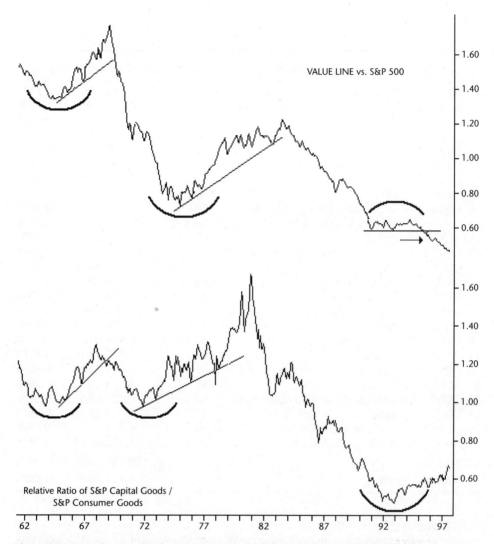

VALUE LINE vs. S&P 500

Relative Ratio of S&P Capital Goods /
S&P Consumer Goods

Figure 2–4   Value Line Relative Strength Compared to S&P Capital/Consumer Ratio.
Chart created with Supercharts® by Omega Research, Inc.

Since 1991, the NASDAQ has turned in an impressive performance as compared to the S&P 500 (Figure 2–5). Based on its old measure as a small stock index, which it no longer is, NASDAQ outperformance might be something to worry about as a sign of speculation. A quick scan back over the past 10 years shows there was no real negative correlation when the NASDAQ depicted an outperformance compared to the S&P. In fact, as Figure 2–5 reveals, strong NASDAQ performance periods were all followed by a stable, if not higher, S&P trend. On the other hand, an underperforming NASDAQ was a precursor for two of the more important market corrections in the 10-year period.[1] Based on these observations the trend should thus be considered in a different light, and even further as a participant in global exposure; (and

Table 2–1
NASDAQ Stocks with Highest Market Capitalization as of 7/23/96

	Symbol	Company Name	Close	Mkt. Cap. (in millions)	Weight
1	MAFT	Microsoft Corp	112⅛	67,078.668	5.75%
2	INTC	Intel Corp	69½	57,156.800	4.90%
3	CSCO	Cisco Sys Inc	47⅛	26,921.288	2.31%
4	ORCL	Oracle Corp	36	23,552.208	2.02%
5	ORNG Y	Orange PLC	14	16,704.842	1.43%
6	MCIC	MCI Communications Corp	22¹⁵⁄₁₆	15,838.344	1.36%
7	AMGN	Amgen Inc	53	14,089.414	1.21%
8	MITS Y	Mitsui & Co Ltd	176	13,667.104	1.17%
9	TCOM A	Tele Communications Inc New	14¼	9,302.486	0.80%
10	SUNW	Sun Microsystems Inc	48¾	8,973.315	0.77%
11	WCOM	Worldcom Inc Ga	21½	8,343.849	0.72%
12	BOAT	Boatmens Bancshares Inc	40	6,288.120	0.54%
13	COMS	3 Com Corp	35⅛	5,868.685	0.50%
14	USBC	U S Bancorp ORE	33¾	5,399.190	0.46%
15	USRX	U S Robotics Corp	63	5,356.134	0.46%
16	FITB	Fifth Third Bancorp	50⅞	5,204.156	0.45%
17	PMTC	Parametric Technology Corp	37⅞	4,796.603	0.41%
18	MFST	MFS Communications Inc	30½	4,776.910	0.41%
19	TLAB	Tellabs Inc	52¾	4,690.530	0.40%
20	ASND	Ascend Communications Inc	41¾	4,643.685	0.40%
21	HBOC	HBO & Co	57	4,604.004	0.39%
22	CSCC	Cascade Communications Corp	52	4,415.996	0.38%
23	SAFC	Safeco Corp	33½	4,222.105	0.36%
24	DELL	Dell Computer Corp	46⅞	4,202.203	0.36%
25	AMAT	Applied Matls Inc	22⅝	4,058.404	0.35%
	TOP 25			**330,155.043**	**28.31%**
	NASDAQ TOTAL			**1,166,101.589**	**100.00%**

its more recent underperformance may have forewarned of the 1997 corrective trend).

Additionally, by 1994, the Value Line RS progression began to look more ominous (Figure 2–3, Arrow B). As the RS consolidation evolved, instead of portraying the "saucer" pattern, or "smile," that is technically representative of accumulation (a base, or bottom) such as can be seen occurred (accompanying capital goods cycles, Figure 2–4), in the two prior consolidations of the mid-1960s and mid-1970s, this RS consolidation began to portray just the opposite—a "frown," or distribution pattern, that indicated a top. This presented a puzzle at the time. But the Value Line provided further evidence substantiating the two-tier global-domestic market thesis. This seemingly aberrant behavior of the smaller stocks may be explained in that the majority of smaller-cap stocks may not be privy to any, much less the extensive global exposure of the DJIA components, or of the larger names of the other

Table 2–2
NASDAQ Stocks with Highest Market Capitalization as of 7/25/97

	Symbol	Company Name	Close	Mkt. Cap. (in millions)	Weight
1	MSFT	Microsoft Corp.	138½	165,923.016	7.96%
2	INTC	Intel Corp	89 3/16	145,821.563	7.00%
3	CSCO	Cisco Sys Inc	79 11/16	52,722.523	2.53%
4	ORCL	Oracle Corp	54¾	35,731.164	1.72%
5	DELL	Dell Computer Corp	163	29,992.000	1.44%
6	WCOM	Worldcom Inc Ga	32 11/16	28,651.443	1.38%
7	PHII	Planet Hollywood Intl Inc	27	26,190.539	1.26%
8	MCIC	MCI Communications Corp	34 13/16	19,068.094	0.92%
9	SUNW	Sun Microsystems Inc	47⅛	17,383.092	0.83%
10	AMAT	Applied Matls Inc	90 3/16	16,331.784	0.78%
11	AMGN	Amgen Inc	59 15/16	15,865.456	0.76%
12	MITS Y	Mitsui & Co Ltd	187¾	14,811.598	0.71%
13	TLAB	Tellabs Inc	61⅛	11,543.456	0.55%
14	COMS	3 Com Corp	56⅝	10,052.693	0.48%
15	FITB	Fifth Third Bancorp	61¾	9,808.370	0.47%
16	USBC	U S Bancorp ORE	65⅜	9,623.200	0.46%
17	TCOM A	Tele Communications Inc	15 29/32	9,515.214	0.46%
18	WAMU	Washington Mut Inc	65 11/16	8,285.952	0.40%
19	HBOC	HBO & Co	77⅞	7,161.541	0.34%
20	CCSI	Costco Cos Inc	33 13/16	7,127.540	0.34%
21	OXHP	Oxford Health Plans Inc	85⅛	6,648.603	0.32%
22	PMTC	Parametric Technology Corp	50 13/16	6,478.035	0.31%
23	CMCS	Comcast Corp	22¾	6,444.665	0.31%
24	PSFT	Peoplesoft Inc	57⅝	6,265.681	0.30%
25	NTRS	Northern Tr Corp	53⅞	6,004.584	0.29%
	TOP 25			673,451.807	32.33%
	NASDAQ TOTAL			2,083,350.410	100.00%

major indices (including the big-cap NASDAQ names). These smaller-stock universes may, therefore, be at a disadvantage in the new global environment and may continue to underperform for the duration of this cycle.

This underperformance is not exclusive to the Value Line, which broke down dramatically into a trend of underperformance, achieving a 35-year low in 1995 (Figure 2–3, Arrow C). Also included are the longer-term charts of the S&P Mid-Cap 400, and the Russell 2000 performance versus the S&P 500 (Figure 2–6). In both cases, the RS structural profile is falling through multiyear support levels to reaction lows from peaks put in place in 1993 and 1994. (Even the "January effect," which traditionally boosts small stocks, can be seen in these charts to have failed again to build strength in 1996.) RS kickback rallies did occur in 1997, as global, big-cap stocks corrected, but there was no evidence of a structural reversal.

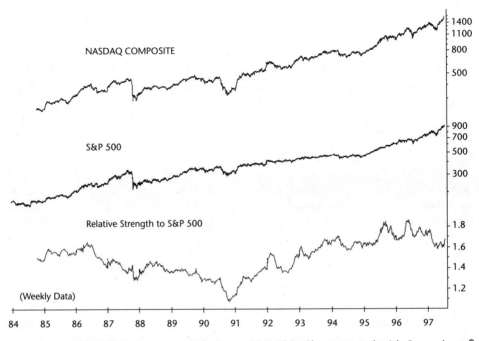

Figure 2–5 NASDAQ Composite Relative to S&P 500. Chart created with Supercharts® by Omega Research, Inc.

Some Mid-Cap 400 names do have global exposure. Their aggregate weight, however, may not be great enough to impact the index's total *relative* performance. Their global penetration also may not have the same success or influence as the larger-cap names in increasing their global market share. As of November 1996, only 5 percent of small manufacturers were involved in international trade. It's a task to establish competitive and profitable operations abroad, especially in Asia and Latin America with several time-consuming stages. The first step is to export. The second (if the product is a success) is to set up a regional office, and third, even establish an on-site inventory warehouse. In a fourth step, the company may choose to give an exclusive manufacturing license in a country.[2]

Offshore expansion is a long and tedious process; it may take time before the global competitive edge of the small- and mid-cap companies make an impact on their performance relative to the already-established, large globally-exposed U.S. companies. Even among those smaller companies that have penetrated global markets, some will naturally do better than others.

There should also be successful smaller U.S. suppliers to the globally-exposed, as well as small-niche domestic market winners, but so far their participation is not great enough to yield an outperformance cycle of their respective indices.

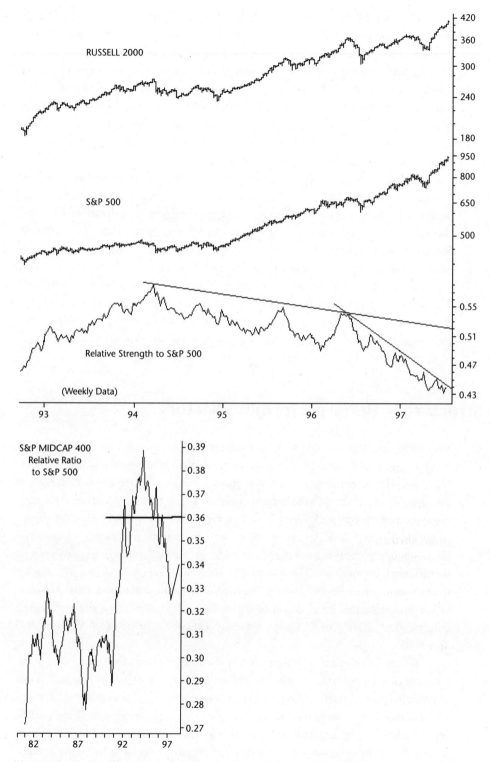

Figure 2–6 Smaller Capitalization Stocks Relative to S&P 500. Chart created with Supercharts® by Omega Research, Inc.

They say history repeats itself, but not exactly in the same way. We are still experiencing the third great bull market of this century. Perhaps the perception that speculative excess fostered by small stocks must come to the fore may be part of what could be different this time; that is, we may experience another "exception to the norm." Since smaller stocks abound in the subdominant tier of domestically-exposed U.S. equities, it may be that only the globally-exposed U.S. smaller stocks will come to the fore and eventually hyperextend, and they may not be recognized from a RS perspective because of their lesser number and influence within a small stock index; or perhaps the current absence of these excesses indicates that there is still further to go for this old bull before these traditional measures of excess appear; or they may appear much *later* due to the difficulties in the process of globalization. Further, the speculative excess may occur differently in this cycle when, for instance, foreign money—given the strengthening/steady dollar—comes into our market to a larger degree. Generally, more conservative foreign investors do not seek out smaller, or speculative stocks, but gravitate to the more liquid, safe havens of the larger-cap issues. Given the (apparent) underlying structure of this particular bull cycle, it may be worthwhile to consider the possibility that the long-held historical relationships of small versus big stocks may evolve differently affected by other underlying equity market forces.

Structurally Underperforming Sectors

Further consideration of the global/domestic thesis evolved in the patterns of many structurally underperforming sectors. In the throes of any bull market, there are always underperforming sectors. In this particular bull market, if one accepts my assumption that this may be a new two-tier market structure composed of globally-exposed U.S. equities (the new growth stocks) versus domestically-exposed U.S. equities, then it might be interesting to examine those groups portraying what appear to be structural relative breakdowns of significant proportions. We would define structural as new multiyear lows that in some cases have followed years of long-term underperforming downtrend progressions. One common thread these groups may share is being composed primarily of U.S. domestically-exposed equities (see Figures 2–7 and 2–8).

It may be relevant when looking at the underperforming groups to make a distinction between those showing absolute risk of a price decline and those in which price is still rising, but less rapidly than the market (therefore underperforming the market). In some cases, the price progressions (at the top of each chart) are stalling or failing, demonstrating potential risk of falling price. In other cases, the price progressions are still in rising trends. The group itself may be underperforming the S&P 500, but the prices of its

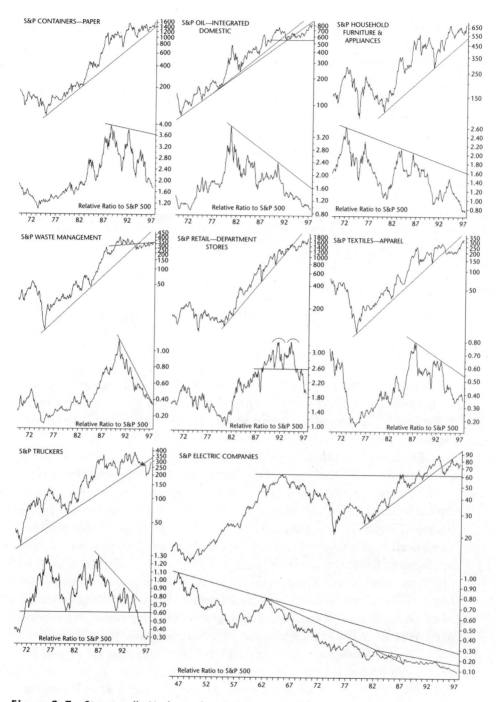

Figure 2–7   Structurally Underperforming Sectors. Chart created with Supercharts® by Omega Research, Inc.

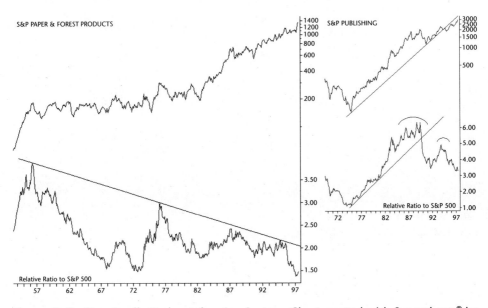

Figure 2–8 Structurally Underperforming Sectors. Chart created with Supercharts® by Omega Research, Inc.

components are still rising and are therefore still contributing to the expansion in breadth, evidenced by the uptrend of the cumulative A-D line, which is maintaining its second structural advance in 70 years to confirm this bull market advance.

For example, in the case of Utilities-Electric, it is clear that although price has maintained an uptrend, in line with a positive structural performance for interest rates throughout this decade, the RS line has been declining for 50 years. The Waste Management group's decline is suffering a 7-year RS low. The RS underperformance of Publishing and Paper & Forest Products has also achieved new historical lows, which we will discuss later in light of new technology.

The situations of Retailers and Textiles, and the precarious trends for Home Building and related areas, speak for themselves as probable reflectors of the domestic tier of consumer U.S. equities. These may continue to underperform structurally as the global tier of U.S. equities maintains its stature.

The Oil-Domestic group has a particularly dramatic picture—a 25-year low in RS has recently been recorded. So far the price progressions are stable (and may even rise), but the more than decade-long lows in RS suggest energy prices may remain flat at best, or at least may not be on the verge of inciting an inflationary trend.

Just as one cannot expect largely globally-exposed U.S. equities to respond in the same way to domestic economic fundamentals, the largely domestically-exposed U.S. equities will, in fact, be buffeted by those fundamental factors at home. The reasons may only become clear over time. Changing demographics and newer technologies may imply slower growth in some areas (as we will explore in subsequent chapters). The reasons may be only speculation. The charts of these domestically-exposed areas, however, tell us that technically they are in structural relative strength decline and, contratrend rallies in relative strength notwithstanding, these pictures suggest these areas are *not* sharing the great upside potential generated by the current major bull cycle. The evolution and impact of even more macroforces affecting these underperforming sectors will be developed in Part Two.

Here is an interesting final point that relates to the structurally bullish technical profile of the overall equity market. Although this deteriorating relative strength study represents 24 of some 102 S&P 500 groups as of February 1996, they comprised only 14.7 percent of the S&P 500 weight, leaving the remaining 85.3 percent of the S&P weight to fuel a continuation of this bull market and its expanding breadth progression.

Why the Globally-Exposed Stocks Are Outperforming

The source of this global versus domestic curiosity revealed itself in the charts during 1993 and 1994. It appeared to me, on a fairly consistent basis, that the charts of the larger, globally-exposed U.S. equities advanced more consistently and had been generally holding up better and/or outperforming their more domestically-exposed counterparts, even in the face of other themes such as Capital/Consumer, large-cap versus small-cap and general domestic equity market weakness. Even though the technical expectation was primarily for a Capital Goods relative advance, by *traditional* broad market measures nonetheless even within the structurally deteriorating Consumer Groups (made up primarily of domestic sectors), there were those globally-exposed Consumer sectors that were bucking the declining trends. Simultaneously, others corrected sharply, then swiftly turned and moved on to new highs, eliminating structural divergences (Figure 2–9).

In the Household Products group, Procter & Gamble is 52 percent globally-exposed and in Beverages-Non-Alcoholic, Coca-Cola (the heavier-weighted name) is 80 percent globally-exposed, compared with Pepsi, at only 22 percent. Similarly, in Personal Care (formerly Cosmetics), Avon Products is 64 percent globally-exposed. If a company is up to 80 percent globally-exposed, we cannot expect it to respond in a purely domestic way to domestic economic fundamentals, to domestic interest rates, domestic inflation, or domestic economic slowdown. The charts have been good indicators of this potential international growth. Even within the Financial sectors, several globally-exposed names "ignored" the 1994 less buoyant trend and advanced

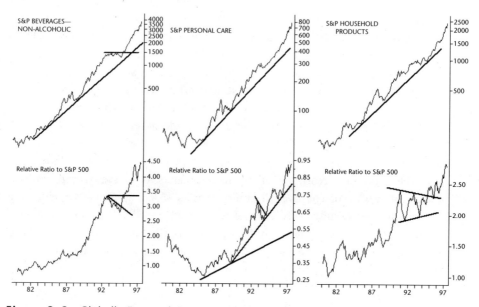

Figure 2–9 Globally-Exposed Consumer Sectors. Chart created with Supercharts® by Omega Research, Inc.

handsomely—developing evidence of the globally-exposed (growth) versus domestically-exposed (underperforming) two-tier market.

As the technical evidence evolved, piquing my interest in this global exposure outperformance, I began to consult fundamental analysts to determine which names in their universes had large global exposures. For definition purposes, I chose an arbitrary level of 30 percent or more global exposure in S&P 500 and S&P 400 stocks. (Global exposure is defined differently among analysts and corporations as sales, revenues, or income.)

The next step was to see if such exposure corresponded to the stronger chart patterns that had been outperforming and breaking out to new all-time highs in price. There did appear to be a strong correlation. A conversation with our Personal Care and Household Products analyst confirmed the global thesis in her universe where all the components were moving in unison. She noted that the multinationals not only outperformed the S&P 500 but had also far outstripped the price action—exactly in line with my technical observations of the more globally-exposed equities. The Personal Care group began its outperformance in 1984 and has not looked back (completely ignoring the theoretical 1992 shift of leadership). In some cases, off-shore participation may not be as large as in others (or as diversified), and some issues had already advanced smartly and were correcting or consolidating those gains. From a technical perspective, however, the chart dynamics of many globally-exposed U.S. equities remain impressive, suggesting the potential for higher prices over time as the percentage of global expansion (increased unit volume growth) for U.S. equities continues to grow. In a possibly related parallel, 1993 was the year our technical universe (Figure 2–10) of globally-exposed U.S. stocks began its trend of outperformance versus both the S&P 500 and small-cap stocks.

For the first time in this century, the world is flooded with developing regions—Latin America, Southeast Asia, China, the Pacific Rim countries, India, Eastern Europe (pending stabilization), and eventually even Africa. All of these countries are hungry for the modernization, industrialization, and technical advancement that the United States and Western European countries have enjoyed for years, and they are gobbling up everything (Capital and/or Consumer Goods) that is forthcoming to propel them to those goals and beyond. Just as the great bull market of 1942–1966 was fueled by domestic post-war economic expansion, so too this cycle may be fueled by economic expansion—only this time it is a "post-Third World" global economic expansion of these now-developing nations and could prove to be another record for longevity and distance traveled.

The basing patterns of the Capital Goods long-term charts in 1993 suggested a comparison to the Capital Goods cycle of 1946–1957. For comparable growth potential today, one need only look at the performance in both the absolute price and the relative strength advances of the Capital Goods

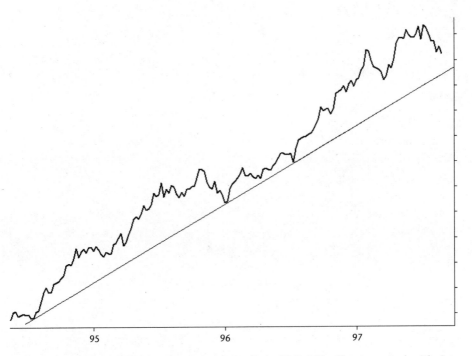

Figure 2–10   Total Global Index Relative Ratio to S&P 500. Chart created with Supercharts® by Omega Research, Inc.

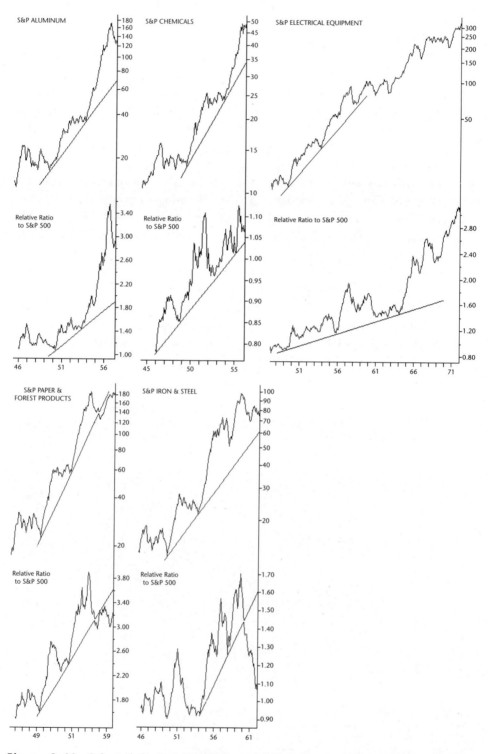

Figure 2–11 Selected Capital Goods Sectors: Performance during 1942–1966 Bull Market Capital Goods Cycle. Chart created with Supercharts® by Omega Research, Inc.

groups during that period (Figure 2–11). Looking at the outperformance of these Capital Goods sectors in the 1950s, one *could* posit that some of these same sectors might repeat their 1950s performance. After all, looking at the 1990s charts of Chemicals, Electrical Equipment, Machinery-Diversified, Manufacturing-Diversified (Figure 2–12), Aluminum, Paper & Forest Products, and Iron & Steel (Figure 2–13), into the 1994 period one could have argued the case for the existence of 10- to 20-year basing processes in the RS for these sectors.

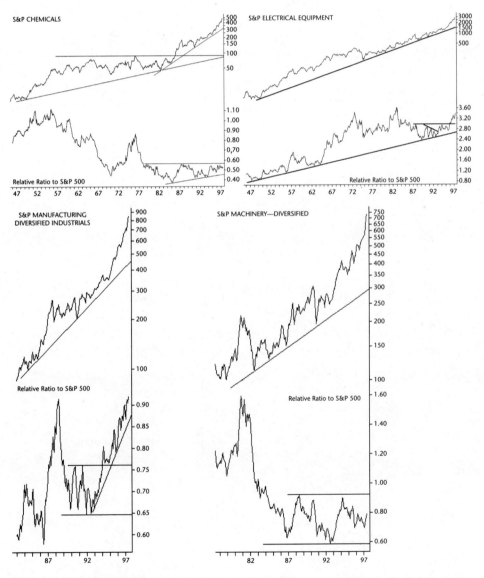

Figure 2–12 Globally-Exposed S&P Capital Goods Sectors. Chart created with Supercharts® by Omega Research, Inc.

Figure 2–13 Potential Relative Strength Bases That Failed. Chart created with Super-charts® by Omega Research, Inc.

But simultaneously, one would have to question the technical configuration of these formations of RS specifically for Aluminum, Paper & Forest Products, and Iron & Steel (Figure 2–13), which seemed also to be tracing out "descending triangular" patterns, a technical formation that generally portends lower levels by virtue of the lower peaks, representing aggressive supply. In fact, it was not until the first of these sectors, Paper & Forest Products broke not up, but down through a 25-year RS support level in 1995, eradicating the potential base, that an even more macrotrend began to suggest itself, one that appeared to be subdividing the Capital Goods tier even more. Following shortly thereafter in early 1996, the Steel sector broke to a 50-year RS low, eradicating its potential base in relative performance. (A base is a consolidation pattern that implies the process of accumulation, buying or demand on the part of investors.) When a consolidation breaks down, the implication is that the pattern represented distribution and a top (selling or supply by the investor) rather than accumulation and a bottom or base. The Aluminum RS remained undecided (until October 1997 when it too broke down). As technology-related evidence emerges that we will discuss later in Part Two, it explains why some of these Capital Goods areas subdivide further and turn out to be not as rewarding as others in light of new, evolving macroeconomic forces.

The U.S. companies (and hence the price patterns of their stocks) reflecting the dynamic, new growth potential are those globally-exposed, positioned to take advantage of enormous global demand; the implication for the continued extension of the U.S. globally-exposed Consumer Goods sectors cannot be ruled out in face of the emerging nations' demands. Many U.S. corporations are already well positioned, deriving a large portion of their revenues from that international exposure, and are still expanding. Others, just beginning, will have greater growth potential over the years to come, perhaps even extending this bull cycle.

The global implication for many U.S. equities (for example, many of the large capitalization names making up the DJIA and other major indices) suggests that price, over the years, may also carry further than might otherwise be expected, having already exceeded my 1994 prediction of 7680 on the Dow. Since this global expansion can be slow and fraught with local bureaucratic, trade-related and economic fits and starts, especially in developing nations (as we have witnessed in Mexico, and more recently in Southeast Asia), it may also turn out to be a cycle with volatile characteristics and long pauses. There will undoubtedly continue to be corrective trends and deep retracements even of globally-exposed stocks, including the technology sectors. Such declines should offer good buying opportunities in the more attractive issues for the next advancing phase in what could be an extended cycle in the globally-exposed tier of U.S. equities. The question "What is going to take the market higher?" may, for the first time, be answered by internationally- or globally-exposed U.S. equities, resulting in this very different two-tier equity market.

Within the context of this global thesis, which fast became a reality, there are a few conceptual considerations:

- By definition, the equity market action may continue to appear "thin," from a *relative strength* (if not price) perspective, with only a portion of total equities participating in this emerging relative strength global leadership tier. The underperformers, as we have seen, represent only a small percentage of total S&P capitalization weight. Hence the potential that the equity market will continue to be pushed higher by more money chasing somewhat fewer outperforming names.

- It is also quite possible that as this global theme progresses, intermarket relationships may be *very* different, and the global tier of U.S. equities may not be as susceptible (as it historically has been) nor respond in the same degree or fashion, to the vagaries of domestic fundamental influences and relationships. This might skew some of the statistical data and technical market indicators, as appears to have been the case in 1994 (when domestic and small caps suffered bear markets while the more globally-exposed major indices experienced only a consolidation of 9.6 percent) and would make stock choices and cycle (Capital/Consumer) subtrend identification within the global tier essential. These domestic influences would be likely to more specifically affect the domestic equities (as seen in the 1994 bear market declines in place for many domestic/small cap stocks).

- Globally-exposed U.S. equities will be more vulnerable to international economic fluctuations, yet also perhaps protected somewhat by the degree of their diversification across a wide spectrum of countries whose individual cycles differ. This corporate diversification may protect investors against a 1994 Mexican-style, and hopefully also the 1997 Far East, disaster as broad multinational exposure provides companies a buffer against such individual country shocks.

- As the potential to more safely diversify internationally by investing at home in well-managed and well-disclosed, globally-exposed U.S. corporate equities (versus the perceived risk of direct foreign investment) becomes recognized by U.S. investors, this realization may encourage and provide impetus for increased investment here at home, thus from yet another perspective, propelling this global tier of the equity market higher. Any evidence of stability in the dollar may eventually entice foreign buyers to our market, as well.

If this global versus domestic thesis continues to be verified by market action, some long-held intermarket relationships may splinter or stumble, and may even bring into question the efficacy of some traditional technical market indicators. The changes in the world over the last decade have been historic and may well influence traditional cycles in very different ways over the next decade, and a new way of perceiving trends may be required.

For example, in Dow Theory, the confirmation or divergence of the Dow Jones Transportation Average (DJTA) and the DJIA has historically represented domestic economic pressures and cycles. The averages are expected to move together as the companies that make the goods and the companies that transport the goods would be economically expected to do. When the DJIA and the DJTA close above a prior rally peak, Dow Theory would project a buy signal; when both averages close below a prior reaction low, Dow Theory renders a sell signal. Yet, with the transports essentially still impacted more by domestically-oriented fluctuations, and the DJIA more heavily impacted by its growing global exposure, it is conceivable that the Dow Theory may not be as consistent or applicable as it has been in the past.

The technical evidence of this Dow Theory de-link was indicated in 1994 by the 22 percent bear market experienced by the DJTA (more domestically oriented), but not confirmed by the 9.6 percent decline in the more global DJIA. This divergence suggests that the so-called "4-year cycle" bear market was seen, as measured by the DJTA, and that the heavy global exposure of the DJIA components may have "protected" it from the 1994 domestic bear pressures.

Dow Outperformance

An interesting and pertinent technical observation occurred in early 1994 when I noticed the developing configuration of the DJIA relative to the S&P 500 (Figure 2–14). Over the past 15 years, a very significant RS base appears to have developed. After 14 years of moving sideways, the Dow/S&P 500 RS has now broken up through, not only the entire base, but also a 34-year downtrend line—a rather major technical statement (similar to the bond yield in 1991 breaking its 35-year trend of rising rates). The more positive bias of the Dow is quite possibly reinforced by the fact that every Dow component represents a U.S. globally-exposed equity name, and this breakout in RS may be another piece of technical evidence that this is a very different equity market environment. By obvious contrast, we can note the breakdown in the RS of the S&P 500 versus the DJIA to a new 15-year low (Figure 2–14, insert). There is a surprising resemblance in the current S&P 500 RS to the initial underperformance trend development for the Dow 35 years ago from 1946 to 1962 (Figure 2–14, left arrows).

Eight months after this observation, and with January 1996 showing a 5.44 percent gain for the Dow and a 3.26 percent gain for the S&P 500, this

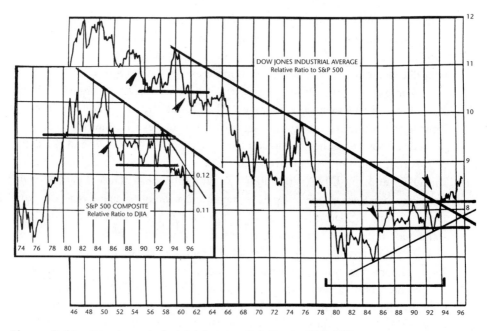

Figure 2–14   Dow Jones Industrial Average Relative to S&P 500.

study seemed worth another look as the DJIA relative strength trend extended. I took month-to-month performance numbers for both the DJIA and the S&P 500 beginning in 1993. (This is the point at which the U.S. globally-exposed equity universe began to show relative outperformance and, in perhaps a not unrelated parallel, it is the same point at which the DJIA relative performance versus the S&P 500 penetrated the 34-year downtrend and simultaneously emerged from a 15-year base into the structural uptrend of outperformance discussed above.) I ran a cumulative monthly performance table for both the DJIA and S&P 500 based solely on *price* to see whether this relative trend was statistically significant. From January 1993, the DJIA advanced 145.88 percent as of July 1997 versus the S&P 500's advance of 115.81 percent, not an insignificant spread (see Table 2–3). There is a technical assumption that moves tend to have relationships to one another: The bigger the base, the higher in space; the bigger the top, the bigger the drop. Thus, the implication of this RS chart comparison is that given the 15-year size of the base and the 34-year duration of the now-broken downtrend, the newly established outperformance trend of the DJIA is still young in its progression, and should continue for some time to come.

Whether within the global tier there is a predominantly Capital Goods cycle or Consumer Goods cycle, or whether there will be an ebb and flow between the globally-exposed Capital and globally-exposed Consumer may not be totally clear yet due to the short time frame as we will examine in Chapter 9 and Chapter 15. One should not underestimate the continued

Table 2–3
DJIA Performance vs. S&P 500 since 1993

Month	DJIA Performance (base: Dec–92)	S&P 500 Performance (base: Dec–92)
Mar–93	4.06%	3.66%
Jun–93	6.51%	3.40%
Sep–93	7.69%	5.33%
Dec–93	13.72%	7.06%
Mar–94	10.15%	2.31%
Jun–94	9.81%	1.96%
Sep–94	16.42%	6.20%
Dec–94	16.16%	5.41%
Mar–95	25.95%	14.92%
Jun–95	38.02%	25.03%
Sep–95	45.08%	34.13%
Dec–95	55.01%	41.36%
Mar–96	69.25%	48.15%
Jun–96	71.29%	53.92%
Sep–96	78.19%	57.75%
Dec–96	95.34%	70.01%
Mar–97	99.43%	73.77%
Jun–97	132.43%	103.15%
Jul–97	145.88%	115.81%

growth potential of select globally-exposed Consumer Goods looking toward the millions of potential consumers in the developing markets. There also may be a number of globally-exposed Consumer equity names that suffer initial structural declines but may not witness the full deterioration of an historical RS cycle decline due to the global growth potential. Those issues may remain buoyant and may not bear the same degree of absolute risk normally expected in a relative cycle decline. This, in fact, occurred in the declines of both the Health Care-Drug sector in 1992 and Electronics-Semiconductors in 1995. Both suffered initial bear market declines, but as sectors, did not follow through with a *second* down leg, traditional in a cyclical bear market three-wave pattern (Figure 2–15). The new growth front will likely see spurts or waves of both global Capital and global Consumer dominance.

As with any performance measure, some stocks within the U.S. equity global universe will perform better than others (based on their varying fundamentals, degree of international diversification and growth potential) and similarly, within the domestic equity universe, not all will do poorly (by virtue of the same fundamental and growth issues). By the same token, both the globally- and domestically-exposed tiers undoubtedly will experience their own bull and bear market cycles in contratrend moves to the global theme as may be in play in late 1997 as this book goes to print.

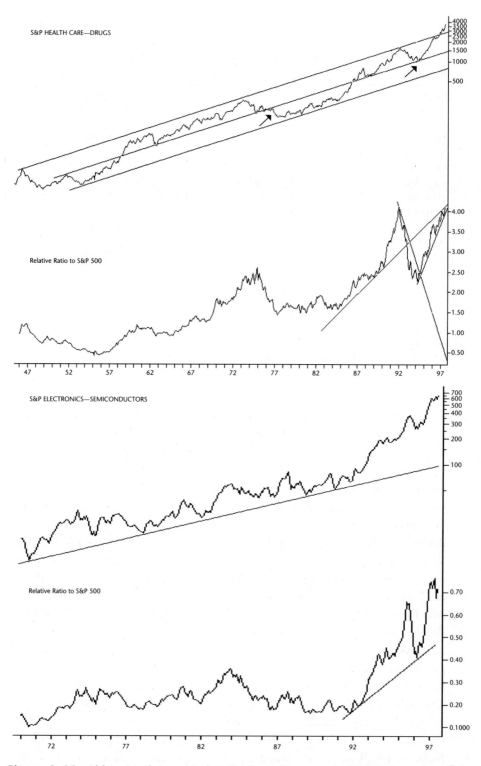

Figure 2–15   Abbreviated Bear Market Decline. Chart created with Supercharts® by Omega Research, Inc.

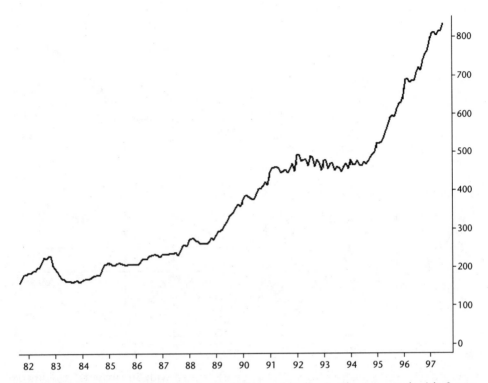

Figure 2–16   Money Market Funds (in Billions of Dollars). Chart created with Super-charts® by Omega Research, Inc.

To further address what will take the market higher, a look at money on the sidelines, so to speak, is quite provocative. We've known for years that money has been accumulating in ever higher aggregates (over $800 billion in 1997) in the nation's money market mutual funds (with more parked in CDs), speculating that one day it might provide fuel for the equity markets. That day may be nearing. Yielding only about 2 percent to 4 percent returns over recent years, the increasing aggregate of money market fund assets (Figure 2–16) would represent an enormous buying potential from the portion of those funds that finds its way into the equity market. Considering this, the speculative phase may not yet even have begun. Seeing 600 million share days was unthinkable just a few years ago. Now the possibility that billion-share days—first seen in October 1997—may become the norm before this bull cycle is over is not out of the question.

Focus on the Dollar

There have been numerous news articles expressing concern about the strengthening U.S. dollar, since mid-1995 (Figure 2–17). The concern about

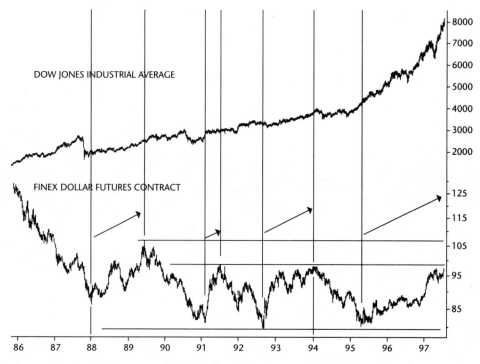

Figure 2–17   Performance of U.S. Dollar. Chart created with Supercharts® by Omega Research, Inc.

the dollar's rise seems to center on its effect on multinational stocks. Since the general focus on multinational stocks might be considered a fairly "young" concept, coming more into focus during the dollar's last down wave of 1994 through early 1995, it is natural that such a worry would emerge as the dollar strengthened from 1995 into 1997. However, this may be too shortsighted a view. The expectation that the strengthening dollar would have a negative impact on the multinationals' profits has not come to pass. Quite the opposite. The dollar has been rising and falling over a 10-year period (Figure 2–17), encompassing the greatest bull market in history; in spite of this, the leaders have been the multinationals.

A study of the dollar's longer-term trend progression is particularly valuable in this case. Our dollar proxy is the FINEX U.S. dollar contract, calculated on a perpetual basis. The contract is most heavily weighted by the German mark and the Japanese yen. Looking at Figure 2–17, the dollar essentially has been in a trading range roughly between 80–85, and 100–105 for the past 10 years. The U.S. equity market, including the globally-exposed U.S. stocks that participated in the 1981–1992 Consumer Goods cycle, has been in a dynamic bull phase for all of that period (interim declines notwithstanding, specifically the identified declines that the U.S. market experienced in 1987, 1990, and 1994). The three identified market declines occurred in periods of a *falling* dollar, albeit the dollar had been declining for a period before the market cracked in 1987 and 1990. The bottom line regarding the U.S. globally-exposed equities is that over this 10 year trading range, they clearly managed to hold their own, and even advance, during the rising cycles for the dollar.

To further the discussion, we have studies in which Alan Shaw correlates the recent effects of the dollar fluctuations on certain Capital Goods and Consumer Goods sectors (Figure 2–18). The Drug group in particular is perceived as always being weak with a strong underlying dollar; but as can be seen in the accompanying charts, there is really no consistent correlation. The shaded areas represent periods within that trading range when the dollar had been strengthening; it is apparent that the chosen sectors, as measured by price, seem to be independent in their trends during a strengthening or weakening environment. One effect of a rising dollar may be beneficial in that foreign investors, heretofore fearful to tread into the U.S. market as the dollar falls (or is perceived to be falling), may be inclined to enter our market against a strong dollar given their under-invested U.S. equity levels.

Perhaps the dramatic growth of exports may offset some dollar strength. The dollar today may have much less impact on the multinationals because of their extensive geographic diversification and foreign production,

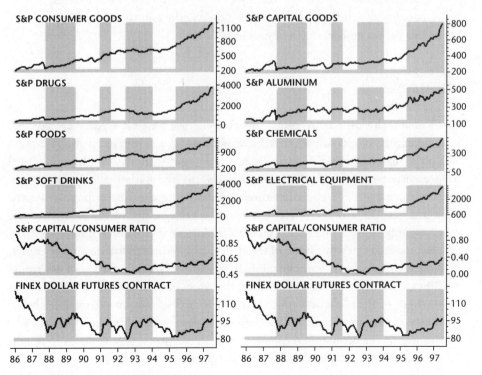

Figure 2–18 Sector Price Performance versus U.S. Dollar. Chart created with Super-charts® by Omega Research, Inc.

affiliates, cross-border mergers, so that currency fluctuations may cancel each other out. The multinational then enters a cause and effect relationship with the economic conditions of the foreign countries in which it is involved. This is always a concern with pockets of crisis (Mexico, the Far East) but diversification among countries plays a somewhat protective role in this, in that all eggs are not in one basket. Perhaps the heavy industrial sectors that find it harder to geographically diversify, or companies without international operations, are more prone to the dollar's cyclical swings. Multinational corporate currency hedges also have made dollar fluctuations less of a factor. The technical configuration of the dollar in 1997 suggests its strength may continue. The dollar advances of 1991 and 1993 within the 10-year progression were sharp advances ("V" bottoms). But the 1995–1997 advance has assumed a more substantial base (a "saucer" bottom). This suggests a stronger technical condition which could imply an ultimate penetration through the top of the 10-year trading range. Were this to occur, our dollar/multinational relationship would be in uncharted waters.

Late 1997 has witnessed a modicum of weakening in the dollar, suggesting an interim pause in its rise. While technically we do not have evidence of a retracement to the trading range lows, it must be remembered that it is when the dollar has weakened that the equity market may have, though has not always, experienced a weakening trend. Given the 1997 market correction, primarily in the global tier, it is possible the equity market may catch its breath before embarking on a new climb.

Summary

From a technical perspective, it appears that we have entered a new two-tier market, one of globally-exposed U.S. equities (the new growth stocks) versus domestically-exposed U.S. equities. This equity market cycle, as defined presently, may be different from any other in our statistical or national history in that it is so globally exposed and serving the largest population the world has seen emerge. We could be embarking on one of the most dynamic growth cycles in our history, which may set another record in distance traveled and longevity by virtue of the post-Third World global economic expansion in unit volume growth for U.S. globally-exposed equities. This would provide another leg of and extend the great bull market from 1982. The strength of the globally-exposed Consumer stocks, however extended, should not be underestimated—the greater the global diversification, the more stable may be the economic response of globally-exposed U.S. equities to the diversity of international fundamental influences.

In light of this new global theme, long-held intermarket relationships may be very different, even significantly altered, and a new way of perceiving trends (even technical and, as we shall examine later, economic trends) may be required. Globally-exposed U.S. equities may not be as influenced by domestic fundamental issues as in the past (nor to the degree that the domestic tier of U.S. equities is influenced by them). Perhaps a somewhat thinner equity market relative strength leadership may prevail, which could continue to skew statistical data (as it did in 1994) until more and more companies expand globally; the heavy global exposure of the DJIA components may have protected it from the domestic bear pressures of 1994 experienced by the broader market issues. We also must remain alert to the macroforces at work around the world, as will be discussed in Part Two.

Chapter

Recent History/Market Projections

As time passed after my original observations in 1993–1994, more technical correlations in the market today versus the past began to catch my eye that seemed to provide intriguing evidence that might confirm the original theses. In the process, the projections of levels to which the equity market might climb over time were raised.

In this chapter, we'll take a closer look at these relationships to the historical data in Chapter 1 as they presented themselves in my evolution of discovery. Focusing on the DJIA 5 percent reversal records and on the cumulative A-D line progressions that occurred during the bull markets of 1921–1929 and 1942–1966, we find support for further extension of the current bull market dating from 1982. Predictions I made during 1995 and 1996 are reviewed to suggest the similarities in the analysis of different periods. Interim technical analytical projections for the Dow are related sequentially. An intriguing analogy to the Nikkei index is also explored. Finally, a comparison of the percentile increase of the three great bull markets of this century yields an even higher potential calculation for our bull market.

History in the Making

By May 1995, it became increasingly evident that we might be living through history in the making. I would like to borrow a piece of statistical information presented in the spring of 1995 by our friends at Lowry's Reports, Inc.[1] whose proprietary measure of Buying Power and Selling Pressure gives a technical appraisal of equities as far back as the 1930s. Lowry noted that "rallies typically undergo a normal, healthy correction of 5 percent or more about every two to three months on average." But in the rally from year-end 1994, no such interim 5 percent correction had yet been experienced. Lowry pointed to several historic periods in which extended rallies took place. Interestingly, these rallies took place from (1) June 1949 to June 1950, for a period of 12 months; (2) September 1953, for a period of 11 months; (3) November 1988, also for 11 months; (4) March 1958, lasting 7 months; (5) October 1960, seven months; and (6) September 1985, 7 months. These extraordinary rallies, uninterrupted by even a 5 percent pullback, all occurred in the bull markets referenced herein. The 1994–1995 trend was exactly this type of extraordinary bull market extension we have been discussing. All the records of these extended advances without even a 5 percent pullback occurred *exclusively* in the current bull market (1982–present) and in the 1942–1966 bull cycle, and provide additional records to those we cited earlier.

The Lowry Report adds further evidence, via these additional 5 percent correction records, of our extraordinary market environment. Without throwing caution to the wind (or suggesting that there could not be a 5 percent retracement), I suggested that if in the spring of 1995 we were to project a similar period of a market advance from the lows of 1994 without a 5 percent correction, based on the 7- to 12-month parameters in the Lowry study, July 1995 would represent 7 months from the December 1994 low, and November through December 1995 would represent the outside extreme of 11 to 12 months. (With the benefit of hindsight, we now know the DJIA continued to rise until May 22, 1996 achieving a level of 5778, for a *new* record of 17 months, before experiencing a 5 percent reversal.)

How Far, How Long?

By July 1995, further observations led me to ask the question: How far, how long could this long-term bull market cycle continue? There are some dynamic advantages to having life-size technical indicators for "wallpaper" in our chart room. One advantage is being able to "walk back through history" and visually catch a trend that is reminiscent of another time. Such an observation may initiate a cascade of questions and comparisons. One such observation on our daily wall allowed me to play devil's advocate in January 1995, suggesting that the 1994 decline might be over. The cumulative NYSE daily A-D line, which almost never portrays anything resembling a bottom, had at the time formed a short-term pattern that appeared to be very similar to a bottoming formation put in place in 1990 (Figure 3–1). If we were to assume that the DJIA 3674 level would remain as the 1994 corrective low of 9.6 percent for the Dow, the actual Dow price decline in both cases (1990 and 1994) would correspond to the first low of the bottoming, or basing, pattern in this daily A-D chart. The "test" of the low (a decline to equal or almost equal the initial low) that occurred after the 1990 bottom came months later, and from higher Dow levels in an ongoing upward trend that extended far into 1991. This suggested to me that the 1994 decline had ended and the Dow was set to march ahead once again.

A further walk through history in July 1995 led my eye first to the lift-off of the A-D line from its 1994 low, (plotted *weekly* on our longer-term weekly wall, see Figure 3–2), and then to the 1949 lift-off of the same cumulative A-D line in almost an exactly similar angle of ascent. And so the process of another possible comparison began.

An analogy of today's market environment to 1946–1956 (Capital Goods cycle) immediately came to mind. The questions of where market behavior in each case may be occurring vis-à-vis the long-term structural cycle of the cumulative A-D line, the shift of leadership studies, and record advances without as much as 5 percent or 10 percent reversals, next came into play. The results of these studies are fascinating.

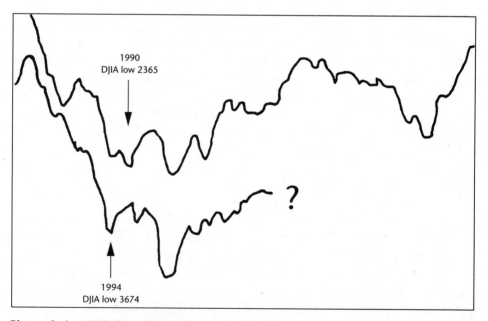

Figure 3–1   NYSE Cumulative Advance-Decline Line.

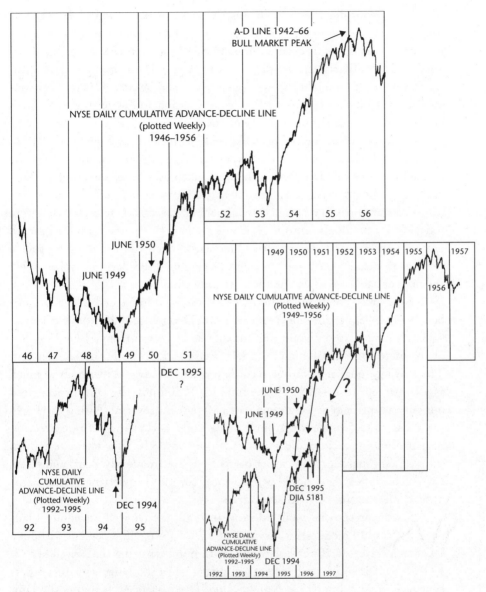

Figure 3–2   NYSE Cumulative Advance-Decline Line.

Taken one at a time (refer to Figure 1–5), first the A-D low in June 1949 came about 3 years after the April 1946 shift of leadership whereby Capital Goods began to outperform the Consumer Goods. In the current trend, the 1994 A-D low occurred 2 years after the traditionally-defined December 1992 apparent shift of leadership.

Second, the relative positions of these two A-D line points, in the context of the structural history of the entire A-D line, is even more interesting (refer to Figure 1–3). The 1949 A-D low occurred at the tail end of the

1946–1950 consolidation, which was the first consolidation after the A–D line broke out of the 1932–1942 10-year base. The breakout in 1950 initiated the second phase of the structural 14-year rise for the A–D line from 1942–1956. Similarly, the lift-off from the 1994 A–D low brought the indicator to within about 6,000 issues of pushing up and out of its 1986–1995 consolidation, which was also the first consolidation following the A–D line's emergence from its 1975–1985 10-year base.

Third, to continue the possible analogy, recall that from June 1949 to June 1950, the U.S. equity market experienced its first record advance (in the available history of the DJIA) without as much as a 5 percent reversal. Discussing the Lowry 5 percent record data in May when we were then 6 months into an advance without as much as a 5 percent reversal, I suggested that were today's market to move into the span of the Lowry 5 percent reversal record periods (which spanned from 7 to 12 months), we could be looking for such a reversal to occur in the July through December 1995 period. By July 1995 the market had, of course, entered that time window.

Now, if we compare the June 1949–1950 A–D line trend to the December 1994–1995 progression (Figure 3–2), December 1995 would correlate with the June 1950 reversal time frame. The DJIA ran from a June 1949 low of 161.60 to a June 1950 high of 228.38, a rise of 66.78 points or 41.3 percent. That advance qualifies for our records for market advances without as much as a 10 percent reversal. From the June 12, 1950 high, the Dow experienced not only a 5 percent reversal, but also a 10 percent reversal, falling to 197.46 for a loss of 13.5 percent. An interesting point is that the entire correction happened in one month, and was over by July 13, 1950. One characteristic of a strong bull market trend is that corrections are frequently sharp and steep, particularly after there have been advances for a record-setting period without any meaningful corrective reversals.

Following the one-month decline in 1950, the Dow advanced until January 5, 1953 (29 months) to a level of 293.79, gaining 48.8 percent without a 10 percent reversal. If we were to play with numbers using the November 23, 1994, low of 3674.63, and project a similar rise in the Dow prior to a 5 percent reversal, a gain of 1506 points would be experienced, bringing the Dow to 5181. Also remember that 1946–1956 represented a record bull market advance, up 222 percent in 10 years without a bear market decline (20 percent or more) and no 4-year cycle. It was the fourth-largest bull run in history. History never repeats itself in exactly the same way, but these are interesting observations and we will see the result shortly.[2]

By December 1995, the rise of the DJIA through the consolidation at 4800 (refer to Figure 1–8) suggested the potential to 5150 as measured by a simple short-term point-and-figure count. Point-and-figure charting captures every whole point intraday reversal, which we plot by hand. Hence, for every point move, a figure is plotted. Charts can be plotted by 1 point (or 1 unit), 3 units, 10 units, or as in this DJIA chart, 50 units to condense time.

Point-and-figure charts lend themselves to the calculation of price targets or projections. (Recall that in technical analysis, one assumption is that moves tend to have relationships to one another. Simplistically, the bigger the base, the higher in space; the bigger the top, the bigger the drop.) From a more intermediate-term measured move in the point-and-figure profile, the suggestion of 5500 could also be put forth. The price progression of the Dow broke out of its point-and-figure upper channel line (a line above and parallel to the uptrend) at a price of 4500. Were that line extended back in time to 1986–1987, the Dow would have penetrated the same upper channel at 1900, after which it would have progressed to 2700 (up 42 percent) before capitulation in 1987. In December 1995, a similar percentage rise from 4500 would project to 6390.

Although we are in the third great bull market of this century, the current cycle trend was still very "long in the tooth" (a record of 61 months) as of December 4, 1995, the second highest record percentage advance (+115 percent) without as much as a 10 percent reversal and approaching the 12-month record advance of 1949–1950 during the second great bull market of the century without as much as a 5 percent reversal.

The 1949–1950 Analogy Holds

Fascinatingly, by December 1995, it became evident that the 1949–1950 analogy had held. It is dangerous when one starts proclaiming "this time it's different" for the equity market. "It is and it isn't," is my response. Today's market is different from the "norm"—the norm being what many careers had experienced, which was market behavior against a backdrop of a secular trend of rising interest rates. But it is not different from the "exceptions to the norm"—the exceptions being the two other great bull markets of this century (1921–1929 and 1942–1966), which were experienced against a backdrop of low/stable interest rates. The task at hand is to try and re-evaluate intermarket relationships and perceive them not as we have in the "norm" periods, but as they were in the referenced exceptions to the norm.

Consider our prior (July 1995) analogy of the A-D line in June 1949 versus that of today, projecting a possible Dow 5181 by December, 1995 (Figure 3–2). Well, believe it or not, in December 1995 the Dow was at 5181 and better. Now with the major market indices appearing to have lifted out of yet another "shelf consolidation" into another upleg extension (advance), the question is, where was the 5 percent correction that should have occurred in the indices prior to the improvement of the technical indicators? There may be an answer very similar to "where was the 1994 bear market, which was seen in the technical indicators and many stocks, but not in the major indices?" That may well be explained by the two-tier market structure today and the concept that the dynamics of many long-held intermarket relationships may need to be revisited and a different way of perceiving them may be required. I had suggested the 1994 bear market was not experienced by the more globally-exposed major indices, but by the secondary smaller cap and more domestically-oriented stocks, many of which have little or no global exposure.

Some interesting calculations for the September through December 1995 statistics relative to its comparable 1949–1950 period extends the July 1995 study above (see Figure 3–2, right insert). After the 12-month June 1949–June 1950 advance (up 41.3 percent) without a 5 percent reversal, from the June 12, 1950 peak of 228.38 to the July 13, 1950 low at 197.46, the Dow experienced a 13.6 percent loss (completing both a 5 percent and a 10 percent reversal for the statistical records). The cumulative A-D line at that time suffered a 3,600 issue decline (following a 15,500 issue advance) for a reduction of 23 percent of the A-D line's advance. This brief one-month pullback was followed by a rise into a first Dow peak on September 13, 1951 at 276.37. The next and final Dow peak of the advance (before another 13 percent reversal) was on January 5, 1953 at 293.79.

As of December 1995, the Dow had risen from its December 1994 low for 12 months (up 30.2 percent) into the September 14, 1995 peak at 4801.80. Its reversal to a low of 4703.82 on October 26, 1995, was only a 2.1 percent decline. But the cumulative A-D line declined 5,334 issues (after an advance of 25,360 issues) for a 21 percent reduction of the A-D line's advance—a relatively similar profile to the A-D loss of 1949–1950. This discrepancy between the 1949–1950 decline in both the Dow and the A-D line versus the minimal 2.1 percent pullback in the Dow, yet with a similarly substantial A-D decline, may be due to the global thesis affecting the DJIA (and the other major large capitalization indices) that protected the indices from the underlying 1994 bear market; once again affecting market action. We may, as in 1994, already have experienced the reversal (though milder) in the more globally-exposed major market indices. And in 1995, with technical indicators confirming, the equity markets could then embark on yet another upleg extension.

Playing with numbers once again, if the Dow, having already mirrored 1949–1950, were again to mirror the 1950–1951 rise of 39.9 percent that occurred following the 1940–1950 reversal, or further, to mirror the 1950–1953 rise of 48.7 percent into the January 5, 1953 high at 293.79, the Dow could then be projected to reach as high as 6580, up 39.9 percent (using the 1994 DJIA 4703.82 low as the lift-off), or 6994.52, up 48.7 percent—ever approaching the 7680 suggested in September 1994, which at the time seemed a heady and distant projection. After 1953 the Dow experienced a 13 percent correction, then rose 90 percent into a 1955 peak without as much as a 10 percent reversal. Given the 1951 equivalent Dow levels above, at 6580 and 6994, and assuming an interim 13 percent decline, the Dow, if it were to continue to mirror the 1949 period, could project to 10,921 and 13,343.

The Analogy Holds Again, Foreshortened

By April 1997, this 1950–1953 analogy had held, though possibly foreshortened. In early 1997, I examined the above study to see where we might be, were the tracking still intact (Figure 3–2, right insert). Well, "believe it or not," the suggested trends appear to have manifested. The Dow achieved the projected gains (calculated off the 4703.82 low of October 26, 1995) to 6994, actually exceeding the target, hitting 7085.16 on March 11, 1997. However, instead of achieving that goal, as in the 3-year period from 1950 to 1953, time contracted to achieve that 46 percent-plus gain in only one year. (Tongue in cheek, perhaps due to the time-saving speed of the new era technology.) Do we dare to play with numbers once again? Dare we anticipate that the recent market weakness could resemble the dip that took place in 1953 after that 46.7 percent gain?

Assuming the outside possibility of a continuation of the analogy, the three-leg decline visible on the chart for the 1953 A-D line was accompanied by a decline from the DJIA's January 5, 1953 high at 293.79, to the September 14, 1953, low at 255.49, for a 13 percent decline over nine months. Recalling our technical definitions, this qualifies as a correction (a move off the high of up to 10 percent is defined as a consolidation, a decline of 10 percent to 20 percent, a correction, and 20 percent or more, a bear market). Were this A-D analogy to hold yet a third time, with the spring 1997 DJIA 9.8 percent decline (10 percent for the S&P 500) a replica of that 1953 decline, the Dow then rose (from the December 1953 low of 255.49) to a high of 521.05 three years later on April 6, 1956. This represented a gain of 103.9 percent. Daring to project forward, if the DJIA were to rise 103 percent over the next three years, then the Dow would increase to 12,512 by the year 2001. These extraordinary numbers also reflect levels calculated from studies we will address in demographics and CPI adjustments as well as in a Nikkei/Dow analogy. All are interesting observations and correlations to contemplate.

Structural Bull Market Confirmations Usher in 1996

The foreshortening cited above may have been anticipated by the February 1996 technical confirmations as the Dow climbed to 5400. The extraordinary U.S. bull market continued to display signs of structural confirmation as 1996 actually got off to a good start from a technical perspective. A structural point to note is that the cumulative daily A-D line moved out to a new multiyear cycle high in its second secular advance. The first, we know, was 1942–1957 during the century's second great bull market. Not only did the A-D surpass the December 1995 cycle peak, but it also surpassed its 1994 cycle peak, which therefore takes the indicator out through an 8-year consolidation phase (refer to Figure 1–3). This action renews the uptrend progression which began with the 1982 A-D low. In comparison to the last major bull market (1942–1966), this phase may again be likened to the 1950 analogy, when the A-D rose out of a 4-year consolidation to advance for another 6 years. Structurally, this A-D breakout argues for a continuation of the bull market progression that has been in effect. (This A-D trend alone negates the views of some skeptics who suggest a comparison of today's equity market to that of the late 1960s/early 1970s when the A-D was well into a 9-year topping process and beginning its structural decline.)

Volume expansion has been a key ingredient in the recent improving indicators. This orderly progressive increase of volume is another signal of the extraordinary strength of this once-in-a-lifetime bull. Volume is the key weapon of the bull (Figure 3–3). As 1994 moved into 1995 and into 1996, it is interesting to note that volume began to establish an uptrending channel that lifted through the entire decade's more consistent horizontal trading pattern, representing this gradual and orderly increase in the volume statistic. These ever-increasing levels of volume are having their effect on the daily volatility

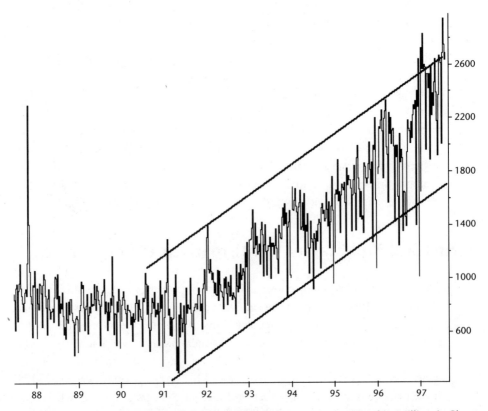

Figure 3–3 Weekly Plot of Daily NYSE Volume (10-Day Moving Total in Millions). Chart created with Supercharts® by Omega Research, Inc.

of the equity market. However, the greater volatility in terms of intraday or daily point advances and declines (to which we are becoming more accustomed) should be put into perspective by considering a 100-point Dow move from 5400 as akin to a one-point move for a $54 stock; a 100-point move from 7800 as akin to a one-point move for a $78 stock. Interest rates continue their long-term decline—the backdrop to this century's third great bull—and remain a strong rationale for the theses set forth here.

Making and breaking records has been characteristic of the three bull markets of the twentieth century. But one has to acknowledge that at some point a reversal will be experienced, even if only as a phase of consolidation (a decline of up to 10 percent off the high). The absolute numbers may be staggering, but the percentages are more modest. January 1996 saw roughly Dow 5400 from a 1995 year-end close of 5117.12, a gain of about 5 percent.

Lowry's data in early 1996 continued to confirm the uptrend (Figure 3–4) as the positive spread between their Buying Power and Selling Pressure indicators achieved a 50-point threshold on June 23, 1995, and by July 13,

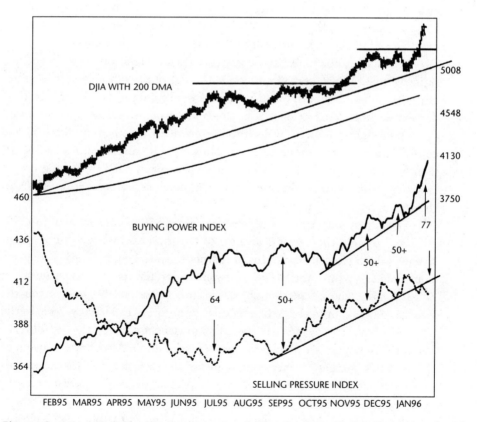

Figure 3–4 Lowry's Buying Power versus Selling Pressure (Daily). Reproduced with permission of Lowry's Reports, Inc., *Lowry's Buy-Sell,* North Palm Beach, Florida.

1995, exceeded that spread to 64 points at a Dow high of 4727.48. Lowry's history shows that "the wider the spread between the two indexes, the longer the rally is likely to persist." According to Lowry, there have been only 26 such occurrences of 50-point-plus spreads in the history of their data. New high levels in the Buying Power generally occur well in advance of a market top. In fact, the statistic generally begins to diverge well before most other indicators, as the market continues to advance: from 2 months to 28 months with a mean average for all 26 cases of approximately 10 months of further rally.

The 64-point spread of Buying Power over Selling Pressure reached in July 1995, undulated below, and expanded again to 50 points or more on September 5, 1995, on December 4, 1995, on January 5, 1996, and, again, on January 19, 1996, continuing to expand to a February 1, 1996 distance of 77 points at the Dow's closing high of 5405.06.

The most interesting finding is that all of the seven rallies that lasted one year or more occurred either in the 1942–1966 bull market or in the 1982–present bull market, adding strong evidence to our record references. While all seven of the 12-month rallies occurred in these two bull markets, they were not the only 50-point spread rallies. (Rallies of shorter duration also occurred in those two particular bull markets.) The time span of the 50-point spread rallies in the 1942–1966 bull cycle ranged from 2 to 28 months; and in the 1982–present bull cycle, from 7 to 17 months.

There does not appear to be any patterned correlation between the duration of these Lowry spread rallies and the size of the subsequent market declines. The four 2-month extended rallies were followed by 11 percent to 16 percent declines (corrections). The 26- and 28-month rallies were followed by 23 percent and 10 percent declines, respectively (one bear market and one consolidation). The market declines following +50-spread rallies lasting 10 months or more ranged from less than 10 percent in 1958 (following one of Lowry's record market advances without as much as a 5 percent reversal), to the 36.1 percent decline of 1987.

If we "play with time," and take the original 50-point spread of June 23, 1995 and project the average advance of the total 26 instances of 50-point spreads, which yielded 10 months of further rally, the equity market progression could carry into April 1996. If it were to stretch for the longer duration of 28 months, the advance might carry into October 1997 and, given the structural breakout in the A-D line, might reinforce the analogy made to the 1950–1953 market advance that lasted 30 months, following the 1950 breakout of the A-D line (see above) to a new reaction high. Also, any extension to the 1996 bull market advance contributes to the recorded data for market advance without as much as a 5 percent or 10 percent reversal. Interestingly, another quick and sharp market decline, primarily in technology stocks was experienced into July 1996, with a second decline in October 1997 closing the 10 percent reversal record.

Dow 8000

For the more speculatively inclined, one could use our DJIA 10 percent filter chart for yet another observation to argue for higher DJIA levels (refer to Figure 1–4). In the prior two great bull markets of the century, each time the DJIA penetrated an "upper channel line," it proceeded to double in price. Having penetrated an upper channel line at the 4000 level, one could have projected the DJIA toward a conceptual target of 8000. Certainly, given some other bull market studies of the Nikkei and demographics, this was not outside the realm of possibility, as 1997 witnessed.

The Dow and the Nikkei . . . An Amazing Fit

Following my bull market extension thesis, Alan Shaw made an extraordinary observation regarding the Nikkei index which might have seemed far-fetched at the time.[3] In looking at the Nikkei's major bull market extension, specifically from 1968, compared to the Dow's uptrend progression, pictured underneath (Figure 3–5), he made a number of observations. First, when attaching trendlines to the semi-log scaled charts, the underlying uptrends of both markets seemed to profile an almost identical rate of change. Obviously, the band of the Dow's advancing "channel" was tighter than the overall trading band that contained the Nikkei for close to 22 years. When looked at over a close to 50-year period, drawn on a semi-log basis, 1968 appears clearly to be the launching year for the big advance that followed.

His second fascinating observation was that the initial upsurge in the Dow Jones, defined from 1982 to 1987, seemed to have a remarkable resemblance to the initial upleg in the Japanese Nikkei from 1968 to 1973. (The periods are bracketed with the A on Figure 3–5.) The 1987 U.S. stock market "crash" resulted in a quick loss of value of about 36 percent. Believe it or not, the 1973–1974 bear market cycle in Tokyo showed just about a 34 percent loss!

These initial observations led to a shifting of the two progressions, trying to "fit" the A periods as closely as possible. The chart illustrates a time shift of between 13 to 14 years to arrive at the resultant "fit." It seemed possible that the U.S. stock market is, in fact, tracing out the course charted by the Japanese stock market some 14 years ago. From 1988 the United States does indeed have a strong resemblance to the 1974 to 1982 period witnessed in the Japanese market. With the Dow soaring some 500 points, on top of the 1995 extraordinary run of about 34 percent, in 1995, Alan suggested that the Dow might be accelerating to the upside like the Nikkei did in 1982–1983.

Trying to reconcile two illustrated trends of supply/demand where the demand factor was the obvious underlying determining force, the study elicits the thought whether there are any trend determining factors present now

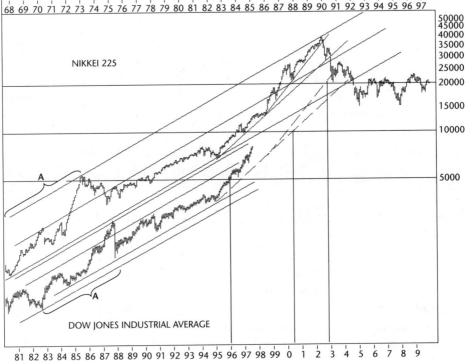

Figure 3–5   Parallel Behavior of Dow Jones Industrial Average and Nikkei 225. Chart created with Supercharts® by Omega Research, Inc.

in the United States that may have been in place in Japan 14 years ago. Interest rates? Inflation? Demographics? Productivity or products of choice? Would the globally-exposed U.S. equity thesis hold for both periods? The extrapolated trends for the Dow are marked by the dashed lines on the chart (Figure 3–5). The first projection would be a Dow level of 10,000 by the year 2000. And then there's the final run for the Dow to nearly 20,000 by the year 2002. And as the study aptly reveals, there could be a few stiff downdrafts along the way, seen in the Nikkei progression as dips of 11 percent, 13 percent, and 18 percent (corrections). At the time the graph suggested one might occur in 1997, however also suggesting the Dow could rise above 6,000 before a 1997 setback.

Secular U.S. Bull Markets of the Twentieth Century

A similar analogy, in which I take some analytical liberties, can be considered by overlaying the three U.S. great bull markets of the twentieth century to evaluate whether or not the rate of ascent of today's bull market is extraordinary or whether there is, in fact, historic precedent.

Let's take a look at the DJIA's great twentieth century bull markets. The first observation is that the angles of ascent of the 1942–1966 and the 1982–present bull markets are somewhat similar so far. The 1920s' bull market was a bit steeper in its 2-year final ascent.

- 1921–1929 — +496.51 percent.
- 1942–1966 — +969.9 percent.
- 1982–present — +962.93 percent (as of August 6, 1997).

August 24, 1921 into the peak September 3, 1929 saw the largest bull market advance of our records (with no bear market interruption), up 496.5 percent over an eight-year period (Figure 3–6). April 28, 1942, to January 18, 1966, saw a 969.9 percent advance over the 24-year bull market cycle (nearly double that of the 1920 cycle) interrupted by three bear markets: 1946 (shift of leadership) off 23.24 percent in 4 months; 1956 (shift of leadership) off 19.4 percent in 6 months; and 1961 off 27.1 percent in 6 months; and at the end of the bull market; the decline of 1966 off 25.2 percent in 8 months.

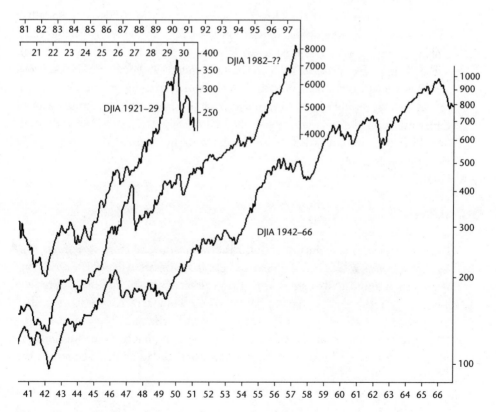

Figure 3–6   The Three Great Secular U.S. Bull Markets of the Twentieth Century. Chart created with Supercharts® by Omega Research, Inc.

Referencing both of the other twentieth-century bull markets, and playing with numbers once again, we note that today's bull market has already exceeded the percentage rise of the 1920s. From the August 12, 1982, low at 776.92, a rise of 496 percent results in Dow 4630.04. If we project an advance equivalent to the 1942–1966 bull cycle, we can project a level of Dow 8312.26. Notice, though, that the century's second bull market (1942–1966) experienced a 473 percentage points greater advance than the century's first (1921–1929), or said another way, a 95 percent larger rise. Assuming our present bull market could exceed the last (and later demographic studies suggest it could): (1) if we add 473 percentage points to 969.9 percent we arrive at a 1442.9 percent potential advance if this bull market (1982–present) were to exceed the last by a similar margin. The result calculates to a Dow level of 11,986.92; (2) if we were to calculate on a comparable percentage gain, a 95 percent greater rise (969 percent + 920 percent) would yield an 1889 percent potential expectation for a total rise off the 1982 low. This would be equivalent to Dow 15,434.56. These numbers resemble the case set forth above in the study of the Nikkei (as well as those later projected in the demographics study); however "far fetched" these may seem, the market's steady advances to date now make them less so.

The comparison of the Dow to the Nikkei of the 1970s and 1980s becomes even more analogous to our own current cycles considering their global expansion (not the least of which was exports to the United States). Astonishingly, from its 1974 low to the December 1989 peak, the Nikkei rose for 15 years without a bear market (a decline of 20 percent or more).

One last number game: Were the Dow to repeat the percentage gain of the entire Nikkei rise from the December 1967 low of 1256 to the 1989 high of 38,915.87, the equivalent Dow level from the August 1982 low of 776 would project to Dow 23,264.

Summary

In this chapter, the evolution of more and more similarities between our bull market beginning in 1982 and the last great bull market of 1942–1966 continues to astound and suggest intriguing precedents for further impressive advances for the equity market. While these comparisons are strong, they must not be viewed in isolation, as the world has changed; they must also be placed in the context of the very different evolving macroforces we shall explore in Part Two, which are reshaping the world today, and consequently, the investment landscape.

Part Two

NEW HORIZONS FOR THE TWENTY-FIRST CENTURY

Chapter

4

Changing Demographics

For the past several years, many traditional intermarket relationships have been experiencing aberrations, puzzling and frustrating market watchers. For example, we have seen long-term relative strength (RS) lows in various sectors and multiyear RS breakdowns in mid-cap and small-capitalization indices. We are having daily conjecture in the media about the occasional "delinking" of stocks and bonds, and of bonds and the Commodities Research Bureau (CRB) index. Is there inflation or not? Are interest rates rising or falling? What about unemployment versus employment? Weaker economy versus stronger?

Some of this confusion conceivably could be explained by the two-tier market thesis: The more domestic focus of the bond market, smaller-cap indices and various sectors, versus the more global focus of other sectors and the Dow Jones Industrial Average and other major indices where the preponderance of stock names are large-capitalization U.S. globally-exposed companies. Many of our intermarket relationships (including economic) may still need to be revisited. There may be questions that each of us in our areas of expertise may need to ask to understand our bull market.

Perhaps it's simply a question of missing the forest for the trees. The daily political and economic "noise" of trading, as well as the traditional way of viewing events, may prevent a longer term vision and understanding of what the charts are really telling us about the macrochanges that could be taking place in our country and around the world for the twenty-first century, of how the behavior of intermarket relationships might once again be "different," or an "exception to the norm" from the way we have known them heretofore; and of how history could be evolving in a different fashion.

In this chapter, we'll take an in-depth look at the first of those macroforces to be considered in this book—the rapidly changing demographic patterns around the world. On the domestic front, we will see that the baby-boom generation is the first of this century not to fully replicate itself, consequently slowing consumption trends and leading to relative underperformance in domestically-oriented Consumer sectors such as Retail Stores and Household Furnishings. At the same time, the movement of aging boomers toward their retirement years will benefit sectors like Financial Services, Health Care and Leisure, among others. Looking at the global picture, we will see that the 80 percent of the world's population that lives outside the United States in emerging nations is dramatically younger, fueling economic and consumer demand around the world. We will see how these demographic profiles may be the factors behind the two-tier market thesis discussed in Chapter 2.

Declining U.S. Demographics

Demographics studies burst open the door to an understanding of why the two-tier equity market has evolved as defined. What is fascinating today is the vast difference not only between the domestic and global demographic profiles, but also between the domestic demographics of today versus that of the past. The demographics in this country (and other developed nations[1]) today are different than at any other time in this century.

The population giving us the bull market of the 1920s nearly doubled to give us the population that led to the bull market of the of the 1940s–1960s, which again nearly doubled to give us today's baby boomers—the largest U.S. population ever—which in turn is impacting the 1982–present bull market. But the baby-boom generation not only *did not* nearly double, it *did not even replicate itself.*

> The 1990s is the first decade to experience a decline in the number of people entering their twenties as well as the number of teenagers. The important factor about this age group is that sometime between the ages of 20 and 29 (the age differs among countries), young adults leave their parents' homes, where they have been sharing goods and services, to establish their own households and begin a new cycle of accumulating consumer goods. The decline in their

numbers now, for the first time, is causing a reduction in the growth of demand for these products. The principal consumers are not there to participate. This phenomenon represents a structural break—not simply a different economic cycle— that will persevere through time.[2]

In other words, the demand for goods associated with family formation, including entry level housing (and its related furnishings and consumer products), should decline in this country during the next cycle. The percent of our society under 18 has dropped from 34 percent in 1970 to 26 percent in 1990.[3] This is different, a first-time-in-this-century phenomenon.

Given the demographic changes in the United States (and other developed nations) with the baby-boom generation being the first of the twentieth century not to replicate itself fully, can we expect consumption trends to be renewed in the same way we have experienced in the past with an almost-double upcoming generation? This new element should be taken into consideration in terms of the overall domestic economic expectations and potential domestic economic dislocations (for individual traditional domestic industries).

Impact on Domestically-Oriented Sectors

This domestic demographic development of maturation in consumer markets (and therefore consumer goods) may reflect what we have been witnessing technically in the long-term structural relative strength (RS) breakdowns and underperformance in many of the domestically-oriented sectors. There have been breakdowns to multiyear lows in RS for such sectors as Building Materials, Home-Building, Household Furnishings and Appliances, Housewares, Containers-Metal & Glass and Containers-Paper, Retail-Department Stores, Retail-General Merchandise, Retail Specialty, and Textiles. As can be seen in Figure 4–1, in which price is represented by the top line, and RS is represented by the bottom line, in some cases these RS breakdowns have been evolving over decades; in others there are definable multiyear "tops" (as in the eight-year RS top in place for Retail-Department Stores). Rallies witnessed over the past year or so have only represented "kickback" rallies which are temporary rallies into the resistance areas (or the original point of breakdown), as in Retailers and Containers, but were then followed by declines to new lows. Some of these sectors have already achieved, or are close to achieving, new all-time RS lows.

Such a development technically may not necessarily mean that an investment area or sector also carries the risk of a price decline, although when relative performance is declining it does imply the potential for such a price risk. Indeed, the charts show that some long-lasting uptrends in price have

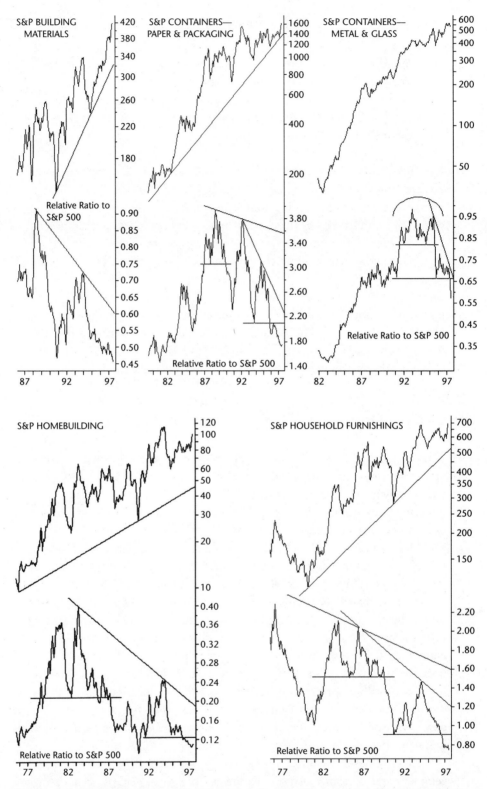

Figure 4–1 Domestic Sectors: Shrinking Relative Demographic Implications. Chart created with Supercharts® by Omega Research, Inc.

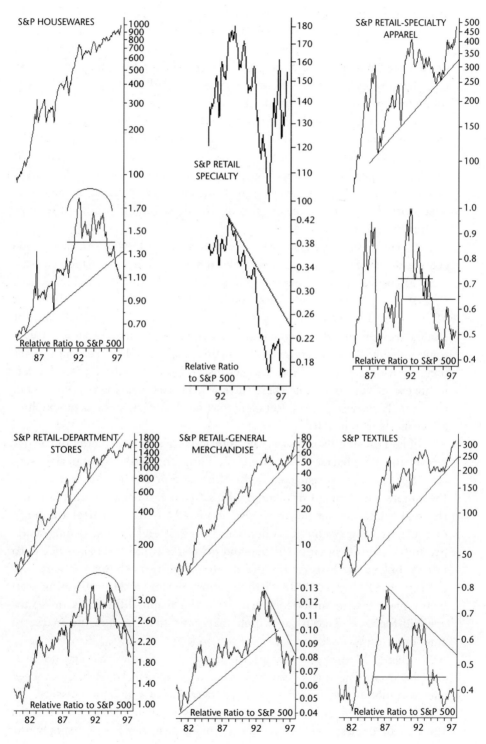

Figure 4–1 Continued.

already been violated and the formation of a structural topping process in price, which can take months to years to form, may well be underway. Recall the principle of technical analysis that trends tend to have relationships to one another in magnitude. Seeing these long-held uptrends in price give way (accompanied by declining and/or faltering RS profiles) suggests that the absolute price risk in these areas may be rising.

But even if the absolute price risk were not to develop, these sectors are clearly no longer bringing sustained reward in terms of outperforming the market, and may be more vulnerable to risk in any market decline which could result in not just a loss of opportunity, but also a loss of capital. These areas may be experiencing the contraction in the consumer markets of the developed world based on the underlying smaller demographic profile of the upcoming generation.

Consider for a moment the retail industry. Looking at the charts, one can see the 8-year RS top in Retail-Department Stores from which the statistic has broken down, bounced up in a kickback rally, failed, and fallen to a new RS low. We have seen endless retail store closings from Fifth Avenue to Main Street. The music industry is another case in point, with the 20 percent annual growth slowed to a standstill; increased store outlets with fewer customers, resulting in bankruptcies, staff cuts, dropping CD prices and a newer focus on formerly ignored music styles just to find sales; all of which has left music executives wondering where the music fans are, leaving the business in a seemingly puzzling crisis. Retailers may need to review the demographics affecting their industries.

The Housing markets may be another casualty, as depicted in the deteriorating RS charts of the Home-Building and Building Materials sectors. Real estate is a basic commodity like food or clothes and is driven by the supply and demand of demographics.[4] Demand began to increase and the real estate market began to rise about 25 to 30 years after the birth of the first baby boomers. When the youngest end of that demographic group finished its buying, the demand pressures lifted and prices began to fall. A look at the historic picture of Housing Starts shows a 26-year declining trend (Figure 4–2) with the most recent cycle performing well below prior cycles; an effect perhaps of the major differences in demographic forces in play today which may now give the housing market a smaller customer base.

There will always be exceptions: efficient companies that may not profile the overall decline of their sectors, or that may be globally-exposed therefore not as prone to domestic demographic or economic pressures, or that have adjusted to the developing changes in their industry, or fill and flourish in domestic niche markets, provide new services, or supply the globally-exposed companies. Conversely, not every company in a growth area will automatically perform well depending on its fundamentals.

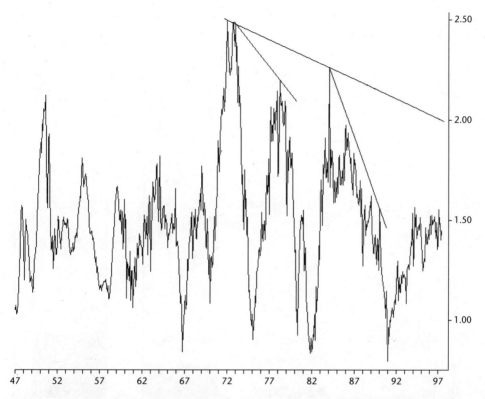

Figure 4–2 Housing Starts (Millions of Units). Chart created with Supercharts® by Omega Research, Inc.

Aging U.S. Population

The other side of the U.S. domestic demographic coin, in contrast to this waning demographic specter, is the baby-boom generation. It is the largest population this country has ever seen and it has created an inflationary bubble at each stage of its life: from Gerber baby foods, to educational facilities, to Levi's jeans, to the incredible housing markets in which real estate reached overvaluations no one believed possible. Today that same population is moving into its next phase of life, saving for retirement. And that is where we are seeing the inflationary bubble, not in the economy but in financial assets, where valuations are at huge premiums, again achieving levels no one believed possible.

The baby-boom generation is just beginning to turn 50 in the late 1990s and over the next 15 years will increase the number of Americans above the age of 65 by more than 20 percent to about 40 million[5] (Figure 4–3). In 2011, the first of the boomers turns 65, rising toward 70 million with life expectancy expanding toward 80.

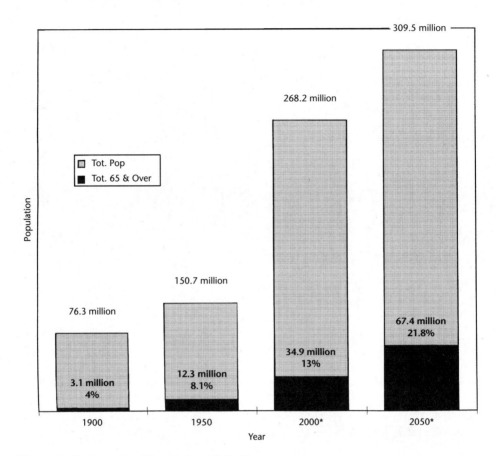

Figure 4–3 Growth of Population 65 & Over.

There may be myriad beneficiaries of their demands, including domestically-exposed stocks in their target areas such as leisure time activities (which conceptually should expand to include golf, cruise, dance, gaming, gardening, vitamin manufacturers, fitness, diet, self-help, home improvement, travel, and books on all of the above); aged-care facilities, services, (including home monitoring and health devices, and the inevitable, funeral services). Additional beneficiaries would include such sectors as Health Care, Cosmetics, Shoes, and Financials (banks, insurance, savings vehicles, mutual funds, brokerage houses). Several of these sectors also fall into the globally-exposed arena and should experience the benefits not only of the aging baby boomers, but also that of the consumer demands of global growth.

The charts (Figure 4–4) for which we have sectors representative of the potential beneficiaries of our aging demographic population, exhibit a rising price trend (top line) as well as a rising (or developing) relative strength trend (lower line): Financials, Footwear (formerly called Shoes), Health Care sectors, and Personal Care (formerly called Cosmetics) pictured later. We will look at the stock market implications in Chapter 5.

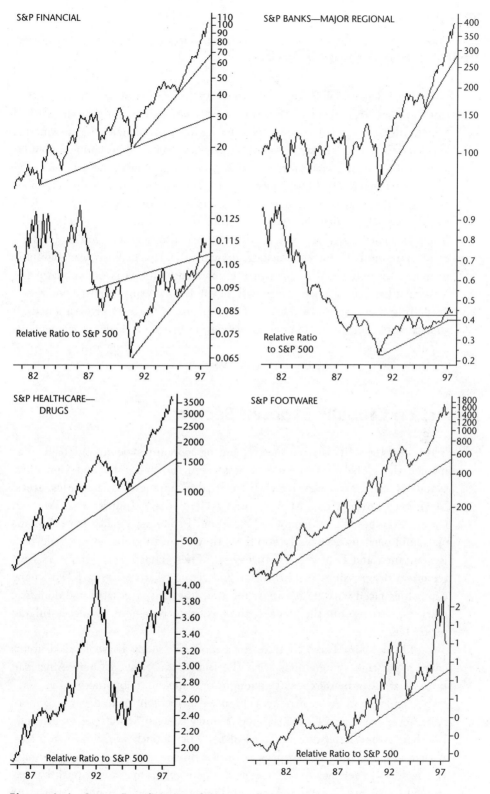

Figure 4–4 Sector Beneficiaries of Aging U.S. Demographics. Chart created with Supercharts® by Omega Research, Inc.

Rising Global Demographics

The global demographic picture is *completely different* from the developed nations. Today, 96 percent of the world's population lives outside the United States, with 80 percent in the emerging nations, particularly Latin America and Asia. Emerging market economies today have tremendous younger populations, with growing labor forces, rising purchasing power and a burgeoning consumer demand. (In Latin America, all age groups are increasing in number and the numbers are even larger in Asia, excluding Japan.[6]) Sixty percent of the world's population lives in Asia alone. Just as the demise of the more youth-oriented domestically-exposed U.S. stocks may also originate in the dramatically changing U.S. domestic demographic profile, this explosive demographic phenomenon being experienced in the emerging nations is undoubtedly the force that has been fueling the growth of the U.S. globally-exposed equities—propelling them, since 1993, into the forefront as the new growth stocks, a first-time phenomenon. The world has never experienced such a tremendous population—potentially some 4.6 billion people—emerging into a trend of consumerism as we have known in the West.

Impact on Globally-Exposed Sectors

The sectors benefiting from these emerging economies' demographic profiles include the globally-exposed U.S. equities of both Capital and Consumer Goods: Chemicals (selectively), Electrical Equipment, Electronics areas, Machinery-Diversified, Manufacturing-Diversified Industrials, Personal Care, Beverages-Non-Alcoholic, Household Products, Health Care, Financials, and perhaps eventually Foods (as they adapt to global ethnic palettes), Restaurants, and Footwear (Figure 4–5). These charts carry more positive technical progressions in both price and rising relative strength. For many companies faced with increasingly mature, stagnant, and saturated domestic markets, moving into the global realm has been tremendously successful and profitable.

Think about Personal Care for a moment: Many Personal Care items carry a prestige synonymous with the image-conscious affluent American lifestyle and can be inexpensive enough for someone in an emerging nation.[7] In particular, note Avon Products (Figure 4–6) which for four years or more has offered women in China the opportunity to earn $1,000 per month selling their cosmetic products instead of $100 per month working in factories. A year ago, a leading newspaper pictured a Burmese woman wading through rice paddies to sell her Avon Products. Their global marketing push has expanded to Malaysia, Thailand, the Philippines, Eastern Europe, Russia, and Japan. The chart is impressive in the size of its base, or accumulation phase,

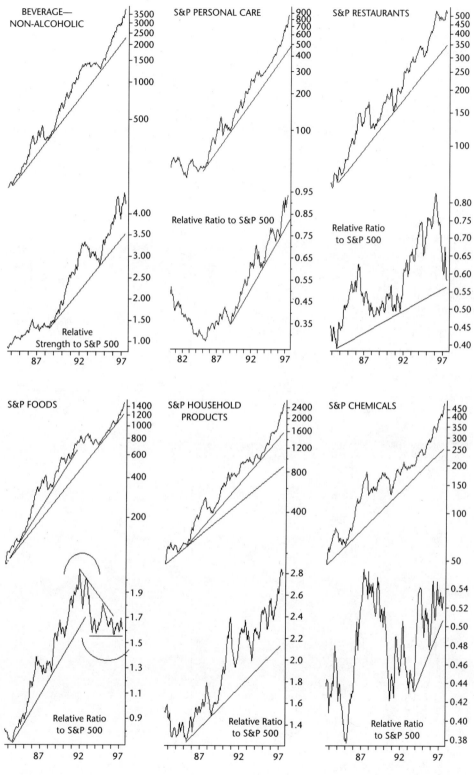

BEVERAGE—
NON-ALCOHOLIC

Relative
Strength to S&P 500

S&P PERSONAL CARE

Relative Ratio to S&P 500

S&P RESTAURANTS

Relative Ratio
to S&P 500

S&P FOODS

Relative Ratio
to S&P 500

S&P HOUSEHOLD
PRODUCTS

Relative Ratio
to S&P 500

S&P CHEMICALS

Relative Ratio
to S&P 500

(continued)

Figure 4–5 Globally-Exposed Sectors: Tremendous Demographic Implications. Chart created with Supercharts® by Omega Research, Inc.

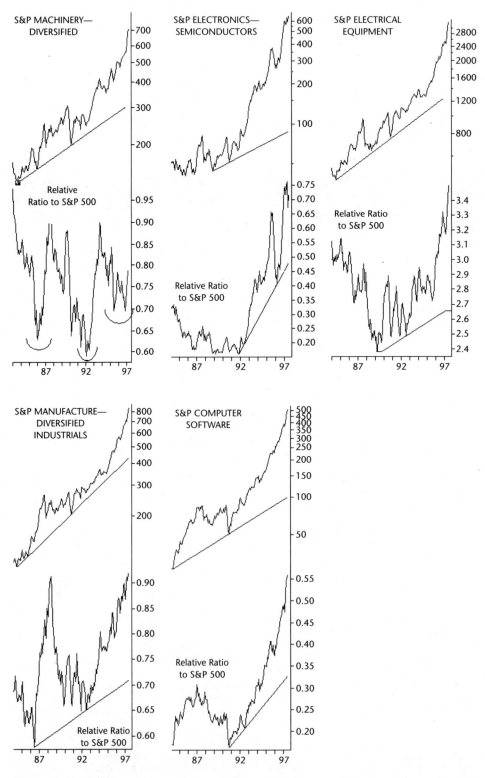

Figure 4–5   Continued.

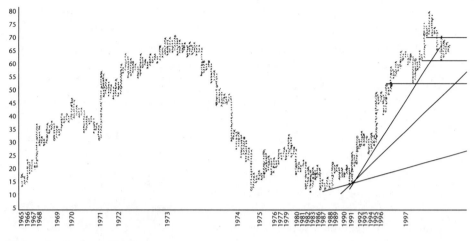

Figure 4–6   Avon Products.

which stretches for 17 years before the uptrend sustained. (Remember the adage, "the bigger the base . . . ") The implications of the emerging consumerism of these nations is tremendous. Never underestimate the vanity of woman, and now even man. There is Gillette, another global Personal Care company catering largely to men. The Personal Care sector has maintained strong price and RS uptrends.

In late 1992 and early 1993, the Foods group, after a 10-year trend of outperforming RS and a price gain of over 1400 percent (during that 1980s' Consumer Goods cycle of dominance), began to profile a negative diverging trend in its RS (refer to Figure 2–1). The price index rose to new highs, but the relative strength failed to do so. The actual breakdown occurred in 1993 and a decline in both price and RS was initiated, breaking a 12-year uptrend in price and a 9-year uptrend in RS. In 1994, a rally took hold that carried the group price to new highs, establishing a renewed uptrend progression. But the RS failed to improve enough to penetrate either the downtrend in force or its resistance level. For the first time in 5 years, the RS finally may be trying to turn up (Figure 4–5).

From the perspective of the globally-exposed U.S. stocks thesis, this group's relative performance had been an enigma and a disappointment, being the only globally-exposed Consumer Goods group that has not turned up to eliminate its RS divergence (as Beverages-Non-Alcoholic and Household Products and Personal Care did in early 1994). In 1995, I expressed this disappointment suggesting that, given diverse global cultures, it may be difficult to impose U.S. foods (cream of tomato soup) on ethnic cultures; that the food companies may be late-comers to the globally-exposed performance scene because they need to adapt to ethnic tastes in the various developing nations the way McDonald's did by introducing "veggie burgers" in India. One gentleman approached me after my presentation and said, "You know, Campbell Soup has created a 'cream of snake' soup for the Far East." Unsure if he were joking, I returned home to discover that not only is there a cream of snake soup, but according to Dow Jones news reports, a duck gizzard soup for China and exotic vegetable soups for Australia. Whether or not this conversion to local taste is what is responsible for the lag in the Foods group relative performance, what cannot be argued is that many of the Food stocks, including Campbell's, emerged from 4-year price consolidations to establish new all-time price highs throughout 1996 and 1997, and re-established uptrend progressions. The RS lag appears to have been due more to the cereal components in the group. But given the large global participation of the major food components, the Foods group RS may be preparing to join the global party.

Considering the demographics of the emerging nations, demand continues to be technically evidenced in the globally-exposed sectors, whose firms are expanding rapidly into these markets as their U.S. domestic demand wanes. No longer able to survive on domestic markets alone, increased overseas demand has become a driving force behind the growing success of many multinational U.S. companies.

But nothing moves in straight lines either up or down. The emerging consumer demand from Latin America (and the even larger one of Asia) will ebb and flow around a plethora of variables within their exploding younger populations. Purchasing power will take time to rise and expand the middle class and will undoubtedly do so faster in areas where women join, or have joined, the workforce. The savings rate, which is larger in Asia (22 percent versus 15 percent in Latin America), and with a few exceptions, reflective of a healthy middle class (less concentration of wealth in a small number of hands), is an important determinant in what products people will buy. A high savings rate that enables an economy to self-fuel its development and education (generally considered better in Asia), is also an important determinant in the character of the labor force and the level of sophistication of products a country can produce.[8]

Demographics and the Two-Tier Market Analysis

The differing demographics of developed and emerging nations stand out as a major driver of what I have been seeing in the charts, and the reason behind the emergence of this two-tier stock market phenomenon. Changes in the unfolding domestic demographic profile (of both the burgeoning baby-boomer needs and the relative, potential deceleration of selected domestic consumption over the next generation) have positive as well as less positive investment implications as they relate to each demographic force and its respective affected sectors in this two-tier phenomenon. The two-tier market character may continue for a time, in which economic growth may not come (initially) in domestic consumer demand for traditional products, nor from the sectors in which we have experienced growth in the past (domestic demand may be focused more on newer technological products). Rather, growth has been/will be fueled primarily by global demand (for both traditional consumer as well as newer technical products), benefiting the globally-exposed U.S. equities—the new growth stocks. On the domestic front, totally new spheres, and as we will discuss, frontiers for which we have (as yet) no industry group identification are and will continue replacing the old.

There may be an implicit element that our domestic environment may result in a two-layer economy: one track struggling with domestic dislocations from the ebbing demographic profile; simultaneously a second track propelled by and benefiting from multifaceted, global demographic trends, burgeoning consumer growth as purchasing power in emerging markets rises, for the products of our globally-exposed U.S. corporations (Capital Goods, Consumer Goods, and new technology). These forces have fueled and lifted our own domestic economy. We may be experiencing a two-tier economy that is resulting in sustained moderate growth, with stronger global industries offsetting the relative waning domestic industry areas.

The two-tier equity market phenomenon may well be a direct result of these evolving domestic and global demographic trends, which should keep these globally-exposed stock market leaders doing well for a long time in both their absolute and relative performance—interim contratrend pullbacks and corrections notwithstanding. The increasing global demographic picture of developing nations' economies, contrary to our relative waning domestic demographic profile, has the strength to fuel consumption and the United States is technologically and strategically poised to provide it; exports are rising (and contributing a growing percentage to our GDP, as we shall explore later). The world has never before experienced such a force of consumer demand.

Summary

In this chapter, we turned our attention to the first of several macrotrends that are shaping the current and future investment climate. We saw how changing demographic patterns, both in the United States and abroad, are favoring the globally-exposed stock sectors and undercutting the domestically-oriented sectors, leading to the two-tier stock market discussed in Chapter 2. While sectors like Home-Building and Retail-Department Stores have endured relative strength breakdowns, globally marketed sectors like Personal Care and Household Products have outperformed and will, no doubt, continue to do so. Other macrotrends will be scrutinized in subsequent chapters, including technology (Chapter 7), inflation (Chapter 10), and agriculture (Chapter 11).

Chapter

Demographics and the Stock Market

In this chapter, we will more closely assess the impact on the stock market of the demographic trends outlined in Chapter 4. The primary purpose of this chapter is to show the direct correlation between the arrival of the aging baby boomers on the shores of their preretirement years and the increasing flow of investment funds into the financial markets with a consequent rise in market values, notwithstanding adjustments for inflation. How far this rise can go and how long it can last is the next subject of inquiry. Assuming a continued low rate of inflation, several projections are made extending to 2004–2011 and beyond, and to Dow levels in excess of 9000. The emergence of financial assets as favored commodities of the savings-inclined aging boomers, is helping to fuel the rise in the market, even to inflationary levels.

A Demographically-Driven Savings/Investment Wave

Most economic studies suggest that as a population ages and members earn more, they tend to save more. This is what is happening in developed countries and is clearly being seen in the United States in our financial markets as more and more preretirement and savings dollars pour in.

As David Cork, Associate Director of Scotia McLeod, stated,

> The baby boom is approaching mid-life and is set to shift gears again. When we are young, we don't invest because we do not have excess capital available. In our middle years we enter our peak earning years. The baby boomers are now closing in on their peak investment years. The boomers, now faced with the prospect of middle age, appear to be entering the next phase in their lives. They are switching from spenders to savers (as a result, less demand for money, we have seen a powerful trend toward reduced interest rates). This leads boomers to their next step, planning for retirement.[1]

There are some interesting historical observations of the effects of an aging demographic profile on structural trends in the stock market. The analogy in Chapter 1 of the 1982-present bull market to the 1942–1966 bull trend has received some additional support from a demographic study (Figure 5–1) that suggests an underlying demographic trend similar to that of 1942–1966: a workforce, 35 years of age and older, rising as a percent of the total workforce. The assumption is that the older the workforce, the greater the productivity rate, the lower the inflation rate, and the higher the savings rate (affecting stocks and bonds). The last rising curve can be assumed to have begun in the 1940s and peaked with the topping of the 1942–1966 bull cycle. The current rising trend began in 1982, just as the present bull market commenced. The curve has been projected by the Bureau of Labor

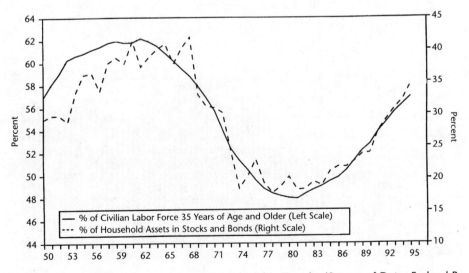

Figure 5–1   Portfolio Investment and Demographic Trends. (Source of Data: Federal Reserve Board, Bureau of Labor Statistics)

Statistics to peak in the year 2004, which implies a theoretical 7-year continuation of this cycle from 1997, contratrend moves notwithstanding.

The following studies add to the points of demographic interest. The Census Bureau has published an age distribution study (Figure 5–2) that graphically depicts the enormous population of baby boomers, who are already beginning to dominate the work cycle of the demographics study cited above. They are a force to be reckoned with, as we know, nearly doubling the population of the preceding generation. There is no precedent for how the flow of this group's financial assets could propel this bull cycle to heights about which we have only speculated. The demographic data certainly qualify as "exceptions to the norm." This aging demographic phenomenon could contribute greatly to the way in which the current secular equity bull market may differ from its predecessors in duration and magnitude.

A third perspective focuses on the relationship of number of births and the equity market adjusted for inflation (S&P 500/CPI); the underlying demographic impact of what could be called a "savings wave" as a population moves toward retirement concerns. Figure 5–2 goes back to 1910 showing the relative generation size based on number of births. Figure 5–3 shows the S&P 500/CPI effect those generations had (are having) on the stock market 43 to 46 years after birth; the demographic effect of the baby boomers at a point when they will presumably contribute not only higher productivity in the workforce (as in the study depicted in Figure 5–1), but also a higher savings rate. Figure 5–3 also implies the impact of the savings ability (much of it going to financial assets) of population cycles on the resulting rise in the equity markets, measured here by the S&P 500/CPI.

The babies of the late 1800s affected the bull market of the 1920s (43–46 years later), and the next generation 43–46 years after birth coincided

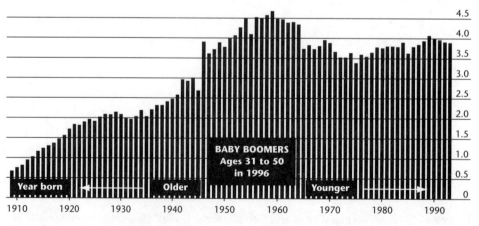

Figure 5–2 The Crowd Marches On. (Source of Data: U.S. Census Bureau)

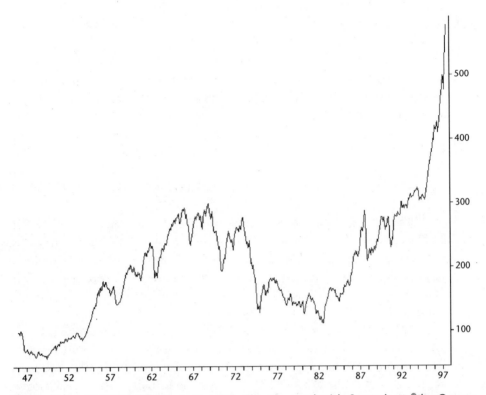

Figure 5-3   S&P 500 Relative to the CPI. Chart created with Supercharts® by Omega Research, Inc.

with and/or affected the depicted bull market in stocks of the 1940s into the 1960s (the century's second great bull market) (Figure 5–3); and the next generation (the baby boomers, nearly double the prior generation) projected 43–46 years later, coincides with and/or is now affecting the third major bull market of the twentieth century. The 1960s bull market outstripped the 1920s bull market rather proportionately to the population increase (Figure 5–2). Based on that, our bull market could generously outstrip that of the 1960s. The demographic profile of the labor force of Figure 5–1 suggests the year 2004 for our bull. More importantly, however, it defines the second half of the final great bull market of our century. One can also see at the right of Figure 5–2 the smaller upcoming generation and suggest that those youngsters may experience the next great bull market representing their generation's savings wave years after birth (peaking in the 2040s). It could perhaps be bigger than 1942–1966, but due to the smaller demographic profile, not quite as extensive as our bull market. (The one variable is immigration flow, which is now the second largest in our history,[2] many of them young and industrious.)

Future Impact of the Savings/Investment Wave

The 50-year history of the S&P 500/CPI (Figure 5–3) shows the beginning of the aforementioned uptrend as beginning in 1950, but in actuality it began in 1942 (not pictured). Assuming a continued low inflation rate for the foreseeable future (using a 2.5 percent annualized CPI), the projection portrayed by the S&P 500/CPI (the *real* S&P), argues for a further extension of this bull market from a temporal perspective (1960 birth peak plus 43–46 years), to around 2003–2006 just for the early wave of boomers, later for the full force and argues for much higher S&P price levels based on the 1920s and the 1950s–1960s occurrences.

The S&P 500/CPI rose 516.5 percent from a calculated level of 48.7 in 1942 to a high of approximately 299.9 in 1968. From a 1982 *real* low of 112.2, the S&P 500/CPI rose 270.5 percent to 415.6 in March 1996. Assuming a *real* advance at least equal to the 1942–1966 rise of 516.5 percent, the S&P 500/CPI on Figure 5–3 would rise to 691.6, which would translate into a nominal S&P 500 level of 1521.5 by the year 2010.

What might we project for the DJIA/CPI (the *real* Dow or the Dow adjusted for inflation) based on this exercise? We are gradually finding studies in our archives that incorporate data not only from the 1942–1966 bull market but also from the 1921–1929 bull market to help discover more analogies to the 1982 bull market. The historical record of the DJIA/CPI from 1914 through 1975 (Figure 5–4) shows that each of the three secular bull markets of the century reflects periods essentially free of a rampant inflationary trend. Some of the statistics we were able to utilize from the archive might be of interest:

- *Bull Market I: 1920–1929*
  The Dow/CPI rose from a December 1920 low at 33.8 to a September 1929 high at 216.3 for a gain of 539.5 percent.

- *Bull Market II: 1942–1966*
  From an April 1942 low at 56.6 to a January 1966 high at 306.4, the Dow/CPI saw a rise of 441.7 percent.

- *Bull Market III: 1982–Present*
  From a *real* Dow August 1982 low at 78.0, if the Dow/CPI were eventually to mirror the 1942–1966 gain of 441.7 percent, it would reach 422.6 on the Constant-Dollar Dow scale; if it rose 539.5 percent, it would reach 498.9. Translating this into actual, or nominal, DJIA points (using the 2.5 percent CPI assumption), we could posit a Dow reading of 9486 to 11198 by the year 2010.

Some of the these projections seem uncanny or "far fetched." Additionally looking at the Dow/CPI, the readings since late 1995 have exceeded both

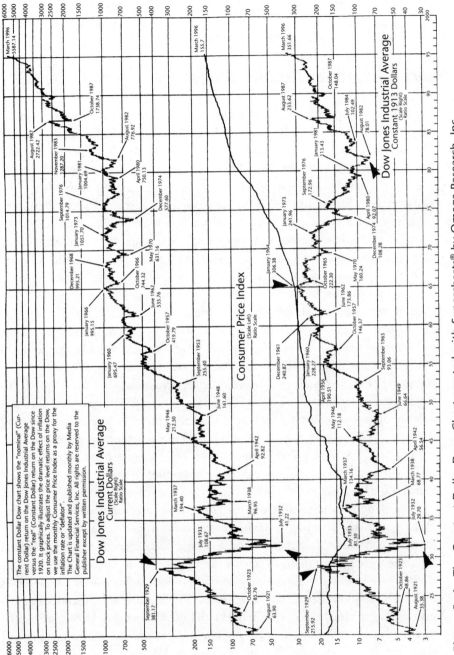

The constant Dollar Dow chart shows the "nominal" (Current Dollar) return on the Dow Jones Industrial Average versus the "real" (Constant Dollar) return on the Dow since 1920. It graphically illustrates the dramatic effect of inflation on stock prices. To adjust the price level returns on the Dow, we use the monthly Consumer Price Index as a proxy for the inflation rate or "deflator".

The Chart is updated and published monthly by Media General Financial Services, Inc. All rights are reserved to the publisher except by written permission.

Dow Jones Industrial Average
Current Dollars
(Scale Right)
Ratio Scale

Consumer Price Index
(Scale Left)
Ratio Scale

Dow Jones Industrial Average
Constant 1913 Dollars
(Scale Right)
Ratio Scale

Figure 5–4 The Constant Dollar Dow. Chart created with Supercharts® by Omega Research, Inc.

the 1966 and 1929 peaks, impressive breakouts which, from a technical perspective, continue to suggest higher equity levels and benign inflation.

Financial Assets as Commodities

Some of the potential implications of our aging demographic profile have been examined in these last few studies. Demographics also influence the movements of money: the young (aged 25–34) borrow and spend; the older (aged 50 plus) save. We have noted that the enormous size of the boomers increased the supply and demand impact on every segment of their life course, and created a demand for money that pushed interest rates and inflation to high levels in this country.[3] The result was an enormous increase in demand for products and businesses accommodating each stage. Incredible overvaluations occurred in many of the hard assets along the way, including housing, gold, and art, pushing up prices and interest rates in response to that demand for money, into an inflationary wave, well beyond any level imaginable by the prior generation. When demand for a commodity increases faster than supply, its price rises, and can, if it rises excessively, create an inflationary trend or bubble in that asset. (On the flip side, when demand decreases prices fall.) Thus the price of many stocks may well outpace the earnings (even the global earnings) of the company in this cycle. Stock prices may, in the course of this impending inflationary bubble in financial assets, reflect more the enormous baby-boom savings demand for stocks than the ability of a company to grow.[4] The financial markets, now responding to these same forces, should be considered, like any hard assets of in-demand quantity of a huge population, as nothing more than a basic commodity[5] responding to the current supply and demand of this large generation.

Moving into preretirement planning, these boomers are saving more. With a smaller upcoming generation, one could assume a lesser demand for money for household formation and a proportionate decline in the demand for money (borrowing). If we have a larger population entering the savings years, again less demand for money. With less need to borrow, more money is looking at fewer available saving vehicles. These alone should contribute to lower interest rates (the cost of money) and debt levels should decline, as the savers compete to lend to a smaller upcoming generation.[6] With more savers than spenders the demand for money should fall, keeping interest rates down for years to come.

As interest rates and inflation are falling in the United States, the money that is not being borrowed needs a savings vehicle. Financial assets, including the stock market, are the recipients of this tremendous demand and are rising as a result, as the boomers funnel larger and larger amounts of money into a relatively finite number of stocks and bonds. The 1990s are seeing the advance signal of this shift with the rapid rise in the price of stocks and bonds, in the daily stock volume, and the enormous proliferation of mutual funds, as those savings are just beginning to build and will continue for over a decade. Just recall the $800 billion-plus still parked in U.S. money market funds. The only place we are feeling inflation is in financial assets—not in the economy at large.

The study of demographics as a predictable quantity—its direction, changes, pressures, and ultimately its effect on each stage of life, the forces of supply and demand that create its directions, and trends—seems critical to the underlying understanding of economics cycles, their conformity and non-conformity to history, as well as the effect on the evolution of macro stock market cycles.

Continuing Rise Fueled by Mounting Savings

Just as our U.S. globally-exposed equity thesis argues for higher stock prices based on the developing nations' economic expansion, these demographic studies appear to support the liquidity argument that a U.S. population, nearly double that of the last great bull market, could contribute to a continued rise in stock prices as the tremendous influx of baby-boomer savings continues into financial assets. A tremendous portion would go to those globally-exposed out-performing stocks, creating apparent overvaluation. The front-end boomers are just turning 50, and generally can be expected to continue to accumulate financial assets until about age 68 (around the year 2014).

Not surprisingly, the profile of financial assets is extremely positive from a technical perspective. Looking at the Financial sector we can make a few observations. First, that the Financial stocks have been in an absolute price uptrend for many years, but until 1992 they were also in an extended trend of underperformance (relative strength to the S&P 500). Since 1992, however, the rally and subsequent neutral performance (in both price and RS) was beginning to come to life (Figure 5–5). The price broke out to a new 6-year high in 1992 and was consolidating; the relative strength had traced out a pattern suggestive of an inverse head-and-shoulders pattern, implying that much higher levels may be at hand. Figure 4–4 shows the follow-through took a couple of more years, but now there is a clear definition of that 9-year base in relative strength. While the price continues to rise, the more important structural message is that the RS progression is just emerging from a 9-year basing configuration which suggests that financial assets may still be in the early stage of what could become a sustained trend of out-performance (contratrend moves notwithstanding).

There is a similar RS pattern for the individual Banking sectors within the financial complex (refer to Figure 4–4), with the added observation that

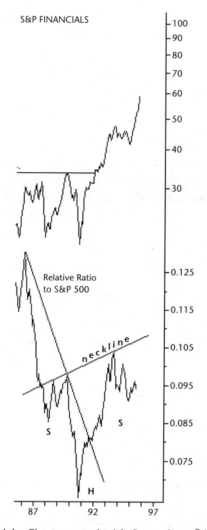

Figure 5–5   S&P Financials. Chart created with Supercharts® by Omega Research, Inc.

the price of the Banks—Major Regional group has also penetrated a 20-year resistance level. All these progressions imply further appreciation is possible in these sectors in the years to come.

In a 1996 study, Alan Shaw suggested that the U.S. financial equity sectors may well be in the midst of a major bull market run.[7] By comparison, this possibility might be related to the major uptrends that profiled the Consumer Goods sectors in the 1980s and in particular, looks like the major decision that the Food group made in 1982, when its price broke out from about 20 years of consolidation, advancing some 1400 percent over 10 years (Figure 5–6). What is of even greater importance is the observation from Figure 4–4 that the Financial group's RS line may only be in the process of developing a

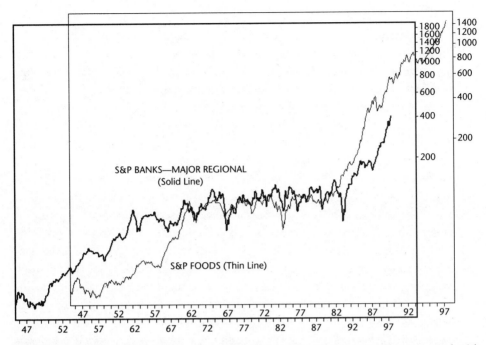

Figure 5–6   S&P Banks—Major Regional Compared to S&P Foods. Chart created with Supercharts® by Omega Research, Inc.

secondary upleg, similar to its price at the top. Along with other interest rate-sensitive equity areas, the financials have responded quite positively to the easing of interest rates, particularly on the long end.

Duration of the Financial Sector Uptrend

It appears that demand/inflation in the "commodities of youth" has ended and may have moved on to the demand/inflation of the traditional "commodity of aging": financial assets, including the stock market. PE ratios may become out of sync because, like any asset which finds itself in an inflationary trend of demand, it may overcome reasonable values as price may outpace companies' respective earnings. On the other hand, this time the emerging nations' demographic demand for the globally-exposed U.S. companies' products may allow valuations to keep pace with money flow for longer than would ordinarily have been thought imaginable, keeping valuations reasonable for a longer period.

Japan is the most rapidly aging country today and most disadvantaged by the imbalance of the structural change in demographics of developed nations with a major decline in their 10- to 19-year-old age group. Most of Japan's population growth is now among those 50 to 80.[8] By 2025, Japan is expected to be one of the oldest nations on the globe with over 25 percent of its population older than 65.[9] The United States still has it boomers growing in the 40 to 59 range. A similar aging demographic profile to ours existed in Japan about a decade prior to our own and, as we have seen, may have been similarly reflected in its soaring stock market trend at that time. Today, Japan's profile may reflect the other side of the demographic mountain.

There will come, we can be sure, an eventual end to this cycle of U.S. financial inflation. But the demographic studies suggest that may not begin until 2004–2010 when the front end of the baby boomers will begin to retire, or further to 2014, when, at age 68 they are calculated to cease acquiring financial assets. There should be at least a decade of continued savings inflow until the bulk of the baby boomers achieve retirement age—at which point money should slowly withdraw from equities and financial asset savings vehicles, including retirement funds and pensions. These demographic influences on the movements of money may then see the stock market slowly drift back to its uninflated value levels. The face of retirement is changing and is a slow process. This decline in savings and this shift of demand may experience variations resulting from any changes that might be made to Social Security age qualification, part-work/part-retirement arrangements, as well as a possible older retirement age as people live and work longer.

The other side of the mountain following the 1929 and 1966 peaks saw quite a market contraction, in Figure 5–4 (in line with the demographic contraction). But our "other side of the mountain" appears different. The valley is not as deep (Figure 5–2) suggesting the decline—however it manifests—may also be different, perhaps more buoyant. Demography being a fluid evolution, it must also be noted that based on current births consisting of late parenting boomers, current 20's babies, and male boomers' second family births—and immigration—the population saving for retirement may increase directly on top of the prior savings wave. (One might add to this the growth of emerging nation populations' middle class needing to save as they age—and our market still the most liquid—the mid-twenty-first century bull experience may be awesome. But it will be for other technical analysts to evaluate.)

But any outflow of money will not be without its technical warning signs. Another glance at the 50-year A-D line (refer to Figure 1–3) shows a 9-year topping process that took place into the 1966 bull market peak, giving plenty of advance signals to the investing community. The study of technical analysis should capture the deterioration and the patterns of distribution (supply) in both price and relative strength performance in individual stocks, sectors, and ultimately in the market indicators, just as it has captured the advance notice of improving stocks, sectors, and evidence of today's bull market. All we need do is follow the warning signals as those trends shift from positive to neutral to negative.

For dyed-in-the-wool skeptics, may I point out the 1929 period on the chart. The A-D line shows a clear 2- to 3-year negative divergence as it declines simultaneously with the rising DJIA price of the late 1920s. We would have had ample warning of deteriorating conditions. We also must remember that new opportunities will evolve even into market declines, because there are always stocks to buy in a bear market, just as there are always stocks to sell in a bull market. Many readers may recall Digital Equipment's 1980s–1990s price progression from a price of 200 to 19 during the greatest bull market of this century (Figure 5–7).

One interesting observation regarding the stock market and the performance of the financial sector should give some comfort as an early warning system to the eventual demise of this secular bull market: In the recorded history of the S&P 500 since 1970, the stock market has never experienced a bear market decline when the financials have been in a rising trend. In other words, the financials have generally led the stock market down (Figure 5–8). This also is reflected by the NYSE cumulative A-D line which, with 40 percent of its issues representing financial vehicles (interest rate sensitive issues, bank stocks, bond funds, and preferred stocks), has always (with the exception of 1977 that makes the rule) since its 1927 origin, given a 4- to 9-months advance notice of an impending severe stock market decline. It has done so by posting a negative divergence progression: As the markets move higher, the A-D line makes lower peaks, failing to confirm the move. This is usually the result of the 40 percent interest rate bias that "sniffs" out potential stock market problems (rising interest rates in particular) in advance, warning that the internal market statistics are weakening under the surface even as the stock market moves to new high levels.

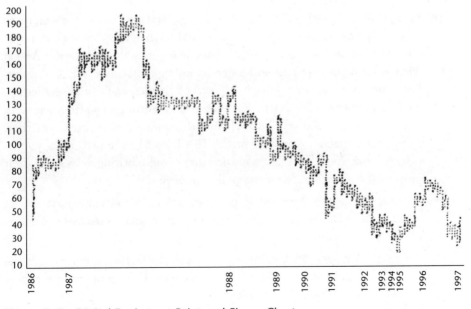

Figure 5–7   Digital Equipment Point-and-Figure Chart.

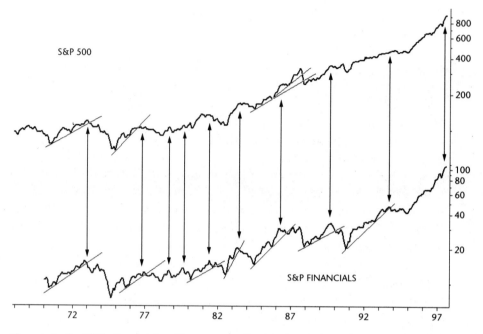

Figure 5-8 S&P Financials. Chart created with Supercharts® by Omega Research, Inc.

Viewing our demographic themes together: The United States, for the first time ever, is experiencing simultaneously the effects of three contemporaneous demographic trend tiers.

- First, the dwindling domestic upcoming generation that may continue to negatively impact consumption and related business sectors such as housing and retailers. To whom will the baby boomers sell their homes? And at what price? A home may no longer be an appreciating asset. The baby-boom supply of housing will greatly exceed the demand of the smaller upcoming generation for existing homes at least through the first decade of the twenty-first century.[10] To whom will commercial realtors rent their aging office space and at what price? To whom will the expanding youth-oriented fast-food franchises, music stores, and clothing stores sell their products? And in what quantity and at what price?

- Second, the largest-ever aging population will bring the impact of its tremendous demand to other domestic sectors and businesses, such as Health Care and Financial Assets.

- Third, the largest global younger generation the world has ever seen is entering some kind of consumerist style economy. How could we not expect things to be different this time?

Summary

This chapter highlighted the source of much of the new investment money that has entered and lifted the stock market in recent years as baby boomers have evolved from their high-spending patterns to retirement-conscious acquisition of financial assets. The stock market, in particular, has seen a decisive boost in valuation. This commodification of financial products will continue to support increased levels in the Financial sectors as boomers address retirement concerns over the next 15 years or more. In fact, the relative strength charts reviewed in this chapter indicate that the period of outperformance by the Financial sectors may still be in its early stages. Yet, a wary eye should be kept on certain technical warning signs for advance notice of any major decline. (Africa should be the next demographic population to emerge into the consumer camp in about a decade, and it may provide yet the next global consumer boom. Today 46 percent of its population is only 15 years old.)

Chapter

The Long-Wave Cycle: A Brief Consideration

A macrofocus of today's stock market and economic trend also may need to include a brief consideration of another, larger, technical, and often controversial historical perspective relating to the Kondratieff Long-Wave Economic Cycle: how equity markets have functioned against the backdrop of that long-wave cycle, and how crosscurrents and frustrations that are continuing to occur in the intermarket arena today may be explained, and what some longer-term, more structural charts may be telling us. Essentially, if the Kondratieff long-wave cycle were extended to the twenty-first century, what might/should be our expectations?

Background of Kondratieff

Nikolai Dmitrievich Kondratieff was born in Russia in 1892 but little more is known of his life until age 25 when he was Russian Deputy Minister of Food in the provisional government toward the end of World War I. His education and intelligence no doubt helped him survive political upheavals, and by 1920 he founded (and directed until 1928) the Moscow Business Conditions Institute. Involved with the Bolshevik elite, he drafted the Soviet 5-year agricultural plan for Lenin's "New Economic Policy," a form of internal free trade that was too moderate for the more doctrinaire Marxists whose influence increased following Lenin's death in 1924.

Out of step with Stalin's politics, Kondratieff turned to academia, not a particularly safe place to be at the time. He became controversial between 1925–1928, because of his research in international economic fluctuations and commodity cycles. He wrote his most influential work, *The Major Economic Cycles*, in 1925, and in 1926 was presented to the Economics Institute of the Russian Association of Social Science Research Institute.

Kondratieff identified the long-wave economic cycle, suggesting that capitalist economies self-correct and renew; that economic cycles undergo a major rise and fall lasting 48 to 60 years. The rising curve was associated with business expansion, inflation, and increasing prosperity; the falling curve with economic contraction, deflation, and a falling standard of living. He concluded that " . . . as long as the principles of the capitalist economy are conserved, each new cycle follows its predecessor with the same regularity with which the different phases succeed each other." Kondratieff was a socialist but also a realist and objective scientist with an intellectual integrity that prevented him from retracting his work even in face of Stalin's oppression of intellectual and scientific discourse. This self-renewing view of capitalism in a Marxist society preaching the collapse of capitalism amounted to heresy. Kondratieff was sent to Siberia in 1930, where he died, unrecognized for his great work.[1]

It wasn't until 1939, when the economist Joseph Schumpeter returned the long-wave cycle to public prominence in his publication of *Business Cycles*, acknowledging that it was Kondratieff who "brought the phenomenon (of long cycles) fully before the scientific community and who systematically analyzed all the material available to him on the assumption of the presence of the long wave, characteristic of the capital process."[2] Schumpeter described long-wave cycles as "gales of creative destruction" as new industry sweeps away the old, and new technology fuels the upsurge and creates new job opportunities. Historic waves include:

- 1780s–1840s Steam power of the industrial revolution.
- 1840s–1890s Railways.
- 1890s–1930s Electric power.
- 1930s–1980s Automobiles.
- 1980s–Present Information and Communication (perhaps the most pervasive and invasive technology ever).

Because Kondratieff was not available to elucidate his own thoughts, all translations and treatises on the subject are interpretations. Kondratieff didn't comment as to the cause of the long wave, suggesting only a relation to the long-term investment cycles linked to replacement of capital equipment like factories.[3]

Since 1939, when his long-wave theory was re-examined, economists have argued about his identification of these economic cycles, attributing the professional doubt over the long wave to the lack of theory as to how such fluctuations could occur. There is apparently agreement that the long-wave cycle includes an over-building in capital sectors and over-expansion that ultimately ends in depression, as industrial plants wear out and a new building era emerges.[4]

How Does the Long Wave Arise?/Implications

The self-reinforcing process of the long-wave expansion is powered by the economic impetus of consumer demand for goods. As demand surges, this leads to economic expansion since capacity is not available to meet demand. With this, low unemployment, rising real wages, and low real interest rates prevail in the rising curve of the long wave.

As production increases, demand increases, more investment is put into growth; debt and optimism rise—which eventually leads to excess, exacerbated by credit extension, inflation, and a debt surge. Eventually over-capacity results as the economy over-builds. Investment opportunities diminish, speculation replaces investment and feeds more inflation, and the long wave crests. As excess capacity grows, imbalances appear and demand erodes, yielding more excess capacity which depresses demand and prices. Unemployment rises, real wages falter, and price wars develop leading to deflation; business failures and defaults follow; and the long-wave down cycle is in force as these imbalances unwind and correct. As prices decline, inflation abates and investment spending is depressed during the downwave. An increase in debtors can lead to bank failures; as prices fall more, increasing liquidation causes the speculative bubble to burst.

Historically, each long-wave downturn has been different and does not imply a 1929-style crash. Long-wave downturns historically also have been periods in which intense technological innovation occurs. The new and superior technologies revolutionize the old technologies and are often incompatible with them. Because significant stress remains in the economy during the downwave, focus is not yet centered on, and cannot incorporate, these innovations. But the stage is set for the next long-wave expansion and, as the downwave troughs, the economy adjusts and absorbs the imbalances. A time of tremendous opportunity emerges as the new technologies come to the fore and power a new economic horizon and a new upwave begins, driving a fresh new economic cycle.[5]

Related to Other Macrotrends

We have been experiencing exactly this new upwave and its accompanying new technology since the 1980s. There is a good chance the economy's potential real growth rate and productivity could increase for the first time since the 1950s and 1960s. The strength and power of a new long-wave upsurge implies that cyclical economic downturns should be milder than average. We have been experiencing this phenomenon as elusive recessions baffle economic seers. Recessions of the 1950s and 1960s were much less severe than those of the 1970s and early 1980s. Recessions during the upwave into the mid-1920s were also less severe than during the subsequent downwave. There also can be a tendency to underestimate the subsequent rebound and the market should stay at historically high valuations. The tendency should be for the long-run performance of the economy and the corporate sector to exceed expectations but this does not rule out sharp stock market corrections to restore value.[6]

The long-wave concept does intermingle with, and may give support to, demographic studies and other macrotrends discussed later in Part Two, relative to the great bull markets of the century. For instance, as we will see in this chapter, the consumer demand which stokes the furnace of a long-wave expansion can be tied to a global demographic profile with tremendous growth potential for world trade, particularly given declining trade barriers. The new long wave is rising on the arc of a new technological information age. When viewed in its relationship to our other macrotrends the long wave can be seen in a much less threatening way. The United States is well-poised within all of these trends to successfully weather the rise and the fall of Kondratieff's cycle.

Long Wave Compared to the DJIA

Reflecting on these long-wave characteristics, perhaps we should focus on several points relative to the DJIA, keeping in mind that the accompanying schematic long-wave chart does not take into account the flexibility of the cycles to be shorter toward 48 years, or longer, toward 60 years; nor does it allow for time variability at crests and troughs (Figure 6–1).

I have overlaid a stock market (DJIA) rise and fall on the abstract long-wave chart. Due to its multidecade duration, we do not have a statistically-large sampling of long waves (only three and-one-half with stock market history) to establish the importance, or lack, of an exact correlation between a particular portion or direction (upwave, downwave, peak, or trough) of the wave and the contemporaneous equity bull market experiences. The pertinent

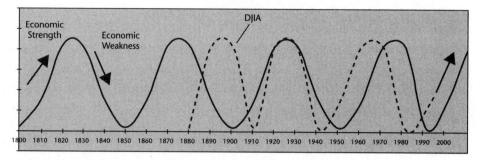

Figure 6–1   Kondratieff's Wave.

point should be that each long wave has experienced a participant secular bull market cycle.

The first important observation here is that both completed secular bull markets of the twentieth century, 1921–1929 and 1942–1966, participated in the waves of their respective Kondratieff cycles (and interestingly, so did the 1870–1890 bull market); further, that 1982–present could be considered a completely new secular bull cycle participating in yet another Kondratieff 48- to 60-year economic cycle, suggesting the validity of the powerful equity market advance we have been experiencing, and also (as suggested previously) that it could continue for years to come.

Secondly, that there is always a major technological revolution in play that drives a new cycle, as there is again today in information and communications.

Thirdly, there is an important global element to the long waves. The up-waves have occurred at times of expanding world trade, again similar, though possibly to a much greater extent today with economic expansion powered this time by the enormity of developing nations. The world has never seem such an enormity of people (with the iron curtain gone and China more open to trade) available for consumption. While the huge transition to a global economy cannot be expected to be without its problems, overall the trend is bullish for growth. U.S. exports have tended to perform better during upwaves than downwaves. The global competition should speed the gains in efficiency, productivity, and ever-new technology. The United States today is the global leader on all these fronts.

Fourthly, the concept "Capitalist Economy" may be key. The developing nations are only beginning their "capitalist-style," or "consumerist-style" economies, so the world's largest population ever is being incorporated into a (long-wave) capitalist-style economic cycle for the first time in history. This is likely to have a major influence on molding the extension and magnitude of both this economic cycle and this secular bull market in their response to such global growth.

A final point is that all downwaves have been different and therefore do not imply a 1930s-style depression. Analyses of the long downwave associated with the 1966 equity market peak had predicted both: (1) depression in the early to mid-1970s;[7] and (reading Kondratieff with his intended flexibility one could have expected) (2) a deflationary spiral 48 to 60 years after 1929, or between 1977 and 1989.[8] Some market observers contend that the last secular bear market decline from the bull market peak of 1966 ended with the low of 1974–1975 (Figure 5–4). Actually, however, the dates January 1967 to August 1982 (not 1974–1975) encompass the years better defining the expected Kondratieff downwave period. It could indeed be argued that those additional years, 1974–1982 (accompanied by rising interest rates and inflation) did, in fact, continue a prolonged downturn and thereby extended the bear market in real terms for the Dow (DJIA/CPI) for a real loss of 74.5 percent (which is comparable to the 1920s actual loss of 89.19 percent, or the then DJIA/CPI loss of 86.27 percent accompanying the downwave of that prior cycle).

Certainly, if one were to have experienced a 75 percent attrition in one's assets it would have felt like a depression. Technical analyst Alan Shaw has defined this possible phenomenon in his presentations over the last decade. It has also been expressed in print as an extended bear market in real terms, equivalent to that of the 1930s' depression.[9] In essence, one could suggest that the downwave for the last Kondratieff long-wave cycle has already experienced its "depression" (as noted by the Dow/CPI data above) and has indeed manifested itself quite differently from the depression of the 1930s. (One could also suggest that it is much too soon to have another "big one"—or long-term equity market decline.)

This interpretation also establishes 1982 (not 1974, as some suggest) as the origin of, and may identify the 1982–present secular bull market as associated with, the emergence of a new Kondratieff long-wave cycle which will carry into the twenty-first century. The global versus domestic U.S. equity, two-tier characteristics that we have attributed to this stock market environment may also affect the evolution of this long wave.

Are Demographics Driving the Long Wave?

In looking for a possible origin of the long-wave cycle, the consideration of demographics—which essentially suggests that consumer demand drives the economic cycle—comes to the fore. Consumer spending normally leads industrial production. When consumer spending declines, industrial production follows suit. When consumer spending picks up, so too does industrial production, which in turn leads capital spending as capacity is increased to accommodate consumer demand.[10] It is, therefore, more than possible that demographics may be the underlying logic behind Kondratieff's 48- to 60-year life cycle for the long wave, which parallels and fits the productive life cycle of man, and would seem to be basic to economic thinking. Demographics (consumer demand) as a major driver for the economy not only contributes to, but also, as we have discussed, may be the primary determinant of the economic cycle and may explain the reasons for the existence of the long-wave phenomenon.

This consumer demand for goods (the major economic driver) might allow an interesting deduction, when juxtaposed to the Kondratieff long-wave economic studies and may fit the Greek form of logic, called the syllogism, to allow the projection of the actual *causation* of the long-wave cycle. Concept:

$$\text{If } A=B \text{ and } B=C, \text{ then } A=C.$$

In other words:

> If demographics (consumer demand) (A) determines (=) the economy (B), and
> if the economy (B) leads (=) the long wave (C), then
> demographics (A) must therefore lead (be the driver of) (=) the long-wave cycle (C).

If we accept the concept, this completely new Kondratieff long-wave cycle may also need to be revisited in terms of its expectations and implications. For the first time in history, this long wave may well function differently, not only as a result of these new technologies and applications leading to the initiation of an entirely new technological long-wave cycle and the dynamics of its force, but also because of the enormous, never before experienced global demand in what is now a much more interconnected and more integrated world.

The declining relative domestic demographic trend of the United States (and other developed nations) alone may not mold this long wave. It may instead overlap, interplay, blend with, the cycles of the developing nations. The character of this long-wave cycle may be dynamically altered with an extension of this bull market, by virtue not only of our demographic profile, but also by this huge consumer awakening of the world's largest participant population (expected to double in 40 years) who have never before been incorporated into a capitalist-style, consumer-demand-driven economic growth cycle. This should continue to have a beneficial effect on the globally-exposed U.S. equities for years. If the 48- to 60-year long-wave economic cycle is in fact reflective of the working life cycle of man, one must also consider what effect an extension of the retirement age in the United States might cause in perhaps also extending the long-wave parameter beyond 60 years—another development economists and cycle market watchers might need to take into the concept of how things may function differently.

Summary

In this chapter, we have seen how an obscure Soviet economist in the 1920s produced an important interpretation of the capitalist business cycle that offers us guidance about the future of today's bull market. The appearance of major new technology has characterized each long-wave cycle as has a demographic surge with an accompanying increase in consumer demand for the new goods. Although the long-wave expansions and contractions have paralleled the rise and slowing of bull markets, the long-wave cycle does not necessarily foreshadow a 1929-style market collapse and a 1930s-style depression. If, for instance, the bear market decline from the bull market peak of 1966 is adjusted for inflation, there was a prolonged downturn concluding in 1982. Working with that date as the commencement of a new long-wave cycle one can project, given the usual 48- to 60-year duration of a cycle, that the current bull market may have a considerable length of time yet to run.

Chapter

The New Technological Era: Observations and Conceptual Thoughts

This chapter will explore the tremendous impact new technology has already had, and will continue to have, on the economy and the consumer and industrial marketplaces. The equally important effect of new technology on the financial market will be considered in the next chapter. Of all the major forces and trends affecting today's investment possibilities, the immediate and relentless changes wrought by *this* new technology are, along with demographics, of primary significance.

We will see that new technology means, more than anything else, *information technology* which creates smart products that boost efficiency and productivity, eliminating "old-tech" jobs along the way. As a result, corporate profitability has been directly bolstered and the retail marketplace has been transformed as consumers respond to the greater capabilities of the new products. New applications become available on an almost daily basis for a variety of uses like the Internet, agriculture, and biomedicine. So rapidly does each new wave of smarter products arrive, that obsolescence seems to have become an almost daily event. The future will belong to those companies that are constantly improving their products and developing new ones.

New Information Technology Is "High-Tech"

Today we are witnessing a new era of technology in information and communication, that is at the heart of, or drives, each new long-wave cycle. But there is a major difference that needs to be reflected on: This is a totally unique technological era with *at least* one significant differing characteristic.

Today's new technological leadership is "high-tech"—an ongoing flow of rarefied information and communication innovations imbued with high-precision, cost-cutting efficiencies that, for the first time ever, is *not* as capital intensive, *not* as labor intensive, *not* as energy intensive, and *not* as industrial as the developed nations of the twentieth century have known heavy industry to be. It is also a wave that has been "*un*employing" people in the traditional industries ("low-tech" or "old-tech") as a result of the new technological advances, as Figure 7–1 shows occurring until late 1996.

It may be an industry cycle unlike any this century has ever known. The result may increase some domestic unsettlement (already presaged by the upcoming new relative demographic profile), and may continue to do so in an evolving fashion over the years. Hence, perhaps a good deal of the confusion in week-to-week domestic economic reports and the equity

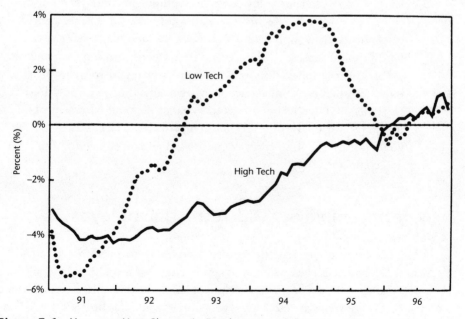

Figure 7–1   Year-over-Year Change in Employment High-Tech versus Low-Tech.

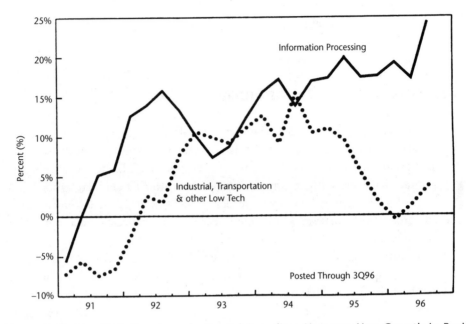

Figure 7–2   Low-Tech Slowdown in Capital Spending: Year-over-Year Growth in Business Equipment Outlays.

market's responses can be attributed to this new high-tech reality (Figure 7–2). As an article in *Business Week* put it:

> In fact, the sharpest slowdown in equipment outlays . . . occurred in low-tech categories, such as industrial machinery and transportation equipment, which make up about 60 percent of hardware purchases. . . . High-tech investment in computers and other information-processing hardware continued to grow at a rapid 19.4 percent annual pace. Low-tech spending is responding to traditional cyclical depressants: weaker demand, slower profits, and lower operating rates. . . . High-tech outlays . . . are driven more by the long-term trend toward enhanced productivity and competitiveness.[1]

"New-Tech" Employs; "Old-Tech" Unemploys

While our corporate restructuring may continue to be harsh, its accomplishment will likely be accelerated by the new technological applications and result in the creation of as-yet-unseen technological industries. By contrast, these "new-tech" industries are employing people at a rapid rate. In 1995–1996, New York City alone reported 4,200 new companies employing people in Web and digital technology.[2] California reported some 57,000 new companies. So when we get simultaneous, seemingly conflicting employment reports as we did in July 1995 of rising *un*employment and rising *new* employment, perhaps it shouldn't be so baffling. There's yet another two-tier phenomenon manifesting itself in the economy, this time in employment—an unemploying "old-tech" tier and an employing "new-tech" tier.

An awareness of the forces of a beginning long-wave technological cycle and a study of history should help us understand the phenomenon of the dislocations of change between one period and another. Historic evidence shows that employment and real income in developed nations has risen continuously due to technological change; job loss is eventually offset by job gains and employment ultimately grows. In a new-tech era, it's the types of jobs that change—not volume—and over the long-term, as new industries are created, the fresh demand for new products and more output creates even more jobs than before. There are always winners and losers but overall every technological revolution has generated as many and more jobs as it destroys, many better paid, which in the long run are the main source of higher living standards. Technology today is more pervasive than in previous cycles and is introduced faster, so more jobs may be lost with less time to retrain, but the demand-generating effects should be stronger.[3] There has already been such a shortage of top software developers that wage wars exist in this new-tech tier; and we have already survived enormous domestic job loss dislocations without a deep recession.

Increased utilization of out-sourcing both eliminates jobs in one company and creates them in others. New employment in start-up companies (many by women and aspiring immigrating people) has been greater than in larger companies. Small business today (over 30 percent owned by women), is the third largest economy in the world after the United States and Japan and is growing faster than it ever has, many started with just phone, fax, and PC, exemplifying the low capital intensity resulting from the new age of networked intelligence. Many of these companies have as few as 50 employees.[4] Most are not low-skilled service jobs but high-value, high-paying jobs, which are desperate for software talent. Labor shortages in high-tech jobs for systems analysts are expected to increase 6.4 percent per year.[5] Qualified labor for hard-to-fill job openings is one of U.S. corporations' biggest problems, often resulting in raising compensation[6] and the new phenomenon of signing bonuses for highly qualified new hires. Young, computer jocks (who have never known a world without PCs) are being hired right out of high school for generous salaries.

The Bureau of Labor Statistics' projection for 1992–2005 expects old-tech job declines in billing posting, calculating, machine, telephone and word processing operators, typists, bank tellers, agents, wholesalers, teachers, distributors, and salesmen. Manufacturing automation technology has reduced

U.S. employment in this (old-tech) area from 39 percent of (total) U.S. employment in 1950 to 17 percent in 1990. The United States has 24 Internet connections per 1,000 people, five times that of Europe, and high-tech industries comprise 40 percent of the U.S. and Japanese manufactured exports versus 33 percent for Britain and 20 percent in Germany. The United States has the comparative advantage, shifting quickly to new-tech, and has enjoyed better job gains.[7]

Information Technology Boosts Efficiency, Productivity, and Profitability

Information technology is not just a sector, it has become the basis of *all* sectors in the new economy; companies and countries that lag will become uncompetitive. High-tech revenues of software firms selling to large international companies grew more than 150 percent from 1988 to 1992 alone—information services up +70 percent. The United States has 66 percent cable utilization rate versus Japan at only 10 percent. The U.S. Department of Commerce reports that information technology has contributed 36 percent of economic growth since 1990 with most new employment in Software & Services. The United States already enjoys a huge $3 billion trade surplus in new-tech, knowledge-related goods and services which is growing five times as fast as old-tech world trade in resources.[8] The technological contribution to enhanced efficiency is making leaps in corporate restructuring productivity: Figure 7–3 shows a major shift that also contributes to this trend of "unemploying" in the mature industries. Looking at the downtrend from the 1966 peak (of the 1942–1966 bull market cycle) to the 1980–1982 lows, now broken (prior to the 1982–present bull market cycle), one can see that from 1980 to 1995 a 15-year base is in place, from which corporate profitability is only just emerging into a major uptrend .

Technological advances allow increased efficiency, and increased productivity, hence increased profits. These radical changes in the way of doing business are already being used, but by only 15 percent of large corporations today leaving enormous room for further diffusion. Virtual financial statements allow corporations to make calculations of risk, return, and liquidity, slashing hours of work. The software can now "mine" the data and transform it strategically to optimize assets and liability; further, payroll, accounts payable, and general ledger can "speak" to each other and share data throughout the corporate system, consolidating the entire corporation across all its geographic areas into one system. In doing so, software now allows "mark to the market" daily recalculations of all corporate forecasts. "Economic Value Added" analysis, and "managing forward" planning (which can shorten closing the corporate books from one month to 24 hours) have increased efficiency and saved up to $100

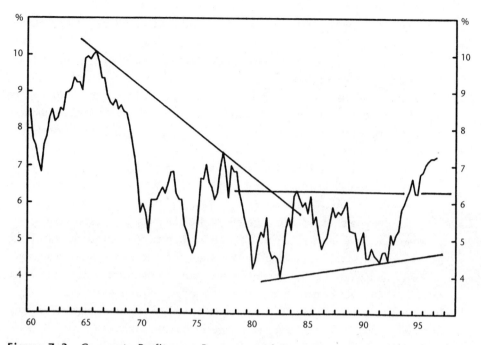

Figure 7–3 Corporate Profits as a Percentage of Gross Domestic Product. (Used with permission of BCA Publications Ltd, *The Bank Credit Analyst*.)

million for a single corporation because the executives spend less in overnight borrowing costs,[9] again lowering demand for capital, which keeps interest rate pressure down. This does create unemployment as duplicate jobs in different geographic areas are eliminated, but customers orders can be cut to 48 hours versus one week processing.

Further, software Paychecks allow employees to view their own records, saving postage charges. The new software offers advantages in processing large amounts of information, making decisions superior to traditional information evaluation, resulting in higher corporate productivity levels. Neural networks recognize patterns, learn and identify changes in huge quantities of data, and have the ability to "learn in real time" from ongoing data flows, quickly identifying fraud and theft patterns.[10] The market for "PCs that think" is huge and growing.

"Demand flow technique" cuts manufacturing cycles in half and trims inventories. General Electric (GE) has taken the just-in-time inventory another step, to shorten manufacturing time, time management technology, and work flow to organize production more efficiently, cutting time and materials waste, and cutting delivery from months to days. (Chrysler can increase production without new factories by eliminating inventory storage; Wal-Mart uses forecast software (CFAR) to eliminate huge inventories of consumer goods sitting idle in warehouses.)[11] Some companies are completely

eliminating inventory warehousing, the middle step and the middle men—
"disintermediation"—through Internet connections between supplier and
purchaser. General Electric is already directly purchasing its spare parts on
the Internet.[12] Even a privately owned mail-order, soon-to-be-global flower
company ships directly from grower to customer.[13] By using computers in
previously unforeseen ways, technology has created a revolution in business
practices, streamlining operations, perhaps even helping to smooth the
bumps in the seemingly elusive business cycle.

Internet and satellite (for larger data transmission) technology allow
24-hour efficiency: Data generated on one side of the globe during the day
can be uplinked and processed on the other while the first sleeps. In this
"virtual" manufacturing environment,[14] simulations, tests, and analysis of
processes are conducted in consultation with others from all parts of the
globe (international cross-functional teams). This leads to the development
of efficient design before expensive and time-consuming investments are
made in exchanges of data, raw materials, model building, and fuel.

Boeing utilized these methods with its 777 aircraft, designed without
physical models, reducing time, raw material use and costs dramatically. Similarly, blade and other engineering designs can use smart software to reverse
the development process: Specify the necessary output expectations and the
software can develop the most efficient blade shape, eliminating costly trial

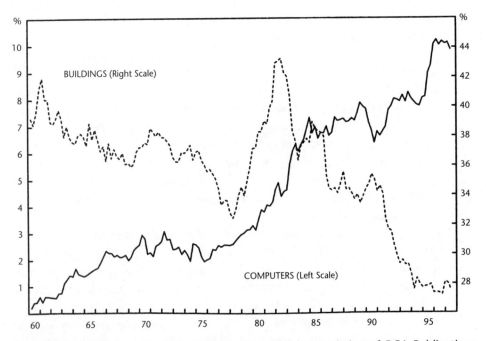

Figure 7–4 Investment Spending Shares. (Used with permission of BCA Publications
Ltd, *The Bank Credit Analyst*.)

and error. GE also has software that checks designs for ease of repair, and an electricity generating version of a GE jet engine for short notice, quick electricity needs, with intercooling efficiency that can be turned on and off quickly for transitory energy demand.[15] Sensors in airline seats may be programmed to respond to pressure and relieve or fill with air for comfort. The banking industry, too, can utilize network banking, reducing transaction processing costs. All levels of governments can save billions by eliminating bureaucracy and poor service with Internet sites for 24-hour consumer information access.

These changes are just embryonic—and so may be their effect on corporate bottom lines. A major part of corporate investment, as can be seen in Figure 7–4, is in computers and other high-tech products.[16] These technological changes and corporate re-engineering may also have a major effect on how we need to re-evaluate normal business cycles and valuations. Old-tool measurements may no longer be adequate. (We'll look at this in Chapter 14.)

Another consideration: If the efficiencies of these less capital-intensive technologies are so cost saving in their ability to lower the corporate need for money, then the corporations which become flush with cash may be able in great degree to finance capital expenditures themselves, again resulting in less external demand for money, keeping interest rates down.

Developing Nations Moving Directly to "New-Tech"

One further observation on the newer technology relates to its role in developed versus developing nations. Developed nations must dismantle the old-tech to replace it with the new, a disruptive, time-consuming process with which the communications industry, for instance, is still involved. Developing nations, never having had the old in place, have the luxury of going directly to the new technology and methods, bypassing the need for reorganization, readjustment, and dislocations that developed nations must undergo to convert. We've seen this with cellular phones in emerging nations that have had no phone lines in place. As just one example, Kunming City in Yunnan Province, China, is erecting hill-top radio transmitting towers for a completely cellular phone system. They and other emerging nations may never know the wired phones of our system.

Also, fascinatingly, solar energy is soaring in developing nations because they have no fuel distribution lines in place. Remember solar energy companies 20 years ago, before the oil giants bought them all up so we'd stop talking about them (Figure 7–5)? Many in the emerging nations are now embracing this less capital- and less fuel-intensive technology as their first, faster, and even less-polluting energy source, ultimately reducing the demand for traditional fuel and its ongoing cost.

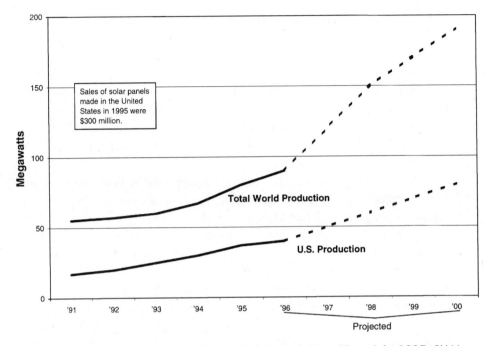

Figure 7–5   Energy Capacity of Solar Panels Sold Each Year. (Copyright 1997. *PV News,* Vol. 16, No. 2.)

One-third of the world's population lives without electricity. Solar power is a thriving U.S. export business as the cost of the technology has come down 50 percent over the decades and is falling 15 percent a year (India representing the largest, with Mexico, Kenya, Indonesia, and Brazil close behind), lighting jungles and deserts and bringing power. Potential markets include China, Vietnam, and South Africa. Tibetan herders already use solar panels of photovoltaic cells for electricity as they travel; Somalian traveling medical clinics refrigerate vaccines with solar panel power.

Solar power needs minimal upkeep: There are no huge delivery or equipment requirements (a man on a mule is sufficient), and one panel can power two light bulbs, a TV, and a radio. Seemingly unrecognized is the solar industry's (new-tech) job creation, as capacity is expected to have doubled by the end of 1997. By 2001 the U.S. Energy Department expects a 70 percent jump in solar exports. Interestingly, this allows 40 percent of the rural population of India to utilize the several hundred dollar systems, opening a market of 240 million people.[17] The subtle underlying point is that they are utilizing a *non*-energy intensive technology to produce their energy needs. As this trend continues to expand, it will lessen the demand expectation for fossil fuels. Because the emerging nations can embrace the new technology immediately, it is possible that their economic progress and growth may be greater, and faster, than might otherwise be expected.

New Technology Pervades the Retail Marketplace

Let's consider some other quietly developing new technologies that also may hold major industry and consumer implications for the twenty-first century. Consumers can now go into select Levi's stores and be electronically scanned for a perfectly fitting pair of jeans. This "apparel on demand" scanning technique can make and deliver custom clothes in less than five days; Italian leather shoes may be fitted the same way—each foot scanned, the shoe individually molded of Italian leather—for one's first comfortable pair of shoes, sold for off-the-shelf prices and delivered directly. Music can now be listened to in the store before purchase, or a medley can be specially assembled, taped, and sold on the spot or downloaded on a PC. What might be the century-long implications?

A potential chain of events could conceptually suggest monumental consequences over the twenty-first century, and may help explain the long-term implications of pertinent stock market sectors' negative chart patterns, as defined technically. As a result of these and other technological developments, there should be less (eventually no) need for inventory (samples would suffice). If there is less need for inventory, there should be less need for enormous commercial retail space to display the inventory. If there is less need for inventory, there is less need for trucks to carry the inventory and less need for fuel (domestic oil) to power the trucks, and to heat or light the no-longer-needed retail space. Could there ultimately be less (or no) need for the many megamalls of America (the fuel to get to them, and the electricity to light and heat them) which may then become the dinosaurs of our generation's excess, incapable of having their sales equaled by a relatively smaller upcoming demographic profile and a much more technologically oriented generation? In the long run, most of these transactions will probably be done at home, electronically on an audio computer: scan oneself, click an icon, send the order to Levi's, or record a tape, pay electronically, and have it delivered by Federal Express.

The Internet, as well as demographics, is remaking the face of retail. "Intelligent Agents" software allows manufacturers to deal directly with customers, enabling consumers to comparative shop on the Internet for the best buy in far-flung geographic locations. Retailers who have survived the bankruptcies of the past decade but who may be missing the demographic and technology warning signs may fail to adapt, further jeopardizing survival. Markets oriented to the youth, for whom the computer is taken for granted, may be the first threatened. To counter this, cosmetic companies are already targeting the 16- to 24-year-olds on the Internet because they don't shop (at department stores) the way their parents do. Some retailers have responded with the "Virtual Emporium": Shoppers can go to the mall and examine merchandise from hundreds of stores online, where vendors buy space at computers set up in "theme departments" with multiple terminals at a kitchen counter or in a children's play area, cafe, or sports bar environment.

Emergence of Smart Products

Technological progress has also developed highly reliable "smart car" navigation systems and computerized mapping (one product tester recently complained that his system took him to "Thirty-seventh and O" in Washington, DC, instead of directly to Georgetown University without realizing that is exactly the correct address). Autos are more fuel-efficient (with 95 percent to 98 percent of pollutants removed catalytically). So even if, as predicted, sport utility vehicles and higher speed limits imply more driving, the efficiency should offset fuel needs with automobiles requiring no more fuel than was used in the 1960s.[18] The developing efficiency of electric vehicle (EV) cars and motor bikes should result in less than half of today's cost of operation (less fuel), not to mention alternative energy sources as they become more cost-efficient (e.g., solar "chemophyll," and fuel cells using chemical catalytic changes in lieu of traditional fuel for electricity; a zinc-air battery for EVs claims to be unmatched for energy with 200 watt-hours of energy per kilo of battery weight or quadruple a traditional lead-acid or twice the powerful, lighter nickel-metal hydride batteries). Some hybrid cars are now equipped to run on alternating fuels, and the possibility of capturing electricity in the combination of hydrogen and oxygen with only water as an emission is in the pipeline.[19] There are microscopic radars and gyroscopes for car safety. Cars today have more computer processing power than the first lunar landing-craft in 1969.[20]

OTHER TECHNOLOGICAL INNOVATIONS

There are negative-free digital cameras that store images on chips for conversion directly to a PC file format that can then be sent out over the e-mail like a postcard.[21] There are photo digital color printers that make postcards; low-cost printers that produce the quality of professional film developers and of high-quality color magazines. Some film developers now offer digitalized versions of negatives on a floppy disk that a PC can read directly. Also in the photo line are infrared cameras that film motion through body heat emission measurement which is translated by computer to 3-D characters that will free virtual reality from all its wires and headgear.[22] The new DV (digital-video) camcorder fits in a pocket; a 3-ounce "wearable" cellular phone and a computer producing a 360-degree view, that can be sent over the Internet to another computer without distortions.

Electroluminescent displays are brighter, viewable from a wider angle than liquid crystal, requiring lower voltages, and are converted to transparent when not energized, so they can be embedded in a window/windshield. A stereo that can fit in your palm uses circular crystals similar to piezoelectric quartz crystals in watches. These tease musical notes out of air for better sound at less cost—Hyper Sonic Sound, the biggest breakthrough for speakers. These crystals can be used in hearing aids, PCs, theaters, and for special effects, putting sound where you want it. They pulsate thousands of times faster than traditional mechanisms emitting two ultrasonic waves at frequencies beyond human or animal hearing. Then they interact, creating a third sonic wave (the difference between the two), a Tartini tone that can be heard with no echoes.[23]

There are now microelectro mechanical systems (MEMS): Japan is developing micromachines from a wider variety of metals and ceramics for more strength and versatility than silicon. Texas Instruments has a chip-sized video of thousands of aluminum mirrors, 16 microns on a side (a micron is one millionth of a meter or 1/100 the diameter of a human hair). Flagellating cilia create microconveyer systems for future microfactories, and develop minuscule motors, batteries, solar cell generators, pumps, and machining techniques. Seiko has a microscopic drill for making holes less than a micron wide (with the help of electrochemical reactions). Micromachines may adopt tricks from insects and become robo-bugs, getting ideas from children for application. Xerox is developing Lilliputian sensors, motors, nozzles, and valves that can gauge heat, light, motion, sound, and respond or adjust as for earthquakes; also a microscopic magnet material one molecule in size to pack data more densely that may open a whole new computing approach, not to mention the one-electron transistors.

Other innovations: e-commerce, e-catalogues, Fastparts software for electronic sales (eliminating middlemen and delays); scanners to eliminate office paper; cellular digital "smart phones" cruise the Net for wireless delivery of e-mail, Cyberspace banking access, take messages and read credit cards and local information on their small screens; wristwatch phones with screens and speech recognition; pagers with Internet access; personal area networks (PANs) the size of credit cards; digital, low-power personal communications service; microcontrollers that serve as brains to everyday appliances making them "smart;" the "smart card" (special purpose computers, on a card); "smart" alarm clocks are expected to download traffic reports and ring when road conditions are most favorable; "smart" refrigerators may reorder food as supplies dwindle; and "smart home" control networks monitor climate controls (both private and industrial), heat, air conditioning, sprinklers, and security; "smart" needles conveying tumor data. Quantum dots store 15,000 times more on a pin head chip; 3-D disks with images stored in 100 layers or one terabyte of data (1000 times as much as ordinary surface disks), enabled by new dyes and high power, pulsed infrared lasers; quantum wire higher-power lasers (reducing the need for telecommunications repeaters); green lasers to read and write denser information; blue-light-emitting diodes (LEDs) that threaten to eliminate the need for electricity with 20-year light bulbs; metal halide light bulbs that use 22 watts for today's 120 watts, in natural white light; these can save $184 over 9,000 hours of use;[24] tracking devices for travelers; satellite-based Global Positioning Systems (GPS) in which a receiver marks and tracks location with an on-screen map;[25] personal digital assistants (PDA), a 1-pound device that reads handwriting, surfs the web, can be used as a

(continued)

digital camera and transmits photos over the Internet, connects to cellular phones and works on the go;[26] voice recognition and text-to-speech capability; faster Internet distribution; titanium anti-scalding devices; so-called "info appliances" including "ubiquitous" wearable computers with a new digital technology making "things that think" (i.e., with a piezoelectric polymer in the heel of a shoe that generates power by walking) that can feed information anywhere and reroute phone calls; PCs now include radio, TV, CD player, answering machine, fax, high-contrast monitors, and hi-fi speakers.

Phone Manager power phone acts like a home switchboard: you can answer or send to voice mail, send voice messages simultaneously to many; display incoming phone number, send to mailbox, conference it, put first call on hold and answer the second or route to voice prompt to hold on; multibox voice mail for each family member; small businesses can send within calling area sale notices to everyone for less than postage; long distance calls can follow you anywhere up to three numbers, e-mail and voice mail delivery. ATTs "Renaissance Network" to support all sort of futuristic services to get your message anywhere in any form: Fax, e-mail, voice; high-speed switched hit higher speed of one terabit (a trillion bits per second) or 10 million conversations for telephones.[27] Low earth orbit satellites, computers in the sky connect to global information; good for long distance pagers, and satellite potential should result in global access wireless phones. Lucent Technologies and Texas Instruments are working on all optical photonic amplifiers that enhance signals without electronics (networking) on a seamless glass fiber.

Even the sporting world is being transformed. The 1996 Olympics sported starting blocks that measure foot force, electronic guns to eliminate millisecond delivery aberrations; lasers to measure runners' acceleration and deceleration; finish line filmless digital cameras; marathoners with transponders that interact with antennas molded in the road to report split times by modem; precision torso placement across finish lines is captured by electronic cameras. (The old traditional finish line tape is now used only to display the names of the corporate sponsors.) The discus returns like bowling balls in robocarts; pole vaulters clear the bar by an exact margin measured by light-emitting diodes in the posts; boxers have accelerometers in punching bags to calculate force of punch. And the swimmers and divers competed under the world's largest (10,000-seat arena) solar roof.

SEMICONDUCTORS

The semiconductor market is expected to more than double by 1999 from 151 billion to 310 billion, accounting for 29 percent of the content of electronic equipment, and Internet growth will require even more building blocks. Wrinkles on silicon wafers can now be removed opening the door to even more progress; smart fabrics may soon detect chemical warfare molecules and snare and lock them in; lightweight plastic polyphosphazene protects from bullets and flames;[28] customized chips for cellular phones, air bags, printers, televisions, "application specific integrated circuits" that manage everything; technology in air bags can release triggers to the cell phone to call EMS by satellite if necessary; there are 3-D graphics multimedia accelerator chips. Computer chips double in speed every 12 months because technology allows smaller and more complex design. In 1997, Intel and IBM, in differing techniques, doubled the speed of their chips; and now molecule-size chips made in test tubes could place the past 30 years transistor production into the size of one beaker!

Vision equipment needs cameras and sophisticated software to see in microscopic detail the inner workings of integrated circuits. Single electron currents from gold atom nuggets precipitated from gaseous fluid, dissolved and painted on silicon wafer nanoclusters, form an ultra-thin conducting film and a laser-gas cleaning process using light energy and an inert gas to remove contamination from surfaces without water and chemicals, and can clean silicon wafers and other semiconductor and industrial materials.[29] Gallium arsenide chips are more expensive but conduct electrons more efficiently with less noise than silicon, and are ideal for certain communications devices like set top cable converters, cellular phones, fiber optic receivers; proton memory chips operate at very low power to extend laptop life; hybrid logic chips provide the brain for appliances, expanding beyond memory chips.

INTERNET APPLICATIONS

Internet-related technology includes audio technology, improving sound quality so music companies can think of new marketing methods; J-Fax "virtual office" converts e-mail to receive fax, voice messages, and world e-mail for the cost of local calls and can set up personal phone numbers in 24 hours, threatening established phone companies' service; "Hyperlinking" software to navigate the web; "intelligent agents" programs to do electronic errands on the Net, go out and bring back to hard drives data of interest to be examined for perusal at one's leisure without online charges; 3-D designs to browse a bookshelf, or buy from a supermarket aisle; "push delivery" doesn't wait for Web site visits, but finds out what information people have shown an interest in and delivers it to their computers; software delivers custom material without extra software, just subscription to information sources; utilities software managing programs which service computers, offer new software products online, eliminating distributors, and can add the latest printer drivers; ever-faster modems accommodate all of the above.

First Virtual allows electronic computer payments by credit card; Java allows ads that move on a screen and take your money using a virtual PIN number, not credit card information; software to protect from online fraud and theft; "electronic wallet" secure transactions payments put on credit cards; and special software enables law enforcement to quickly track gun purchase records and trace their origin to crack multiple cases left unsolved. Brokers now have online access as do their clients, also using a PIN number; some even have a two-way PC video to work with clients online to try out different financial possibilities; mutual funds too are connecting with clients interactively online. E-commerce can be a mall for an online corporate procurement system. Some are set up for specific industries, like car dealerships and banks, linking them together for instant loan

(continued)

processing; energy networks link oil companies to share data. IBM's "world avenue" is a virtual mall where merchants list products and the system brings up appropriate merchandise.

AGRICULTURAL APPLICATIONS

In the agricultural realm, there is a gene in rye that allows it to tolerate high aluminum levels in soil that could be transferred to wheat, allowing it to grow in billions of acres worldwide where it can't today because of the heavy aluminum content that kills wheat. Genetic engineering for resistant crops has the potential impact of reducing the use of chemicals to fight pests; in alleviating the hidden stresses of pesticides and nitrates in drinking water, and the additional cost of water treatment. There are also computer and satellite technology for farm equipment and fertilizer delivery and new agricultural "till-free" methods which may change or lessen farm equipment requirements; water conservation and filtration technology for agricultural and industrial use. Crop products immune to weed chemicals create cheaper farming and larger yields; soybeans, rice, beets, and canola; the technology is capable of producing in crops insect resistance, disease resistance, yield enhancement, and other desirable quality traits.[30] Biodegradable herbicides reduce a hundred fold the need per acre. There is a weevil that keeps water hyacinths under control in Africa thus eliminating the snails causing river blindness. Canola oil genetically altered to resist heat, lubricates engines; corn and soy can also be genetically altered for heat stability. Cucumber roots can be protected from fungal rot by coating the seeds with beneficial bacteria, ultimately displacing the need for fungicides—also in the works for corn, squash, and other crops.

There is a genetic marker for "beautiful buttocks" or meatier hindquarters on sheep. One may also increase the cancer fighting compound in milk by raising the unsaturated fat in cow's feed. Bright light pulses can kill bacteria, molds, yeasts, and salmonella with ozone gas. Vegetable firefighters made from waxes of several plants and water create a foam-coating material so they can't burn or release vapors, also lowering temperatures to below the flash point of flammable material, thus using less water for less property damage; they are nontoxic and biodegradable. Nature's benefits include the heat of a lotus: as the plant begins to bloom it begins heating, up to 85 to 96 degrees; energy output is equivalent to one watt; skunk cabbage heat melts ice to protect its bloom; both can be harnessed.

BIOMEDICAL APPLICATIONS

Technology extends to the biomedical field as well. Computers and biology are combined for diagnosis; microelectronics contribute to genetic analysis; lotions to deactivate biowarfare agents by disabling them are in the pipeline; Teflon-coated cancer cells to prevent metastases; retrieving hemoglobin from outdated blood, purifying and stabilizing it for reuse; drug delivery such as skin patches or mouth mucosa (below tongue) delivery of testosterone, estrogen, nitroglycerin, and so on; faster, better methods, strip cell material to get to the pure DNA in 2 hours instead of 48, creating/affecting growth of genomics, clinical diagnostics and gene therapy; hospital clothes with anti-microbial additives kill bacteria and fungi on contact, even through washes; 30 years of one's sensory experiences may be captured on a single chip in the brain: X-ray lithography drastically shrinks circuits on memory chips. By 2025, one chip may store 10 terabytes (one million times today's storage) to tap electric impulses of the brain's optical, auditory, olfactory, kinesthetic (touch), and taste nerves. Dentistry now has air microabrasion—no drilling. Hypodermic needles now retract like turtles to prevent accidental punctures; 3-D imaging for helping plastic surgeons in replacement modeling; a silicon chip planted in the eye may provide enough detail for the vision impaired, with a healthy optic nerve, to read the newspaper; and a minimally invasive coronary artery bypass is in practice.

The medical industry has micromachines that pass through narrow pipes or vessels or through blood and hunt for cracks; microcatheters and endoscopes, using metals that change shape with heat, snake themselves through vessels with microcameras and scissors for non-invasive surgery; medical "watches" on the wrist to monitor blood pressure, inject medicines as needed; and medical swipe cards could give instant access to medical history from anywhere; even genesplicing to achieve indigo colored dye without the noxious chemicals of current processes.

Summary

This chapter highlighted the leading role played by new technology, primarily semiconductor-based information technology, in reshaping the business and consumer worlds. Smarter products have made greater productivity and profitability possible. (The related topic of how to measure information age productivity will be discussed in Chapter 14.)

We also saw how developing nations are bypassing the "old-tech" and moving directly to "new-tech," thereby creating lively markets for the newest products of the companies with the type of global exposure discussed in Chapter 2. We reviewed a number of those innovative products and their applications. It is important, however, to keep in mind that these are but a few of the myriad technological discoveries that are published on an almost daily basis; by the time you read this book, half of this technology will probably already be obsolete, superseded by even newer, faster more efficient systems. It's the mindset that matters.

Chapter

Old-Tech and
New-Tech:
Need for New Sectors

Despite the many advances in information technology (new-tech) products discussed in the preceding chapter, a number of essentially static industries and market sectors have continued to produce and sell products. These old-tech firms have experienced stock price underperformance in relative strength (RS) compared to the new-tech sectors. In this chapter, we will identify some of the old-tech sectors and examine the reasons for their relative underperformance.

Due to their more recent appearance, the new-tech areas of the economy have been more difficult to track. The existing Standard & Poor's group component sectors do not effectively reflect new-tech activity and progress. Accordingly, we will propose the development of new sectors to more accurately portray actual groups resulting in growth and profitability. Identifying appropriate new sectors is invaluable for comprehending the changes taking place in the economy. A related problem—how to better measure productivity in the new-tech knowledge economy—will be discussed in Chapter 14.

Old-Tech Sectors Underperforming the Stock Market

New technologies may have long-term implications for the future of many old-tech sectors underperforming the stock market. From a longer-term technical structural basis we are seeing up to 50-year breakdowns in RS to the S&P 500 (Figure 8–1) for industries such as Aluminums, Paper and Forest Products, Waste Management, Domestic Oil, Engineering and Construction, Publishing, Truckers, Trucks & Parts, Steels and Electric Utilities; and as discussed, structural breakdowns in some smaller-cap indices like the Mid-Cap 400, Russell 2000, and Value Line—contratrend rallies (such as occurred in 1997) notwithstanding. As described earlier, not all of these underperforming sectors portray price risk yet, although once the RS declines, price too, can eventually follow.

The charts of these old-tech sectors have been profiling multiyear patterns of underperformance, in some cases accompanied by price declines. The concept of old-tech may be at the root of these underperformance trends; simultaneously, domestic exposure also may be a factor for some. The Domestic Oil group; Truckers and Waste Management have up to 12-year breakdowns and their price trends are also beginning to falter. Auto Parts is profiling a 10-year trend of underperformance. Engineering & Construction has followed suit. Iron & Steel has fallen to a 50-year RS low along with Aluminums and Paper & Forest Products, all structural breakdowns (and the Autos, not pictured, is vulnerable to follow suit). The Electric Utilities group continues in a 50-year relative underperformance trend; its price broke a 14-year uptrend in 1994. This industry is just beginning its struggle with deregulation, cost efficiency, consolidations, and competitive issues, including consortiums of smaller companies wrangling for cheaper power—all of this added to the new technologies of jet engines and fuel cells. The RS low may reflect the current investment disadvantage now affecting this industry. It may well take years before those adjustments take hold, ultimately reflecting a better relative market performance.

It was actually when the Paper & Forest Product group broke to a 25-year low in 1995 that I began to question whether something very different might be occurring in a more macrosense. I went back to the charts to look for clues of what might be evolving differently. Let's reflect a moment on that earlier perspective in 1994, discussed in Part One, in which these more industrial sectors seemed to portray the possible technical potential of basing formations. Recall the outside possibility that those RS configurations also looked like possible descending triangular formations. One of the more dramatic charts of the Iron & Steel sector followed the Paper & Forest Products, registering a 36-year RS low; the ominous chart for Aluminum joined the trend. (Even Metals & Mining and Gold & Precious Metals sectors experienced a 3-year relative strength low in the summer of 1996 corresponding

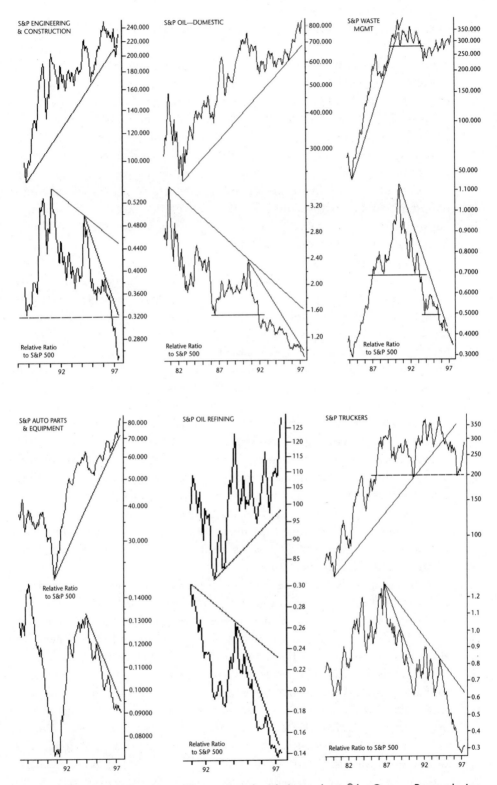

Figure 8–1   Old-Tech Sectors. Chart created with Supercharts® by Omega Research, Inc.

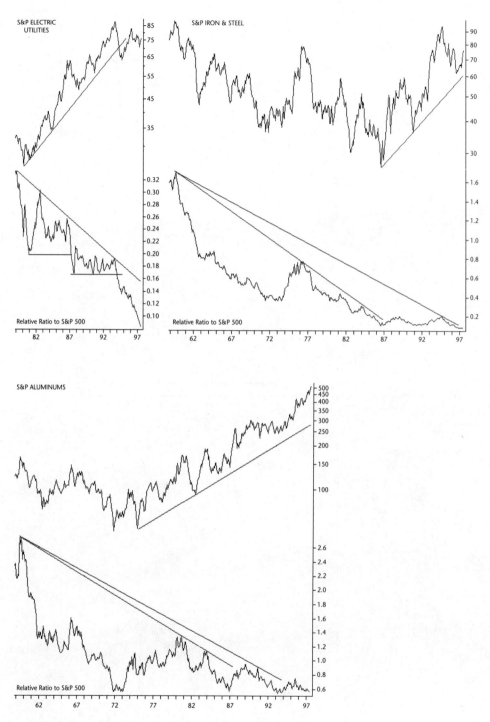

Figure 8–1   Continued.

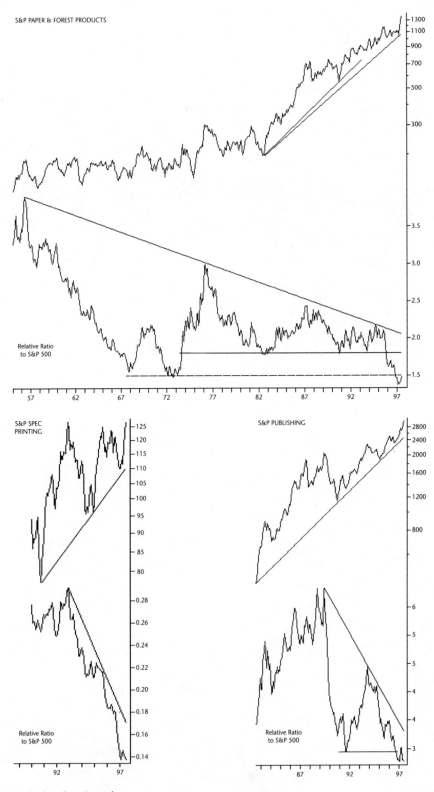

Figure 8-1   Continued.

with the Base Metals drop to new lows on the London Metal Exchange in September 1996.[1]) Could these industries be going out of business? Of course not, but the laggard RS progressions in many of these old-tech industries versus the dynamic relative profiles for the new-tech related sectors began to suggest the possibility that these old-tech sectors may no longer represent the same size piece of the total economic pie going forward for the United States, as they have historically in the old heavy industrial era.

New-Tech Replacing Old-Tech

The old-tech relative underperformance of Paper & Forest Products, Publishing, and Specialty Printing may result not just from their large domestic focus, but also may be reflecting technological advances in communications; the Internet; Intranet; e-mail; e-commerce; e-catalogues; e-airline ticketing; e-rent a cars; online tracking and tracing of packages; Oasis online (paper-free) stock settlement; e-quarterly reports; e-taxes; e-401K transactions done by voice response; Healtheon Corp. development of online (paper-free) health and insurance bills and claims; e-banking; e-pay (which could save $900 million per year in billing postage alone); all virtually eliminating a large demand for some print and paper products, many in triplicate. General Electric is already doing 10 percent of its commerce on the Internet. Federal Express is nearly paper-free.

And this is just in the embryonic stage. Only a small fraction (8–12 percent) of major U.S. corporations have dipped a toe in the Internet commerce waters. If we think about the emerging nations, they have the ability to *begin* their enterprises electronically—bypassing the old, going directly to the new technologies.

There are e-bookstores like Amazon.com and barnesandnoble.com; e-zines: newsstands on the web; libraries and library science have been transformed by the Internet, and librarians, now called "cybrarians," navigate knowledge, with no more card catalogues, resulting in more information related jobs.[2] We are moving from "the numbing pace of paper (in triplicate) to the lightning speed of electrons in a new era of friction-free markets."[3] Data, text, audio, and video—the paper users—are all now available as computer digital documents. Book publishing has a unique additional problem of "gone today, here tomorrow," or growing returns—trying to fill megastores' inventory without attention to demographic changes; computer inventory monitoring, effecting swifter returns; and the question of quality books may all be contributing factors.

Steel and Aluminum may have their own problems with the advent of new metals like carbon fiber, which is lighter than aluminum and stronger than steel, or the steel-like composite of carbon dioxide-infused cement that can also reduce atmospheric CO_2. Other alternatives include auto design integration and plastic replacing formerly metal parts, and polyester and glass fiber composites in lieu of metal for quality bicycles at a fraction of the cost. Even railroads are using lighter materials like fiberglass. Boeing's new fighter design utilizes the first all-composite wing made of thermoplastic composite (cutting the weight significantly), technology easily transferable to commercial planes.[4] A new composite of alumina and ceramic withstands deep sea pressures up to 16,000 pounds per square inch.[5] Steel, already representing a much smaller portion of national GDP, along with aluminum, nickel, and other basic materials (Figure 8–2), may be affected, as other formerly unavailable materials like titanium are being explored, and by slowing demand (perhaps a demographic phenomenon?) in the developed nations.[6] The use of aluminum cans is declining; glass bottled fruit drinks and glass shaped plastic bottles are cutting into the soft drink can market. In addition, available supplies are growing as emerging nations develop their own natural resources—creating overcapacity, as in 1997 in Southeast Asia.

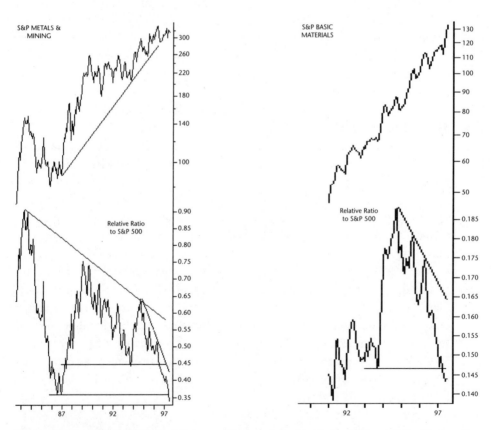

Figure 8–2   Old-Tech Related Sectors. Chart created with Supercharts® by Omega Research, Inc.

WATER FILTRATION TECHNOLOGY FOR INDUSTRIAL/COMMERCIAL USE: A HUGE INDUSTRY ON ITS OWN

There are special molecules to remove metal and radioactive water impurities, as well as de-ionization systems and electrodialysis modules. Ceramic membrane filtration dramatically reduces bacteria levels in water and milk, and is used in the chemical/steel, pharmaceutical, and medical industries. Reverse osmosis removes salt and contaminants and along with electrodialysis contributes to the desalination processes already used in South Africa, the Caribbean, the Czech Republic, and the Middle and Far East. Ceramic gas filters provide high water purification for semiconductor and pharmaceutical needs. Membrane and ion exchange remove microcontamination essential to purify water for the microelectronics, food and beverage industries. Electrolytic recovery, adsorption filtration, and precipitation technology is used for metal finishing and electronics industries. Municipal waste can now be mined for metal, extracting more than 50 percent of waste metal;[*] silver recovery systems exist in the biosolids technology.

Wet air oxidation systems destroy complex organics and/or reduce them to carbon dioxide and water or other biodegradable forms. Molecular bonding technology is used for remediation of soils and sludges contaminated with heavy metal, converting the metals back to their natural nonleachable state. Exchange resins and membranes are replacing chemical-intensive water purification methods. Reactive membranes act as catalysts to allow different size/weight molecules through. Aqueous remediation uses ultraviolet (UV) methods to disinfect waste water for re-use (by rapidly decomposing contaminants like chlorinated solvents, sulfonates, bitriles, and other highly oxidized materials) and can aid in altering genetic material to render bacteria, viruses, and microorganisms infertile; embalming fluid technology no longer pollutes the water. Paper bleaching with oxygen eliminates chlorine. High resolution technologies measure residual chlorine more efficiently to prevent over-use. Gas-phase chemical reduction process destroys high concentration polychlorinated biphenyls (PCBs) by removing hydrogen chloride water and particulates; landfill leachate treatment systems; growing water treatment for runoff and contaminated waste water from hazardous and municipal solid waste landfills; and ozone injection treatment breaks down industrial contaminants for safe effluent into sewer systems. Amine-coated ceramic granules are being used to recover emulsified hydrocarbons from liquid waste streams for the petrochemical industry's re-use. Biosolids management can now pelletize the eight million dry metric tons of solid waste produced annually in the United States, reducing it to a low volume fertilizer product.[†]

Mill sludge is used as an oil spill absorbent; paper sludge and ash are used as building materials replacing cement and reducing tons of waste products. A weed that produces an herbicidal product biodegrades in four days. New biodegradable corn-based cutlery that looks like plastic has been created. There are small pulse power beams to clean diesel exhausts, yielding pure nitrogen and oxygen instead of toxins. There are manganese batteries that eliminate the toxins and the cost of lithium batteries.

[*] Otis Port, *Business Week*, October 21, 1996.
[†] *The Environmental Business Journal, Vol. IX,* No. 2/3, February/March 1996. Water filtration source information courtesy of Richard Heckman, CEO, and Timothy Traff, Director, United States Filter Corp.

The Domestic Oil group has a particularly dramatic picture with a recently recorded 15-year low in RS. As far back as January 1992 the domestic oils experienced nearly a 10-year low in RS which has since extended to a 15-year low in RS, portending a structural continuation of the negatively diverging RS trend. There is as yet no sign of RS stabilization—no evidence that the trend has stopped declining. (A statistic can't go up until it stops going down. And that evidence is not yet in place.) The more than decade-long lows in RS suggest energy prices may remain within a manageable trading range, at best, or at least may not be on the verge of inciting inflationary pressures. Added to the aforementioned energy-saving technologies, domestic demand for solar power in a variety of forms is rising: solar heliostats (sun-tracking mirrors) are producing steam for large scale generators. Technological developments like carbon aerogel provide enormous surface for electric charge storing devices called aerocapacitors which can be used in electric utility grids or on trains to soak up braking energy and re-use it to help a train accelerate again.[7] Could this declining, structural RS progression of the Domestic Oil sector perhaps reflect a less fuel-dependent, alternate energy, new-tech era as well as domestic demographic changes?

The Waste Management sector as it stands today may no longer be applicable, and the group's decline may reflect the possibility that the current methods may be futile. How much can we bury? With 80 percent of the world's population coming into a consumerist lifestyle like ours, we can't afford to bury it any more. New technological advancement, such as the discovery of chemical or agricultural agents, which neutralize rather than displace pollution, are available today. Pollution technology is utilizing vegetation, such as sunflowers, to remove radioactive metals from soil and water; the plants remove the waste through their roots. Water hyacinths have been used for some time now to clean industrial waste—including phosphorous, nitrogen, and ammonia—from water supplies.

The Need for New Sectors

None of these possibilities, however, are reflected in the S&P group components as defined today. We are to a degree working with old tools, unable to measure performance in these growing areas. The implications of such technological revolution and national downsizing in the way of doing business may be enormous over the next generations. Many sectors as defined today may no longer be pertinent and/or may need to be redefined. The need for new sectors to represent what is on the forefront of change is glaring (Figure 8–3). Totally new spheres and frontiers for which we have (as yet) no sector identification, may join or replace the old, as we adapt from the older to newer industries and technologies in this exciting era. Mutual funds have

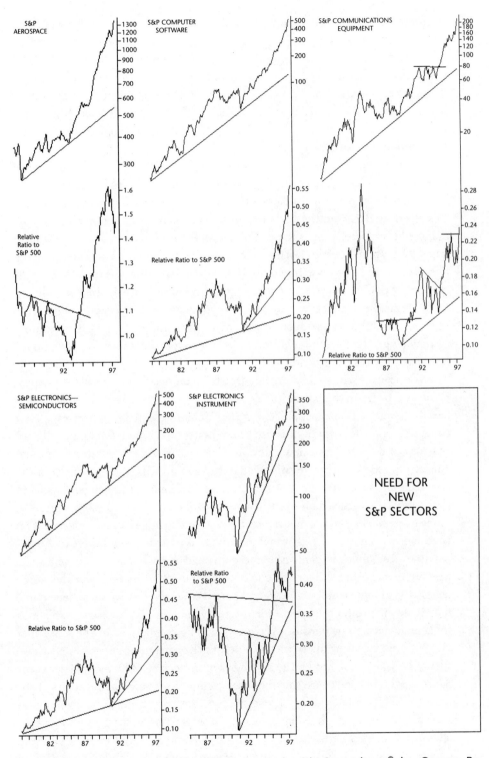

Figure 8–3 New-Tech Sectors. Chart created with Supercharts® by Omega Research, Inc.

begun to fill the gap with categories like Micro-cap (which would cover many tiny stocks representing the newer technologies not included in the existing small-cap), Medical delivery, and Agriculture. Standard & Poor's eliminated the Gaming sector and has had to reinstate it just as demographic trends bring it into focus. The Fertilizer sector was eliminated, just as agriculture looms large in the future (as we will see in Chapter 11). In fact, S&P redefined some sectors in July, 1996; the exercise, however, appears not to have been taken far enough.

The groups we perceive technically to be in RS decline may be telling us that the leaders of yesterday may not be the leaders of today or tomorrow. They may need to be technologically transformed or re-directed if they are to survive at all. From the little we have mentioned about new-tech frontiers, one could project sectors such as Pollution Technology and Water Filtration (the global annual cost to purify industrial-use water and waste water is rising over $350 billion as we will explore in Chapter 10), Fiber Optics, Web Technology, and Outsourcing (which is growing dramatically in centralizing technological manufacture, lowering component costs through volume discounts, streamlining product design, marketing and sales, and is expanding to include product assembly); sectors for servicing the aging domestic population as well as Energy Alternatives.

Education will be key. Although we have no sector to measure its performance or growth, education is critical for survival in this knowledge-based economy. Those people losing their jobs in old-tech industries cannot expect to find them again in those same industries. Education and a willingness of old dogs to learn new tricks is essential in today's environment, and education itself must constantly change to keep up with rapid changes in the new technologies. An aspect of the frenetic development of the new-tech era is the rapidity with which even new technology becomes obsolete—often in months, or weeks, days or hours. Technology companies can no longer rest on their laurels and expect next year's earnings to pour in from last year's product line. Technology companies are continually challenged to develop the new technology and skills their customers are demanding to effect their own necessary changes and to stay competitive. Today's revenues may come mostly from products that didn't exist a year ago. Technology companies today may need to be considered more like drug companies, in the sense that if they don't have products in the pipeline they may not survive, and those surviving today may not be the survivors of tomorrow. The technology companies surviving today are the ones that are making their *own* products obsolete as quickly as technology allows. To do that they need to be able to hire and utilize the best educated workers; those companies with the most successful recruitment will have a significant advantage. (And many are taking on the education of unskilled, often formerly unemployable, for less-skilled jobs, contributing to a falling unemployment level.)

Telecommunications Sector: The Challenge of Rapid Change

The rapid evolution of communications technology has also affected the Telecommunications sectors. While there is not the extensive price history available for these groups as there is for others, what history there is has seen breakdowns in relative performance (Figure 8–4). The Telephone sector has fallen to an all-time RS low, and the long-term RS negative divergence versus price is apparent. The Cellular and Long Distance sectors have followed suit, due perhaps to the currently free telephone calls, faxes, and so on, available through Internet access. The factors affecting these technological sectors may reflect the internal dislocations involving deregulation, reorganization, as well as dismantling the old to make way for the new, and the distractions from technological progress that these focuses have caused. The PCS combines

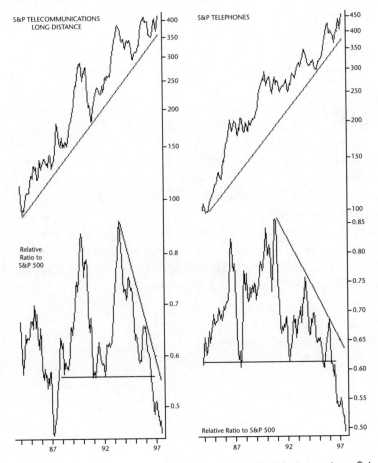

Figure 8–4 Telecommunication Sector. Chart created with Supercharts® by Omega Research, Inc.

paging, caller ID, voice mail, call forwarding, and lower rates than cellular; it is threatening the wireless business with new-tech obsolescence.

Cable TV is also vulnerable in the expensive race to upgrade to hybrid fibers with interactive capabilities, as the telephone companies invade this territory, rushing into their own upgrades in the competition from wireless and cable and the faster Internet access modems on cable. Direct TV eliminates the need for cable entirely and is becoming more cost effective. Broadcasting is not immune either, with the advent of Audionet, the Internet's largest broadcaster (in lieu of local limited range radio). Distance is no longer an issue: One can receive a broadcast from anywhere. The Internet providers make the money selling time to all local stations.

Technically we would look for stabilization in the relative performance to precede any sustainable advance in these areas. Not surprisingly, the long-term price uptrends at the time of this writing remain intact. No doubt there will be a separation of the wheat from the chaff and more consolidations in these and other sectors as witnessed during the 1995–1996 correction in the technology sectors: Some companies merely consolidated to emerge a year later to new highs (like Microsoft and Intel) without suffering the secondary declines to new lows usually associated with bear markets; others experienced protracted bear markets for declines up to 75 percent.

Summary

One of the primary difficulties in identifying new-tech stock groups has been the lack of relevant S&P group component sectors. At the same time, many of the existing sectors comprise old-tech areas that, on an RS basis, are underperforming. In this chapter we scanned the old-tech/new-tech changeover and proposed new sectors that would reflect that irreversible evolution. In light of this old-tech and new-tech two-tier perspective we may need to revisit one of our long-held analytical tools, the Capital/Consumer ratio, which we will do in the next chapter.

Chapter

Revisiting the Capital/Consumer Ratio

In this chapter, we will take a second look at the Capital/Consumer (C/C) ratio to assess its validity today. As we discussed in Chapter 1, the C/C ratio defines the relative outperformance/underperformance between the Capital and Consumer Goods sectors at a given point in time, and we reviewed the shift in leadership from Capital to Consumer in 1982 and its relationship to a contemporaneous market decline. We also reviewed the 1992 shift back toward Capital Goods dominance although this changeover has been more ambiguous than its predecessors in view of the macrotrends we have been discussing. We will now examine whether the historic long-term bias toward Capital Goods cycles has shifted in favor of a bias toward Consumer Goods cycles, and whether the S&P Capital Goods component group has become outdated in view of the two-tier global market, new tech/old tech developments and the major demographic trends outlined thus far. A clear understanding of the actual C/C ratio has been important in forming an accurate technical picture of the underlying trend for investment purposes.

Capital Goods Breakdown; Consumer Goods Breakout

Further observations from a macrotechnical perspective appear to support the evidence suggesting a move away from the old-tech heavy industrial, capital-intensive, energy-intensive, labor-intensive cycles of the twentieth century. Looking at the Capital Goods sector by itself (Figure 9–1), notice the RS experienced a multiyear breakdown in 1989 to a level unprecedented in the history of the S&P data. A break of a 40-year support level should be considered a major technical statement, comparable to the 30-year break through resistance in 1981 by the Foods group. A good portion of the 2-decade decline in RS for Capital Goods reflects the 27-year RS decline for the old heavy-weighted S&P Computer Systems sector (now called Computer Hardware—see Figure 9–2). Anyone who bought and held this sector any time between 1968 and 1992 underperformed the stock market. Digital

Figure 9–1   S&P Capital Goods Relative to S&P 500. Chart created with Supercharts® by Omega Research, Inc.

Figure 9–2 S&P Computer Hardware Relative to S&P 500. Chart created with Super-charts® by Omega Research, Inc.

Equipment, for example, traveled from a price of 200 to a price of 19 in the greatest bull market of our lifetime (refer to Figure 5–8).

Contrast this to the outperforming Consumer Goods from 1981–1992 (Figure 9–3). If one accepts the old-tech thesis, the relative breakdown for the traditional Capital Goods sectors should not come as a surprise. Since 1992, the Capital Goods index has experienced a positive RS trend. This is no doubt due to the heavy weight of the outperforming Electrical Equipment and Manufacturing—Diversified Industrial groups in its composition. But the rally is still contained under the support break of 1989.

The flip side directs us to the RS profile of the Consumer Goods group which experienced a 42-year *breakout* in 1982 similar to the Capital

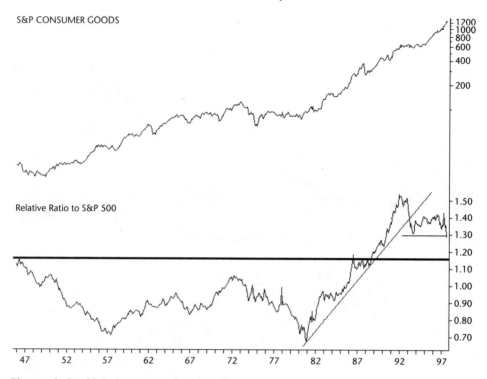

Figure 9–3 S&P Consumer Goods Relative to S&P 500. Chart created with Super-charts® by Omega Research, Inc.

Goods RS *breakdown*. Having advanced substantially in its initial rise following the breakout, this Consumer Goods performance may need to digest its gains, even pulling back to its breakout level—a normal technical expectation before continuing up.

A Possible Trend Reversal in Leadership

In light of the evolving macrothemes, and the delinking, or changes, that have been taking place since 1993 in traditional expectations of intermarket relationships, I think there may be a serious structural change developing in the C/C ratio, perhaps partially due to global forces and partially due to the ratio's current, less applicable, composition. For years, we have used this measure of the S&P Capital Goods to the S&P Consumer Goods for identifying shifts in stock market outperformance leadership from one of these market segments to the other. In doing so we have been able to identify structural changes and guide investment decisions into the next area of stock market leadership or outperformance (as set forth in Part One).

Throughout the 60-year history of this C/C ratio (Figure 9–4) there are several observations of its behavior apart from those discussed related to bull markets: When the ratio line is rising there is a Capital Goods sector

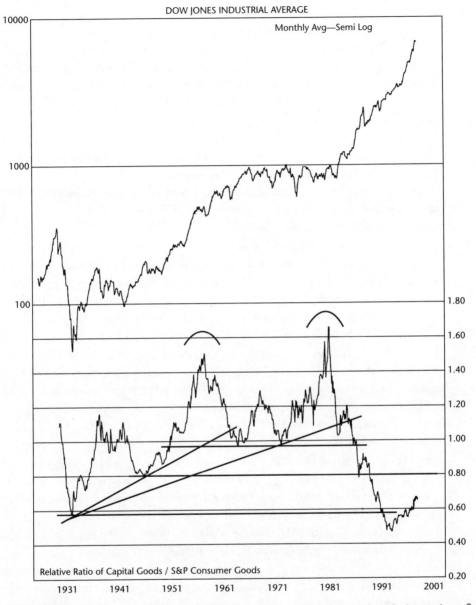

DOW JONES INDUSTRIAL AVERAGE

Monthly Avg—Semi Log

Relative Ratio of Capital Goods / S&P Consumer Goods

Figure 9–4 Capital Goods/Consumer Goods Ratio. Chart created with Supercharts®
by Omega Research, Inc.

dominance in the stock market and when the line is declining it represents a
Consumer Goods sector dominance. The first technical observation is that
from the beginning of the available data, while their cycles have clearly alter-
nated throughout history, one could submit that a defined upward bias toward Capital Goods cycles was in effect until 1981. That bias, it could be
argued, is manifested in the chart by the preponderance of slightly more extended Capital Goods cycles than Consumer cycles. In other words, looking

back at Figure 1–5, not only has there been an alternation of Capital and Consumer cycles, as well as an apparent "set" of longer Capital and Consumer cycles followed by a "set" of shorter Capital and Consumer cycles, but the Capital Goods cycles (Figure 9–4) on the whole were more extended in magnitude, distance traveled, and duration than the aggregate Consumer Goods cycles from 1929–1981. Also, each consecutive Capital Goods cycle took hold, or re-initiated, at a slightly higher point on the chart (defined by the uptrend line) suggesting a stronger bias toward, dominance of, or demand for, the Capital Goods sectors overall from the longer term perspective; this perhaps reflective of, or corroborating the predominance of the U.S. industrial economic forces of the decades in that era. But now one can see that a dramatic major shift may well have taken place. The long-term C/C ratio chart may relate to, and argue for, the macroconcepts set forth herein.

Since the 1981 peak, several serious technical parameters have been violated that suggest the former bias in favor of Capital Goods may have now changed. The first observation is the break of the Capital Goods cycle relative dominance uptrends: The first 30-year uptrend was violated in 1963–1965 (coincident with the ending of the last secular bull market); the second 50-year uptrend was broken in 1982, confirmed in 1985. The longer a trend has been in force, the more important its violation. The years from 1951–1983 could be considered the "top" (the flattening, slowing momentum) of that relative industrial cycle leadership; the 34-year "support" level violation in 1985, another multiyear breach, completed the top. What was in formation at that time, having begun in 1981, was an extraordinary Consumer Goods relative cycle which not only broke that 34-year support level but also violated a 42-year support level in 1988, and a 58-year support level in 1990, carrying the C/C ratio to a 61-year low in December, 1992. A technician who saw this chart without a title might be prompted to ask the following technical questions: Has the (long-term) trend been violated? *Yes.* Are there signs of distribution evident? *Yes, a double/triple top pattern.* Is it enough to imply more than a minor movement might ensue? *Yes.* Has readable support been violated? *Yes.* Finally, has the stock initiated a downtrend? *It seems so.* This last question is still outstanding and will depend on the magnitude both of the current relative Capital Goods cycle and the magnitude of the next Consumer Goods relative cycle over the years to come. (The Southeast Asian crisis of late 1997 may slow growth and precipitate the shift of this Capital cycle into the next Consumer cycle.) The possibility of a major trend reversal exists.

I think there are several important considerations here. The magnitude of the Consumer Goods cycle from 1981–1992 is the longest in the history of the C/C ratio. The Capital Goods relative cycle initiated in 1992 has been feeble by comparison, and so far looks like a "kickback" rally. By kickback rally, I mean a temporary rally toward the resistance level (the level of the former support break). The apparent macrocycle shift may be initiating a profile of an extended series of cycles in which the relative Capital Goods dominance may carry the *less* dynamic characteristics of duration and distance traveled (as the Consumer Goods relative cycles had experienced from 1933 to 1983); also, the relative Consumer Goods cycles may now continue to exceed expectations of both distance traveled and duration as the twenty-first century unfolds.

Has the historical relative bias in the industrial era of the United States, toward Capital Goods cycles, as we have known them, shifted to a structural bias in favor of Consumer Goods cycles? Reflecting on this in light of some of the concepts presented in these pages, the following helpful questions might also be asked: Given the emergence of 60 percent of the world's population in Asia alone into some form of a capitalist- or consumerist-style economy, and given the resulting outperformance of the globally-exposed Consumer Goods (particularly Consumer Staples) stocks and sectors, might this apparent new bias toward Consumer Goods cycles represent a *major* structural shift given these demographic forces? Further, if the concept set forth regarding the relative underperformance of old-tech sectors today (versus new-tech sectors) may, in fact, imply that many of these older heavy industrial sectors may share a smaller piece of the U.S. economic pie (and most of these are the groups which S&P currently defines in its Capital Goods sector), isn't it then possible, given that definition, that these old-tech sectors could contribute to a relative smaller magnitude in the performance of the Capital Goods sectors versus the more potent global Consumers Goods sectors?

Revision of S&P Sectors

The sector changes that S&P has made (or neglected to make) in its major sector revisions of July 1996 could also be another factor in these trend observations. In their new calculation of Capital Goods, the Computer Hardware group was eliminated. (However, we have been maintaining it in our own calculation of the C/C ratio on the chart for historical consistency.) But technology sectors as a whole (which today actually constitute the Capital Goods sectors of the exploding new-tech economy) are *not* included by S&P in its Capital Goods definition. Hence, this entire new-tech arena, as it proliferates into a much larger piece of our economic pie, does not have its growing weight represented in the S&P C/C ratio. This indeed may contribute to and help to explain these technical observations regarding the C/C ratio. Without technology included, the C/C ratio may cease to represent today's major forces of the Capital Goods new-tech economic contribution and therefore may be faltering against the more globally-exposed strengthening Consumer Goods components, in terms of apparent relative dominance. We may continue to see this bias in the future as the C/C ratio remains antiquated with only old-tech components in the Capital Goods sector definition. The structural "break-down" in the C/C ratio, given the above composition, may also be reflecting that these old-tech Capital Goods Sectors may not be as active economic participants in the Information and Communications era going forward, as they have been in the past Industrial era. Therefore, this C/C ratio may be another intermarket relationship that needs to be revisited today in light of new technological developments. The C/C ratio may not be as pertinent today (without the inclusion of technology in its rapidly expanding domestic and globally-exposed implications) to our economy as it has been historically in measuring the full relative balance of the Capital or Consumer cycles in the stock market today.

Summary

We are experiencing the initiation of an entirely new, knowledge-based technological cycle (even a new long-wave cycle) consisting primarily of communication, information (networked intelligence), electronics, catalytic, and precision technology which renders efficiency to existing processes and defines new frontiers, and we are witnessing the dynamics of its force. It cannot be disputed that the communication and information technology is a new horizon in which innovation is key and evolution into burgeoning new technologies is just beginning. We are clearly seeing a demise of the old heavy manufacturing in this country (despite the industrial needs of emerging nations, whose industrialization will benefit immediately from new-tech processes). The two-tier cycles of technology (the ending old-tech, the beginning new-tech) discussed in Chapter 7, and of demographics (one waning, one waxing) discussed in Chapter 4, have never been experienced simultaneously before in this country, and may be resulting in a two-tier economy (as we shall explore in Chapters 13 and 14). Once again, we need to be alert to these and other alterations that can occur as a result of unique dynamics. These changes in trend should be more accurately reflected by S&P in the C/C ratio so that the ratio cycles may be a more effective analytical instrument in the formulation of investment decisions.

Chapter

10

Looking for Inflation in All the Wrong Places

As equity investors, we are all concerned, if not consumed, with the question of the liklihood of inflation. We touched on this subject in the first chapter, noting the stable/low-inflation environment in force since 1982 and the technical indications of its likely continuation. Our efforts to track the future of inflation, however, must take into account the many changes that are reshaping the world economy and investment possibilities. Just as the U.S. stock market should now be viewed from the two-tier global/domestic perspective, and growth prospects should be assessed as influenced by demographic trends, so should inflation be interpreted in light of these and the new technological innovations. In this chapter, we will consider the new places to look for inflation and where not to look.

The raw materials of today's evolving technology are vastly different and less inflationary than yesterday's steel and coal. Water has become a major component to manufacturing processes and its scarcity (in a pure form) is converting this material resource into an essential commodity. Even the cost of primary fuels like oil and gas has been transformed by market and supply trends. All of these developments warrant a re-evaluation of our traditional means of measuring inflation.

A Fresh Look at the CRB

What macro implications might the new technological era have on our perception of another intermarket relationship? How might we again be missing the forest for the trees. Perhaps we should explore the charts and bring into question the validity of the Commodity Research Bureau/Bridge Futures Price Index (CRB)[1] as we have known it. (The CRB Index represents a basket of 21 actively traded commodity markets and is the most widely watched barometer of general commodity price trends and thus also of domestic inflationary potential. It includes grains, livestock, agricultural products, metals, and the energy markets, among others, and is considered to be the commodity markets' equivalent of the DJIA). A different way of perceiving it may be required, given the new dynamics of the two-tier environment/bull market within the framework of an altogether new technological cycle.

Our technical research has shown no signs of an inflationary trend on the domestic economic front since 1982 as measured by at least one indicator, the real, inflation-adjusted Dow (DJIA/CPI—refer to Figure 1–8). The DJIA/CPI has progressed dramatically over the past decade, not only fulfilling the target in 1982 of the reverse head and shoulders bottoming formation as projected, but has also advanced to equal and eventually surpass the 1967 peak—thus rising through a 30-year resistance level. It is very difficult to make a case for the return of inflation any time soon. There are as yet no signs of a reversal in this trend and considering the duration of the uptrend since 1982, the technical expectation would be to see signs of a topping process well in advance of a structural shift of trend: the break of an uptrend, or the break of support, or a nonconfirming negative divergence. None of these is currently visible. The same inflation observation can be made for the PPI (Figure 1–10), which continues to slip to new lows.

However, examining another indicator, the history of the CRB (Figure 10–1), one can note that an important 14-year downtrend has been penetrated. Clearly, the multiyear trend for the CRB has stopped going down. It can further be noted that the CRB has also begun to rise to put in place a 6-year high from which it may pull back toward its breakout level, a normal technical expectation. However, the CRB, though having risen, has not seen an aggregate significant rise in raw industrial material prices.

If we are indeed experiencing a new technological, electronic, communications, and information industry revolution, perhaps the deep-cyclical, heavy-industry leadership of the last cycle may not be where we should be expecting to see today's expansion and outperformance. One reason may lie in the upcoming shrinking relative U.S. demographic profile today. But even more, today's U.S. cycle appears to be the beginning of an *entirely new* technological frontier that, from the charts, does not appear to be dependent on

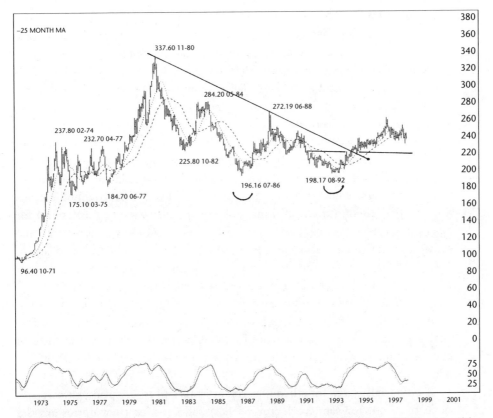

Figure 10–1 Commodity Research Bureau/Bridge Futures Price Index (CRB)—Monthly. Chart courtesy of Commodity Trend Service (1-800-331-1069).

the capital-intensive, heavy machinery, deep cyclical base, and its related raw materials that this country has known in its Industrial era.

Today's New Raw Materials

In reflecting on the raw material components of the CRB, one may need to ask whether the CRB as it stands today adequately represents the raw materials of today's new technological cycle? Are they (copper, gold, platinum, and crude oil, for example) pertinent to today's new industries and, what might the CRB be telling us that we are failing to perceive? The next question is, of course, if not these raw materials, which ones? In an effort to try to answer the question of what raw materials are pertinent to today's industries and technologies, I consulted the (then) Smith Barney technology-related and communications fundamental analysts as well as numerous corporate reports. The results were both surprising and compelling.

For example, the semiconductor industry utilizes silicon which is made from sand. Shortages would be due to capacity, not raw material availability. The metals used only for etching include gold and precious metals, high grade iron, steel, and copper (electricity conductors); rubber is used for connectors, and polyurethane (chemicals) for nonmagnetic housing of the computer unit; plastic (chemicals again); and some steel and aluminum. The semiconductor process involves catalysts of chemical washes (ethylene glycol, ethers, methylene chloride, nickel); electronic chemicals; hydroxyl amines; hydrochloric acid; and gases (from air) such as silane, nitrogen, helium, hydrogen, and argon. Electronic components need Teflon, plastics (from chemicals), polymers, some steel, copper, and aluminum. The communications areas utilize silicon (sand); minimal gold and copper wiring; glass (sand) for fiber optic cables to convey light pulsed for audio and video; gases (from air) separated by the chemical companies. Lasers use, guess what, sand again, light, and beryllium. The raw material and energy costs of the new-tech processes are well below those of the old-tech processes.

Also used are strategic metals such as titanium, itrium, rhodium, telurey, gallium, and arsenic, which could, under political duress, experience shortages (supply comes from Russia and South Africa). But other less expensive materials could substitute with near-equivalent conductability, if necessary.

Essentially, *sand* for silicon, lasers, crystals and fiber optics; gases, separated from *air*, for semiconductor washes; and *light* for fiber optics are the *new* pertinent raw materials.

The analysts' consensus was that there is "no cost," as compared to past costs, to the raw materials of today's technological profile. Almost none of the above, except for precious metals, are components of the CRB index today. So not only does the CRB represent the raw materials of the last industrial cycle (old-tech), but the raw materials of this cycle (new-tech) sand, air, and light, even if they *were* included, are so low cost as to be essentially free, and therefore "not inflationary" compared to the raw materials of the past. This could be contributing to the maintenance of our low inflation economy.

Today, it appears the metals may play a much smaller role in the domestic economic profile as reflected in their structural chart progressions. Multiyear breakdowns have occurred in the metals themselves in 1996 and we know the Basic Materials, Metals & Mining (refer to Figure 8–2), and Gold & Precious Metals (Figure 10–2) sectors suffered breakdowns. Some rallying has occurred in a few metals but price levels, so far, have only returned to near resistance levels or downtrend lines and then moved lower. Gold has established a multiyear downtrend. There is also the consideration of the opening of the world, with the end of the cold war, and the access that now exists to resources around the world that were not as available for free trade. Natural resources, also being developed at a rapid rate in emerging

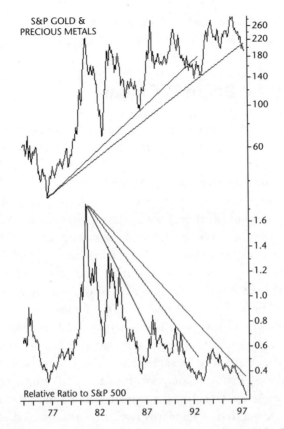

Figure 10-2 S&P Gold and Precious Metals Relative to S&P 500. Chart created with Supercharts® by Omega Research, Inc.

nations, create more available and accessible supplies to the marketplace creating an almost unlimited source or, more realistically, a less finite supply; add to this the new-tech metal recovery techniques. It may well be that the CRB no longer reflects the engine of the technological sectors of this new industry leadership and may require new components.

Therefore, those deep cyclical leaders that were at the forefront of the last two industrial cycles also may be dinosaurs of this new age, which would account for the multiyear technical declines that we see in place for those particular sectors. It is not to say that they don't have a role today, but since they are not the primary focus of this cycle they are exhibiting relative underperformance, and may not reap the same rewards of today's leadership industries. Perhaps, the industrialization of developing nations will also be modified by these catalytic and other technological and alternate energy innovations to streamline their process, efficiency, and costs. The result may be to bypass many old-tech, capital-intensive methods and/or utilize the newer materials and technology. This may imply lower demand for the "traditional" raw materials and heavy industries than otherwise would have been expected based on what was experienced in the U.S. industrial cycle.

The Agricultural Boom Is Global

On the other hand, it may well be that we simply are *not* perceiving what the CRB *is* telling us today about another force of the emerging cycle and this new era. There is one component in the CRB index that has been rising dramatically and uncharacteristically: Agriculture.

It was the agricultural components (which constitute over 50 percent of the weighted total of the index) that, in early 1996, rose dramatically. Farmers in the United States have been making money for the first time in years and agricultural exports have been increasing since 1994, hitting a record in 1996. Short-term observers cited weather and inventory variations. But a more probing question that should be asked in examining the CRB index is: Are we indeed looking for inflation in all the wrong places? Are we missing a message about the character of this macrocycle? Has the perception of the CRB as a measure of domestic inflation changed? Is it possible that our two-tier market thesis may also be applicable to the dynamics of the CRB?

That the agricultural components of the CRB are soaring should come as no surprise. As societies become more developed and urbanized, and as disposable income and living standards rise, there is increased demand for more and better food. This is indeed happening with 80 percent of the world's population residing in these developing nations (including Asia, and Eastern Europe with Poland, the Czech Republic and Hungary, as leaders). The United States, as one of the largest agricultural producers, provides 25 percent of the world's agricultural products. Our agricultural exports are hitting record levels (up 7 percent in 1996) representing 33 percent of what we produce. Agriculture is doing so well in this country that government subsidies and set-aside programs are being phased out, and farmers are finally working in a free market economy.

We are seeing multiyear (up to two-decade) breakouts and all-time highs in agricultural products, particularly grains (Figures 10–3a & b and 10–4). The significance of this implies the price rise may be more than an aberration due to weather (an explanation that the daily economic news forecasters bandy about with every raindrop, frost and sunbeam). Nor is it politically influenced like the oil markets.

Looking at the long-term corn and wheat charts, the potential for a major change of trend is compelling. Could this represent the emergence of a secular bull market for grains? Corn prices have emerged through a 22-year, wide-range of trading swings; wheat, 15 years. The charts for oats and soybeans profile breakouts from 5-year trading ranges that resemble potent

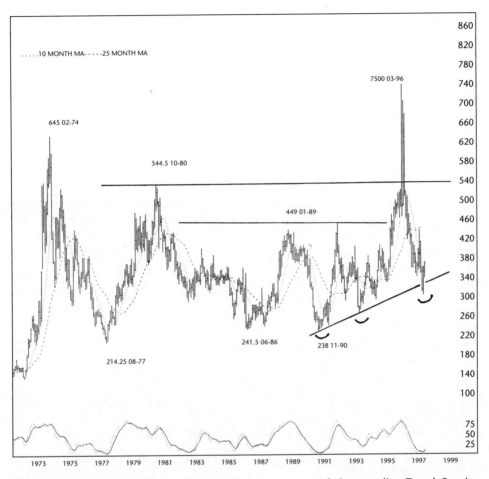

Figure 10–3a   CBT Wheat—Monthly. Chart courtesy of Commodity Trend Service (800-331-1069).

technical basing configurations, and imply a shift of trend from a neutral trading to a more upwardly biased range. I'm not suggesting that the inherent volatility of the commodity is changing. But I *am* suggesting that the *trend* of that volatility may be shifting, from a multiyear horizontal range of volatility to a new structural uptrending range in which prices register higher highs, and as they have been doing for several years, higher lows (which represents aggressive demand). Volatile commodity swings and El Niño notwithstanding, the price action of these charts today technically suggests the establishment of a new structural long-term uptrend which may result in higher, more upwardly biased trading parameters. From a technical perspective, the larger the base, the greater the upside potential over time. Pullbacks, such as occurred in 1996, would be a normal technical expectation, as disbelief abounds regarding the long-term implications of this phenomenon as more than a

Figure 10–3b Corn—Monthly. Chart courtesy of Commodity Trend Service (800-331-1069).

one-shot event. Those retracements appear to be ending, as the prices stabilize at yet another in a series of higher lows.

This may well be only the beginning of the trend. In 1888 there were 1.5 billion people on earth. By 1988 there were 5 billion, and by 2050 there will be over 8 billion, with most of the increase coming in the rapidly growing areas of the emerging nations[2] (Figure 10–5). And, global life expectancy has risen from 46 years to an expected 80 years by the 2020s. The developing nations have a younger demographic profile, prime for expansion and expenditures; the Asian developing nations constitute 60 percent of the world's population. In the early twenty-first century China alone would need the equivalent of an entire year's world grain shipment to feed 21 percent of the world's population; China became a net importer of grain in 1994 as it refocuses on industry.

India, the world's largest democracy, is the second largest population after China and is increasing 2 percent a year; it has a developed industrial

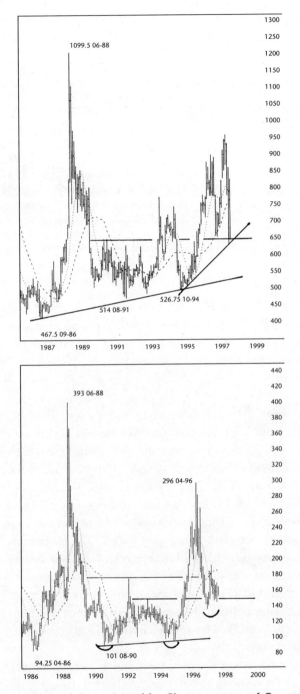

Figure 10–4 Soybeans and Oats—Monthly. Chart courtesy of Commodity Trend Service (800-331-1069).

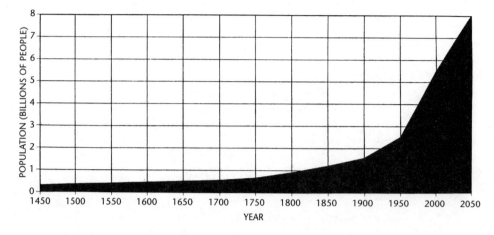

Figure 10–5   Global Population Growth. Used with permission of U.S. Filter Corp.

structure as well as an impoverished majority untouched by the twentieth century. India has been a pioneer in fertilizer and irrigation techniques and has been self-sufficient in food, but its margin of safety is eroding as the population approaches 1 billion. In Kenya, food production has fallen far behind population growth. (Politicians in some poor countries bribe with food for votes.)

The study of populations and food shows shifts in consumption at stages as incomes improve. Currently 45 percent of the world's population is about to rise to its next food consumption level. Scientific advances and genetic alterations (as discussed in Chapter 7) have enabled food production to triple over 50 years. The United States is at the forefront of this trend. Some chemical companies (Monsanto and DuPont for example) are redefining themselves to address the agricultural trend as well as its technological industrial "green" potential. Major corporate CEOs are turning from chemical-based to renewable plant materials (like a cornstarch polyester) for less polluting, less energy intensive products. The demand for food has been rising 5 percent a year for 10 years but productivity per hectare is only growing at 1½ percent/year. The United States additionally is losing 1 million acres a year to ruralization (addressed in Chapter 11). The agricultural implications of the world's population are enormous.

If inflation pressures are to be found anywhere, as agricultural supplies shrink due to enormous global demand (blight, drought, sunspots, El Niño, and other natural factors), isn't it likely that these pressures will eventually and perhaps permanently be manifested in agricultural products? The dramatic breakout through these significant multiyear bases for grains suggests a long-term trend and the possibility of enormous upside potential over the years to come (into the twenty-first century).

Hence, the CRB not only does *not* reflect the raw materials of today's U.S. technological focus, but what the CRB does reflect (agricultural products) as the potential secular inflation components, appears to be more related to the global economic tier of consumer demand than to the domestic economic tier; therefore perhaps no longer a barometer of *domestic* inflation pressures.

Water: The New Commodity

Water is a huge, impending twenty-first century issue both globally and domestically.[3] Water is the most valuable finite resource on the globe—the necessity of life. Yet water is already scarce today, with shortages in 80 countries affecting 40 percent of the world's population, on a globe with over 5 billion inhabitants. The twenty-first century will be challenged to accommodate the dramatically growing population.

The amount of water on the planet remains constant. Only 2.5 percent of the world's water is fresh (97.5 percent is salt) and over two-thirds of that fresh water is locked in glaciers and deep fossil aquifers. This leaves a mere 0.7 percent of the world's total water as accessible fresh water in lakes, rivers, and shallower aquifers—and only this amount is renewed by rain and snow. The amount of potable water is decreasing; the quality of this useable supply is shrinking and deteriorating due to contamination[4] and must be shared by a growing global population. More than 50 percent of the world's population lacks adequate sanitation; 1.2 billion people, more than one-fifth the population in the world, don't have safe water to drink. In the emerging countries, 66 percent of the population has no access to toilets, or water for washing, even in many hospitals; drinking water often cannot be distinguished from wastewater. In these countries, people are affected by water-borne disease from fecal contamination, resulting in contraction of parasitic flukes, protozoa, intestinal worms, and cholera; this looms large as a growing threat, bearing pain, diarrhea, dengue, malaria, river blindness, lethargy, anemia, and—for children—poor cognitive development and often death.[5] The World Health Organization estimates over 5 million people die each year from contaminated water diseases (this on top of illnesses from industrial pollutants).

The sheer quantity and variety of waste discharged into the fresh water sources have overloaded and outstripped nature's ability to break down the harmful elements. Commercial chemicals, particularly the chlorinate organic chemicals, have been spread by air and water and are found everywhere in living tissue. Heavy metals, lead, mercury, arsenic, and cadmium are deadly; copper, silver, zinc, and chromium also kill aquatic life; mining streams are barren for centuries after. Cancer, nerve disorders, birth defects, mercury poisoning, endocrine disruptions, and learning disabilities are the results in humans and animals. Fertilizer runoffs accelerate algae growth, cutting down oxygen supply in water and suffocating its inhabitants, and breeding organisms that lead to fish kills. Drainage into oceans is increasing toxic red tide algae blooms. High nitrate content in drinking water decreases the oxygen-carrying properties of hemoglobin in our blood, a particular threat to infants. We all know about acid rain. Illness from unsanitary environments are easily communicated today over long distances and are cropping up in developed nations. Ill health results in economic stagnation, bloated health costs and affects the entire global economy. Water availability per capita has dropped 37 percent since 1970, and the population is expected to soar in the next 50 years.

Water use for agriculture, industry, and domestic consumption has been increasing more than twice as fast as population growth in the twentieth century. Water shortages, including those from contamination are crippling agriculture and industry. The link between water and crops is critical as agriculture uses 87 percent of available global fresh water. As the population grows, the link between water and agriculture becomes more critical, and more expensive. Increasing numbers of regions are outstripping their local water supply: Twenty percent of crop production already is seriously reduced due to salinization of the land as water evaporates in arid and semi-arid regions, and also due to water erosion and water logging. "Low water stress" results in countries that use 10 percent of available fresh water reserves; "moderate water stress" using up to 20 percent; "medium to high water stress" if withdrawals rise to 40 percent of available water; and "high stress" over 40 percent. By 2025, two-thirds of the population will have moderate to high water stress and 50 percent will experience serious difficulties because of poverty. Water scarcity becomes a limiting factor to economic growth, and high stress countries may need to choose less water-intensive industries than agriculture and may begin to import food.

As competition for water rises, water management will be critical to global peace. The expected population increase estimates a 50 percent to 100 percent increase in water just for food production (meat production requires significantly more water than grains and vegetables). Most of the new population growth will be in the developing nations, with an increase in urban areas from 37 percent in 1995 to 56 percent of the population by 2025, which displaces both people and water supplies from agriculture and creates urgent need for sanitation. In 1995, the world had 321 cities with populations over one million, including 125 mega-cities of 10 to 20 million—and the mega-cities are expected to double in 20 years. The implication for inflation of food and water in the twenty-first century becomes clearer.

In addition to usage, about 60 percent of drinking water supplies in emerging nation cities (if they have pipes at all) are lost by illegal taps into the system or leakage through rusty pipes; this compares with an average 12 percent of waste in the water systems of Britain and the United States. Underground water sources are being pumped out faster than nature can replenish them. Over-pumping has seen worldwide water tables drop by tens of meters with serious effects: Rivers are drying up and vital aquatic ecosystems are disappearing, and competition for dwindling supplies is increasing. In Asia, water is being increasingly drawn down for expanding industrial production, rising living standards and growing populations. Most of these countries may have even more severe water problems by the year 2025. The proliferation of wells could dry up underground water sources in Bangladesh, India, and Pakistan. The lack of water and debilitation from disease will make it more difficult for a country to compete for pure water-consuming high-tech industry and foreign investment to enhance productivity, consequently limiting economic and social development. The World Bank has warned that heavy reliance on underground water to serve industrial needs cannot go on indefinitely.

- China already is governmentally re-allocating water from agriculture to industry because 300 Chinese cities are short of water. Almost 25 percent of the world's population lives on only 8 percent of the world's waterways. The Huai River (second largest after the Yellow River) is the most polluted with untreated industrial effluent. Most small scale towns and villages do not have even basic waste water treatment. Eighty percent of the Huai's water is undrinkable and too toxic for crops. Only 3 percent of homes are connected to treatment facilities. The water table under Beijing has dropped 6.5 feet per year for the past decade and one-third of the city's wells have dried up. The world's largest dam under construction in China is in debate as potentially the world's largest cesspool.

- Much of Bangladesh's water is contaminated by the naturally occurring arsenic-rich pyrite mineral, causing arsenic-related black body spots, tumors, and gangrene.

- In India, 350 million people are below the official poverty line; 70 percent have no access to toilets; 30 percent with no water, leaving India with one of the highest water-related illness and mortality rates in the world.

- Jakarta's water utility can only supply 50 percent of the needs—and most shallow wells are contaminated by human waste and ammonia, a few with heavy metals, including mercury.

- In the Philippines, safe drinking water may be scarce in Manila in 5 years. Only 10 percent of 800,000 households are connected to the sewer systems. The rest goes into the water supply.

- Singapore is rich enough to buy its water and is exploring its first desalination plant (an energy-intensive process costing 8 to 10 times that of treated water, but, over time desalination may become cost effective).

- A 4-year drought in Spain has caused consumption of 75 percent of the country's water reserve and agriculture production has dropped up to 50 percent.

- In Mexico, heavy pumping of aquifers under Mexico City is causing the city to sink 22 inches every 60 years, 12 inches a year in some areas. The Cathedral in Mexico City is cracking from this overpumping. Many rural areas have no pipes and people pay one quarter of their earnings for water; their mortality rates are 10 times that of developed nations.

- The countries of the former Eastern bloc have the residue of five decades of communism, when poisons were never allowed to stand in the way of production. These are still infusing the air and water with waste far in excess of international standards. Toxic drugs contaminate ground water; raw sewage fills the rivers and coastal waters.

- In Prague, an underground reservoir of sulfuric acid threatens to leach from a uranium mine into an aquifer supplying the city's water.

- In Kazakhstan, the Amu Dar'ya and Syr Dar'ya Rivers have drained the Aral Sea, once the fourth largest inland body of water on the globe, to feed 30 cotton fields with tons of chemical fertilizers. By 1990, the Aral Sea had lost two-thirds of its volume, and the runoff of agricultural chemicals and raw sewage and salts leave tremendous health hazards for ground water, drinking, and irrigating and runoffs into the sea. Infant mortality is 50 to 60 per 1,000.

- Russia's crown jewel, Lake Baikal, holds one-fifth of the planet's fresh water and has more water than all of North America's Great Lakes combined (it supplies 80 percent of the water to the former Soviet Union). This "pearl" of Siberia has been polluted by heavy industrial dumping over the years.

- In the Middle East, from the plains of Anatolia to the eastern Sahara, rivers are the lifeblood of this arid region, where growing nations compete for a shrinking water supply. With accelerating population, expanding agriculture and industry, water is replacing oil as the region's most problematic commodity.

- Turkey has huge water resources from the upper regions of the Euphrates River and has been harnessing these resources with dams to fill a reservoir 10 times the size of the Sea of Galilee. This, however, deprives downstream countries of water.

- Syria and Iraq, farther downstream, are heavily dependent on the Euphrates and are affected by these Turkish dams. Syria uses kerosene lamps several hours a day already; Iraq's agricultural land, one step farther downstream, receives the Euphrates saline runoffs from the fields upstream. In Syria, the bedouins' well-drilling is lowering the water table by as much as six inches a year—emptying desert water holes.

- Jordan has already overpumped its aquifers. Agriculture is poor and water is rationed.

- Israel, with the Sea of Galilee, is well advanced in water conservation and purification, recycling two-thirds of its water and utilizing drip irrigation (eliminating evaporation by delivery directly to the roots). But Israel still exceeds its renewable supply by 15 percent and drains one-fourth of the water from occupied territories.

- In Egypt, the Nile provides 98 percent of the country's water needs, but is laden with agricultural chemicals, industrial waste, untreated sewage, and waterborne parasites such as schistosomiasis, a freshwater worm of Africa. The dams, as well as water usage, are sinking the once agriculturally priceless Nile Delta that relied on upstream sediment for renewal. Plans may evolve to build desalination plants.

- Other nations, comprising 10 percent of Africa, are dependent on the Nile for water. Their increased usage could deplete and jeopardize Egypt's downstream supplies. Lake Tanganyika and Lake Victoria in Africa are two of the world's largest lakes, but African raw sewage is a serious problem, contaminating even shallow aquifers.

- Kuwait has little fresh water but has the money and energy for desalination plants.

- Saudi Arabia is a leader in desalination, producing 30 percent of the world's desalinated water supply. It also pumps fossil water deep within the earth, posing geologic structural problems that could eventually cause ground level collapse.

- In Latin America, raw sewage and industrial waste typically flow untreated into the water supply.

- In the United States, in San Antonio, the Edwards aquifer has such heavy manufacturing demands that some endangered species are threatened. A water reuse program for "effluents" is under consideration.

- In California, one of every ten public drinking wells is contaminated by toxic solvent used in dry cleaning. The health consequences make water a life-and-death issue for millions of people.

- In the "Cadillac Desert,"[6] the Colorado River, shared by seven states and Mexico, nourished the explosive growth of the Southwestern United States. But due to overindulgence, the river no longer reaches the Gulf of California (damaging the delta's spawning grounds); it trickles down to nothing in the desert. The same can be said for the Salt and Gila rivers which used to converge west of Phoenix, but now run dry east of the city due to withdrawals for irrigation.

- Stretching from Texas to South Dakota, the Ogallala aquifer supplies regions all along its extent and is North America's largest—90 percent of its water has helped increase agricultural yields from Nebraska to Texas producing $20 billion a year in food and fiber on about 15 million acres. Now parts are running dry from overpumping and levels have dropped up to 10 inches. The downward percolation of agricultural chemicals has also adulterated portions of the Ogallala. Fully 95 percent of America's fresh water exists underground and by 2020 the Ogallala aquifer will have fallen 23 percent from overdraft. (For every gallon pumped out only a tea cup is replenished naturally.)

- Deep below the Mojave Desert, the large Fenner Basin aquifer is pumped up to 30,000 acre-feet[7] of water/year for crops—also running a deficit/depletion course.

Yet there is also virtually no industrial or consumer business that can exist without water. Every manufacturing process needs purified water, using from minimal amounts to millions of gallons per day. Treated water is the principle soft drink ingredient; it takes seven gallons of treated water to process one bushel of corn to sweeten 400 bottles of soft drinks and that's without the water in the bottles. A ton of Belgian chocolate uses 4,000 gallons of purified water. A gallon of French wine uses three gallons. One ton of steel uses 23,000 gallons. But electronic manufacturing is the most staggering statistic. Electronics manufacturing can use up to 150 gallons of highly, highly, purified water in *one* rinse cycle . . . for *one* microchip. With silicon growth in 1996 into a $350 billion chip/microprocessor era, and global computing power doubling every 2 years, we are looking at an era when everything we touch will have a chip in it.[8] Imagine the water requirements just to support this technology.

Water delivery is a $55 billion a year business in the United States and we get 85 percent of that water from municipal companies that run a more costly and often less pure operation than private companies. Industry further purifies the water it receives from municipalities to remove salt, chlorine, minerals, and protozoa. Filtration is a process technology that must be customized to meet myriad needs. High end filtration is used not just for industry, but also to recycle water and treat waste water before it is released back into the environment so that it doesn't contaminate existing supplies. The United States spends 10 times as much to assure an adequate clear drinking water supply as does the rest of the world, yet 45 million of its people still drink contaminated water.

The annual world cost of purifying water, treating waste water, filtering and separating processes was over $335 billion in 1995 rising to over $500 billion a year by the year 2000. The cost to purify water just for U.S. human consumption alone is $30 billion and $80 billion a year worldwide. The United States uses 150 gallons of water per day, per person—other areas of the world use only a fraction of that. The bottled water and home filtration market is still young, yet exceeds $2 billion. The World Bank estimates up to

$800 billion is needed for water purification to avoid severe water shortages in Latin America and other emerging markets.

The Asian water industry is now worth $16 billion and is expanding rapidly. The water/waste water needs in Asia are huge and expenditures are anticipated to increase $6.3 billion in Asia by 2000. European environmental directives will cost $150 billion of investment for purification; $100 billion for sewer/sludge treatment.

The unit price of water is rising 5 percent to 6 percent per year (Figure 10–6). Global population growth, economic expansion, scarcity of water, contamination of water resources, and concern about quality will exponentially increase the need for worldwide filtration. The Middle East already is bartering oil for water. The spectrum of water's future on this globe is both fascinating and troubling. It might be interesting to reflect that we already pay the same amount for a gallon of water that we pay for a gallon of gasoline. We will not be fighting wars for oil in the twenty-first century—we will be fighting wars for water.

Water needs to be recognized as a precious commodity with a market value set by the forces of supply and demand. There should be a futures market for water and if we want to add something meaningful to the CRB, that represents inflationary potential in this country (and across the world) in the twenty-first century, let's add water! (It may become the world's new gold or oil.)

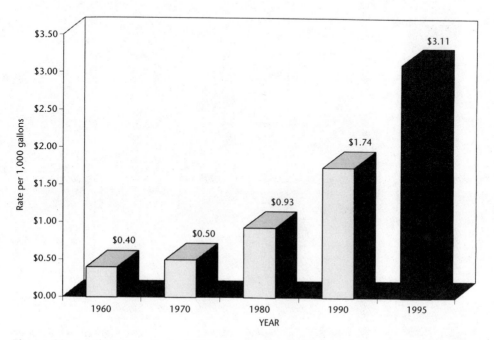

Figure 10–6 The Rising Cost of Water Usage. Used with permission of U.S. Filter Corp.

Oil Component

The energy complex, another CRB component, also needs to be addressed. From a sector perspective, we have seen that even as the price rises the Domestic Oil sector RS has fallen to a 15-year low. There is as yet no sign of stabilization—no technical evidence that the trend has stopped declining. The demographic U.S. implication, increasing access to world supplies, and the technological considerations discussed may play a role here. The International Oil sector, for several years now, even as the crude oil price has zigzagged from its 1994 lows, has shown a trend of flat, or a neutral, in-line market performance (RS) (see Figure 10–7). The stock prices of the international oil companies have been advancing (with the expectation the market could still double from 1996 levels, a market performing sector would still be rewarding). Oil price has gyrated in a wide range perhaps due to the perceived tight supply of cost saving "just-in-time" inventory and the spiking effect of continuing momentary concerns and speculations, maintaining the volatile nature of the energy markets, in their balance between supply and demand. Yet there appears to be little suggestion of impending inflation from

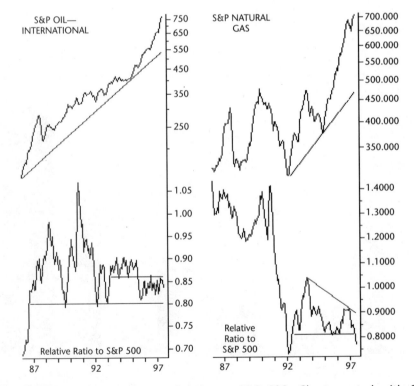

Figure 10–7   S&P Energy Sectors Relative to S&P 500. Chart created with Supercharts® by Omega Research, Inc.

this source. When the CRB began its 1993 advance (reference Figure 10–1), the price of crude oil was plunging to a multiyear low and did *not* contribute to the 1993 surge in the CRB, the surge being primarily due to the grains. The RS of the oil sectors does not reflect the intermittent price strength for the oil commodity. The Natural Gas sector, after trying to stabilize for a 5-year period in its RS progression, suggesting the possible future reversal of the 15-year downtrend, weakened again in 1997.

Even within this weakness, an interesting statistic shows a shift in the sources of energy consumption over the past 17 years and a projection through the year 2000: Overall consumption of petroleum is decreasing, while overall consumption of natural gas is on the rise (Figure 10–8).

In spite of foreign industrialization and potential automotive demand, especially in India and China, there are plentiful reserves in many of the emerging nations and in the former Soviet Union, heretofore inaccessible, which are now becoming available to the rest of the world. In the nineteenth century Azerbaijan was the world's largest source of oil. Combined with the oil of Kazakhstan and Turkmenistan, reserves more than rival those of Saudi Arabia not to mention the huge reserves of Siberia. In particular, the reserves in Kazakhstan are already being developed by Chevron, and we can only guess at what will be discovered in China. Similar development is in

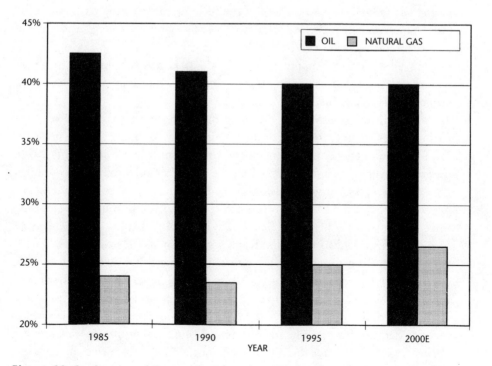

Figure 10–8 Sources of Energy Consumption. Used with permission of the Independent Petroleum Association of America.

place in Angola, Congo, Columbia, the Gulf of Thailand, off the shores of Malaysia, Australia,[9] and Sakhalin, north of Japan. As post-Third World nations develop their own oil reserves, overcapacity and excess supply have already begun to take place. (U.S. oil imports have risen above 1970 levels yet the average price per gallon is reportedly down by seven cents.)

Technology is also at the heart of the energy industry today. Production costs are dramatically lower due to the new technology available from 3-D seismic, CAT, and MRI imaging applications; multidirectional drilling; and high-tech extraction techniques, stabilizing prices and raising yields from 35 percent to 70 percent in geographical areas once abandoned. These supply implications, given the lower new-tech fuel demands, do not suggest inflationary pressures will emerge from the world's oil fields.

The implication of major technological advances reducing fuel usage (including telecommuting) should not be underestimated, in the face of rising supply. From solar energy to the fuel savings discussed in Chapter 7, industrial technology is reducing fuel consumption. Consider the Boeing 777 which uses 30 percent less fuel, and with its computerized manufacture eliminating raw materials and energy needed for test-model development. Consider other alternate energy in the pipeline such as Xenon gas providing 10 times more thrust for rocket launchings; and the potential of a neutron beam to blast nuclear waste producing tremendous energy (and in the process dissipating the radioactivity). Because of the technology, growing corporate eco-efficiency and their recycling (of up to $2/3$ of raw material needs), and alternate energy advances, price gyrations may not relate in the same meaningful way to the available reserve supply. Crude oil, along with other old-tech, may play a much smaller role in the domestic economic profile, a smaller piece of the economic pie in the future.

In addition, one Middle East analyst[10] believes that there are conceptual mistakes in predictions of dramatic oil price rises being used to pressure local political settlements again—due to the lessons learned during the 1970s oil crises. In spite of industrialization, the Mid-East oil-producing countries are a one crop economy and must sell what they have. They hold an interest in expanding their client base—to prolong the life of the product and to minimize incentives of other countries to develop their reserves. The 1970's rise in oil prices worked to their disadvantage because, as oil prices rose, worldwide conservation programs were put in place, lowering demand. Alternate energy sources were sought along with energy efficiency and self-sufficiency; and other countries developed their own resources further. The result was that Arab production *fell* after the 1970s price rise, creating local recessions and less demand for oil. The ultimate conclusion: Rising prices were against their best interest. After the initial shock of the Gulf War, prices moderated, Saudi production increased, opening the question as to whether, with the supply implications today, oil prices can rise above a moderate trading range: Hence, the lower long-term influence on an advancing CRB progression and a lower influence on domestic inflation pressures, at least as related to supply and demand.

Role of Chemicals

Chemical processes play a role in this technological wave, and may be reflected in the positive technical configuration of the Chemical group and its RS. Recalling Figure 2–14, I was struck with the similarity between the chart of the DJIA relative to the S&P 500, and the current progression of the Chemical group's RS (Figure 10–9).

First, the major Chemical group, like the DJIA, is made up primarily of globally-exposed U.S. equity names, one possible reason for the RS similarity. Second, many Chemical companies are operating more cost effectively and are somewhat less vulnerable to the familiar cyclical swings.[11] Third, the technological revolution is allowing the industry to make small, much more specific "catalytic" changes to existing production capabilities (rather than costly rebuilding) to move their processes and products into the new technological age, and into global markets. Fourth, there are also strong growing

Figure 10–9   Relative Performance of S&P Chemicals Sector Compared to the Relative Performance of the DJIA. Chart created with Supercharts® by Omega Research, Inc.

A QUALITY OF LIFE TAKEN FOR GRANTED

By 1960, the world's consumption of grain had more than doubled, but actual grain plantings increased by only 2.6 percent—due to the benefits of chemical advances in fertilizers, pest, and fungicides (the latter controlling deadly microbes); the addition of nitrate preservatives ended large botulism death rates; refrigeration relies on chemical coolants allowing global transportation and local preservation of food. In developing nations, 50 percent of food grain is lost (and misuse of agrichemicals is a serious environmental problem); yet developed nations waste has dropped to 3 percent to 4 percent due to chemical benefits.

The chemical business bridges a gap between consumer demand and limited natural resources: Housing is highly dependent on chemicals: 40 percent of its materials are manmade; eight percent of an average car is now made of plastic, saving 0.5 liters of fuel per 100 km.[12] One barrel of oil can be transformed into polyester for equivalent wool output of 280 sheep (that need to eat) or a 1.4 hectare cotton crop. Land resources might not exist to replace the manmade with natural.

Chemical companies convert gases for industrial use: Oxygen for cleaner efficiency in the steel and glass industry; krypton for lasers, lighting and thermal windows; hydrogen as the clean engine fuel of the next century, emitting only water, or used as a refrigerant; carbon dioxide in the food and beverage industries. Chemicals are used to recycle paper and plastics; form the research basis for new bacteria/fungus killing materials; and for self-cleaning clothing.

Zeolites, volcanic rock minerals with catalytic chemical properties, are valuable gasoline savers—the amount of gasoline from a barrel of crude oil doubled (refineries decreased) when zeolites replaced the old catalysts. They are also used to transform methane to methanol to gasoline in countries, such as New Zealand, with gas but not oil resources; and to convert propane and butane to high quality fuels making lead-free gasoline less costly.

Chlorine may be considered at the heart of the chemical industry. It is used to break, and make, molecular bonds for new molecules—60 percent of chemical output is dependent on chlorine. Agricultural pesticides need disinfectants using chlorine; sulfur dioxide, ozone, and ammonia; protecting lead pipes utilizes phosphoric acid. Chemicals help industry to meet the rising water hygiene standards. "Multiple barrier method of water treatment" relies on several chemical additives for: coagulation removal (ferric sulfate; chloride and aluminum chloride); pH adjusters (lime; sulfuric acid) to help coagulants work; and activated carbon and ozone.

Water purification is the biggest single market.[13] Chemical companies can reduce thousands of gallons of toxic waste dumping, spending 1 percent of that cost to dispose of it on-site by injecting ozone to break down contaminants for safe disposal directly into the sewer system. Treating waste on-site with business' new voluntary standards ushers in a new technological era of environmental cleanup, tracking raw material use, generation, treatment and disposal of hazardous wastes, which is now more cost-effective for the companies than polluting and cleaning up.[14]

The critically important chemicals called catalysts, once poorly understood, are responsible for the linking molecular bonds that create thousands of different plastics. The code has been cracked and now at least one class of catalysts, single-site catalysts, are clearly understood and can be fine-tuned to make plastics with customized properties of toughness, stretchiness, heat resistance, weight, absorbency, conductability, and magnetism; to be made more environmentally friendly (even eliminating some chlorine-based use) and at a lower cost for what may be the "most significant polymer catalyst advancement in 50 years."[15]

agricultural and alternate eco-material trends in most of the large chemical companies. Quite possibly, the Chemical group RS chart might be suggesting a shift back to more of a "growth" industry, in contrast to many old-tech sectors. (However, this profile does not yet extend to the other Chemical-Diversified or Chemical Specialty sectors with declining RS profiles, which may still be affected by old-tech related or excess chemical commodity supply issues and whose business is being usurped by big oil companies with greater cost efficiencies.) The DJIA's upward thrust of outperformance versus the S&P 500 has taken the progression out of a 35-year downtrend, and a 15-year base and the Chemical group appears poised to follow suit. Interestingly, both RS progressions have followed similar peak-and-trough pathways from about 1954, to their final lows in 1985, followed by a more neutral basing process for 15 years. (S&P's recent removal of Monsanto—the second largest component weight—from the Chemical group, due to its redefinition as a bio-ag company, could somewhat alter this chemical observation.)

Summary

In this chapter, we have seen that this new technological wave, in comparison to the more capital-intensive Industrial Revolution, appears to have a lower capital and raw material investment requirement. And the small, relatively low-cost technological catalytic changes to existing processes can adapt the already-in-place capital infrastructure of old industries to the more efficient technological process to meet new current needs. The new processes run with lower raw material and energy usage—hence, a smaller capital outlay.

As the importance of the old-tech industries becomes increasingly outstripped by rising new-tech enterprises, methods and materials, we can no longer expect to find the same measure of inflation in all the old familiar places. As investors we need to obtain an accurate reading on the level of inflation where it matters today—in the new-tech and global areas. The CRB, as presently constructed, fails to register the impact of the low cost, new-tech raw materials, and presents through its agricultural component a reading that is more truly global than domestic. Pending recomposition of the CRB, we can better assess inflation by keeping in mind the vast growth in the world and the implications for essentials such as agricultural products, water, and the ongoing and changing role to be played by chemicals. In the next chapter, we will consider the future directions in which U.S. agriculture is trending as a result of this growing world demand.

Chapter

11

New Agricultural Direction for the United States

So far in this book we have concentrated on the impact of the macrotrends of technology, demographics, low interest rates, low inflation, and long-wave cycles upon the stock market. We will now step back a bit from that focus and examine the effect of two of those trends on the no-longer-static U.S. agriculture industry. By examining whether agriculture will be similarly stimulated by these trends, we begin to form an awareness, if not an understanding, of the future influence of agriculture in the U.S. economy and stock markets. In doing so, we will build on the concept introduced in the last chapter: that the growth in American agriculture is being driven by continually increased demand, both corporate and consumer, domestic and global.

Global Food Demand Boosts U.S. Agriculture

For some time now, agriculture has not represented the predominant U.S. domestic economic activity as the norm of the last century (in what was an industrially-driven, capital-intensive economy). But, in light of the new global involvement in economic forces, we may be addressing a new era, one even projecting a shift of wealth to the agricultural producers (away from the consumers) in this country over the twenty-first century due to this enormous growing global demand.

America began as a predominantly rural culture and economy. In the 1820s, the government ensured a broad-based land ownership. Industrialization and urbanization created a commercial food system that grew to international proportions. With World War I, the farm population began to decline, and by the 1990s only 2 percent of the population is living and working on farms. This long-term decline may be ending, however, as emerging nations continue to develop along with their demand for more food. China has 21 percent of the world's population with only 7 percent of the world's arable land, and the world is becoming more dependent on grain from North America.[1]

Farmers in the United States are making enough money on their crops to question the need for further government subsidies or the withholding of 10 percent of farmland from planting. Exports are soaring. U.S. farmers are on the leading edge in agricultural biotechnology—transgenic hybrids, insect and drought-resistant crops, beneficial bacteria use, and pivot irrigation technology. With the aid of their PCs and site-specific satellite connections to improve plantings and pinpoint the source of global demand, farmers are obtaining yield enhancement ranging from 10 percent to 50 percent and are feeding the emerging nations' populations.

As the disposable income of emerging nations grows, their spending power grows, and food quantity and quality demands increase. China, as only one example, is having trouble keeping people on the farms to produce food as masses flock to the cities and rapid industrialization takes thousands of acres of agricultural land (rice paddies) out of production. Water, already scarce, is now governmentally allotted to Chinese industry (instead of agriculture). Growth in GDP results in more demand for food and also increased diversion of land away from farming in favor of industrial uses. Thus, the process of a developing economy by definition puts a squeeze on its ability to generate food. China's growing demand for food for its 1.2 billion people is only in its early stages. The United States is seeing a return to production of inactive land.[2] Given the potential for world population growth the long-term U.S. agricultural horizons seem bright[3] as U.S. farmland represents 25 percent of the world's productive capacity.[4]

Is it possible that the United States is on the verge of *converting* from a century-long, capital-intensive, heavy industrial economy to a *new secular,* twenty-first century trend toward a precision technological, electronic economy and a new global agricultural economy? I don't mean to suggest that we are reverting to an agrarian or pastoral culture, but rather I am talking about progressing, not only to *a new high-technological* society, but also to *a new high-tech agricultural* society that feeds the world (again two-tier, as we continue to replace old technology with new).

Biotechnology and Related Technologies Raise Farm Demand

Not only is the United States a leader, as we saw in Chapter 7, in biotech (genetic) advancement in crops of all descriptions (much of it done by selected chemical companies), but also there are some important technological trends in their early stages in other industries that also suggest agricultural demands will expand.

The drug industry, for example, has unveiled the "Biotech Goat." Using genetic engineering, "transgenic" animals are successfully producing monoclonal antibodies that deliver chemotherapy cancer drugs directly to breast, colon, and lung tumors at a fraction of the cost of drug synthesis factories. A drug company spokesman was quoted, "If we can make drugs with herds of goats rather than a whole new plant" and do it for half the price, there is "an unlimited supply" of the product; "if you need more, increase the number of animals." Where do you suppose this is done? Transgenic *farms* with "the best hay money can buy."[5] Pigs, apparently, are next on the list of transgenic animals; if it's a success, we can assume this cost-saving advance will spread, along with the need for land.

The United States is already researching the planting, even selling, of various nutrient-rich grains from Africa (pearl millet, fonio, sorghum, and tef)[6] that grow fast and can live in small plots of poor soil in arid land. Further, biogenetic advances are being made in creating higher nutrient corn and higher oil-producing corn and in creating longer, better roots for existing crops to survive on less water, an effort that could make less favorable land agriculturally productive. Saving water is being reflected in the new "xeriscaping," or dry, techniques to reduce the 50 percent of U.S. drinking water that now goes to irrigate gardens and landscapes.

Remembering the land and water pollution technologies discussed earlier, these seem to be coming to the fore just in time to clean up the land for more agriculture, tree, fish, and goat farms. It is fascinating and ironic that many of the advanced technologies on the forefront of this era are being utilized to purify basic land and water just as they will be needed to meet global agricultural/consumer demand. Water, indeed, qualifies as a new and important CRB component into the next century. (But as desalination becomes cost effective over the century, due to shortages of available fresh water, the prognosis for the seas will be increased salination, further jeopardizing the already shrinking fish supply.)

Fish, including salmon raised on farms has doubled in the last decade due to depletion of "wild" stocks of fish. Already, half the shrimp sold in this country is from farms; catfish has replaced cotton as the Mississippi crop; scallops and crawfish raised in China are imported here in tons, threatening our local fish farmer business. It has captured the interest of multinational corporations, including food producers and drug companies. Genetic altering to meet the needs of customer tastes—more/less fat, omega three fatty acids, and pigmentation. Purity and drug usage can be problems—ponds on former farmland can be high in pesticides; inefficient feed use and concentration of fish waste can pollute water. It can take two pounds of feed to create a pound of farm fish—50 percent of that can come from wild fish, depleting the natural resource.[7] Abalone farms feed on kelp and provide a vegetarian aquatic farm environment for a univalve in high demand especially in the Far East.

De-Urbanization Is Resettling Rural Land

The emerging nations today are developmentally where the United States was early in the twentieth century, in the process of urbanization, but in the 1990s the United States is already witnessing and undergoing an opposite trend. Technological advancements (computers, cellular phones, modems) are increasingly allowing people to escape the stresses and deteriorating lifestyle of the cities and migrate to the country, where they can conduct business in their homes, free from urban hassle—a trend of *de-urbanization*. Corporations, too, are helping to break down the rationale for large, centralized (urban and suburban) headquarters as improved software runs operations from anywhere through PCs instead of costly mainframes—helping regional economies to grow into ex-urban areas. (Crime is already documented as falling in cities and rising in rural areas.) Even though the macrodemographic housing cycle is down versus 30 years ago, the geographic movements show increases in ruralization. (Rural housing may be reflecting demand for *new locations*, rather than a greater U.S. demographic population.) Could the profile of this cycle witness the *de-urbanization* of America, accompanied by a shift of our U.S. domestic economy base? Might that perhaps also be what the declines in the deep cyclical and domestically oriented sector charts and the breakouts from mammoth multiyear bases in agricultural products are indicating?

The demand for land appears to be a trend just entering its growth phase. It is not an overnight process. If it takes multigenerational cycles of the twenty-first century to achieve its peak, it will progress through our children's and their children's generation and beyond, just as it took multi-generations to fulfill the maturation of the industrial revolution.

Summary

If this trend is correct, farm and rural land usage could expand to meet both domestic and export demands for commodities and research demands for biotechnological growth. These agricultural and technological de-urbanizing trends, along with the aforementioned technological long-term view of retailing space, also could carry a negative implication: That some established urban real estate markets might witness a slow demise as the trend of de-urbanization continues through the coming century. Could it be that farm and rural land will climb in value and become the next inflationary hard asset for future generations? (In a flight of fantasy, could one even project that our children's children will witness the full circle return of the malls of America to farmland?)

Part Three

UNSCRAMBLING THE PUZZLES

Chapter

Asking Questions

In Part One, the two-tier global market thesis was presented as the new architecture of the stock market. In Part Two, we examined a number of macrotrends that are impacting and shaping the future of the market and reshaping many, long-established intermarket relationships. A different way of perceiving them may be required, and in Part Three, starting with this chapter, we will set this process in motion by asking an array of forward-looking questions to enable us to probe beneath the surface of daily events and long-held doctrines to see what may really be occurring in this fast-evolving market arena. In Chapters 13 and 14 we will seek answers to some of the questions posed, or at least refine our question-asking process to better grapple with today's increasingly complex issues.

Reassessing Intermarket Relationships

It is not just equity intermarket relationships that need review, given the two-tier equity thesis but also many of our *economic* intermarket relationships may need to be re-visited and adapted for validity in today's world. We need to examine how the behavior of economic intermarket relationships might function in a slightly different fashion from their historical norms.

Missing the forest for the trees is easy unless we step back from the edge of the woods to look at the bigger picture, the longer-term vision and understanding of what the charts may really be telling us about the underlying changes taking place. For a technical analyst, the study of history plays an important role: Identifying the potential long-term trend can and does impact interpretations, assumptions, and decisions (even on the very short-term fluctuations within those dominant trends). The 1985 identification of the 35-year secular shift of interest rates from a rising to a falling trend was critical. Historical evidence of a similar underlying structure allowed my analogy to the 1942–1966 bull market period, and further to the demographic, technological sea changes, and their critical effect on every aspect not only of the equity market, but also of economic behavior.

It bears repeating that we cannot base our analysis and expectations of stock market or economic behavior for one extended period on studies and statistics defining behavior and expectations of another structural period. Thus, we cannot expect the stock market or the economy to be interpreted or to function in an environment of falling interest rates and low inflation in the same way it would against a backdrop of rising interest rates and rising inflation (such as existed from 1967–1981) or perhaps even against low/stable rates and inflation (as we will explore in light of the new-tech forces). We cannot expect intermarket relationships to be similar in dissimilar periods. Nor can we expect companies that are 80 percent globally exposed to respond to domestic economic fundamentals, interest rates, inflation, or economic slowdown in the same way as domestically-exposed companies would. The macrofactors we have discussed (the two-tier global versus domestic equity market structure, demographics, technology, and agriculture implications) are completely unique and are bringing their own specific influence to bear on the expectations and behavior of today's markets *and* economy.

Question-Asking Process

The daily chattering and numbers noise over the strength or weakness in the U.S. economy may also cause us to miss larger trends. What may we be failing to perceive in light of the very different underlying structures in today's world and how are they impacting economic results differently? What is not being evaluated in light of these changes? Are interpretations being made on the rules of the old domestic economic structure rather than based on new ones that may better represent the new global and technological forces? What is not being measured? How might employment, wage structures, inflationary or non-inflationary pressures, exports, global trade, and imports be different today as a result of the new macrodemographic and technological global realities impacting every economic statistic? What new tools, new vocabularies, and new formulas may we need to use in the economic realm to capture the effects of these changes and the technological rapidity with which they are manifesting themselves and tangentially affecting every area of our lives?

Ultimately, how will all of these issues continue to impact the stock market? The key may be to try and ask relevant questions that probe the underlying structure of today's U.S. economy (which can no longer be isolated from the emerging global economy), and as a result, to foresee how things may behave as an "exception to the norm" in this cycle. For instance:

- The Information and Communications Technological Revolution (IT) is not only different from earlier technological revolutions because it is less capital-intensive, less energy-intensive, less labor-intensive, less industrial, and the new raw materials (sand, air, light) driving the economy forward are "free" (or at least plentiful and accessible) relative to the old industrial era, but also because the "fuel" of one tier of the economy has changed—from fossil fuel to the fuel of knowledge—thus carrying vastly different economic implications for productivity and inflation than previously experienced.

- Given the utterly novel electron economy, are we looking for productivity measures in all the wrong places; *materially* mismeasuring economic growth and productivity given the immeasurable intangibles of the electron benefits? Could technology, still only minimally diffused, impact overall profit trends to such a degree (aided further by the low new-tech commodity prices) that we might need to employ the laws of physics into economic models to quantify the growing *electron* intangibles of today's productivity? We will attempt to do so in Chapter 14.

- Isn't it possible that if interest rates are raised to allay inflation risk in face of better than expected earnings (driven primarily by the trickle-down effect from the globally-exposed growth phenomenon companies), that a rise in interest rates could boomerang; that this could more severely strain many of the already flailing domestically oriented (demographically affected) and old-tech industries while having little impact on the multinationals (where the expanding growth has come from global, not domestic, demand)? Changes in domestic economic fundamentals, like interest rates, inflation, and a slower economy, should have less influence on the highly globally-exposed companies. By the same token, it will be global forces, and fundamentals such as the 1997 upset of Southeast Asia, that will impact the globally-exposed companies. Any such temporary slowdowns inevitably will trickle down to slow our economy proportionately.

- Could higher wages have a much less inflationary impact today, even delinking from the traditional NAIRU labor/inflation formula, since the rise in high-tech productivity (going largely unmeasured) is more than offsetting the slower wage gains, pushing down unit labor costs even in old-tech sectors? Additionally, might the relative U.S. demographic decline be a perfect fit for the fewer jobs resulting from technology gains? Might this reduction in total number of workers needed per corporation offset a slightly higher wage for those who *are* working, canceling out the traditional wage inflation expectation? Additionally couldn't the jobs, relocated to rural lower cost areas, effectively raise the wage report, while actually lowering the actual wage of what a corporation would pay in a similar urban position, skewing reporting? Should wages be as great a concern today given the potential for global wage (and price) equalization as skilled lower cost labor floods the markets from the former Eastern bloc and emerging nations? As technology diffusion increases, global transborder access to those workers increases; (they are even being sought out for immigration to fill the unskilled labor pool needs).

- Due to the relative declining domestic demographic changes, should "full employment" be interpreted with different economic expectations and consequences? Could full employment be de-linking from its heretofore inflationary trend due to our first-ever, declining demographic profile (fewer workers), the rise of a less labor-intensive technology (fewer workers needed), and the global access to labor? Might not the worker/job mechanism now fit like a gear: As fewer workers come online for fewer jobs, full employment may achieve an *equilibrium* we've never known before in this country with heretofore nearly double upcoming generations entering the workforce. (We explore this in Chapter 14.)

- Should the U.S. economy itself be viewed as two-tier (old-tech, new-tech), and should employment numbers be similarly considered?

- Should the measure of low inventories (in face of rising global demand) be interpreted differently in light of the new technology applications that smooth the business cycles (shorten lead times and balance demand) by keeping inventory "on demand" rather than backlogged (and costly to hold) in a low inflation environment? Should inventory-to-sales numbers, the lowest in two decades, come as a surprise given these new methods and, therefore, *not* reflect the dire economic business cycle implications they have in prior heavy industrial, and higher inflation, cycles? (Considering the new technology is only 15 percent diffused through U.S. corporations, this benefit should only improve.)

- Could the CPI be invalid if the productivity measure is missing economic activity? Therefore, if we can't judge whether the economy is slowing or speeding, how can we know how fast the economy can grow before igniting inflation? And if food and water are becoming more important, shouldn't we include them in regular reporting?

- The PPI 12-month rate of change shows no signs of *domestic* inflation. Could this be reflective of the "low cost" raw materials of new technology (sand, air, and light), and of old-tech producer materials (and their increasing supply) representing a smaller piece of the domestic economic pie as technology becomes the major driver? Therefore, couldn't the discrepancy of softness in industrial commodity prices in face of strong manufacturing numbers reflect the old-tech tier's diminishing proportion to the entire U.S. manufacturing economy, and the new-tech tier's rising share?

- Could oil prices remain benign as well, reflecting lower energy technologies, increased fuel efficiency, extractive skills, alternative energy, corporate eco-consciousness, decreased new-tech energy demands, and the huge reserve development in Eastern Europe and in emerging nations?

- A rising dollar, in its 10-year trading range, appears *not* to weigh negatively on the globally-exposed companies which continue to grow profits, considering: the degree to which a stronger dollar makes foreign investment less expensive; and the large degree to which intrafirm global affiliate transfers (making imports cheaper, and many not included in the trading numbers), as well as increased corporate hedging, cancel currency risks.

- Should corporate results, valuations, and over-valuations be measured and interpreted in a falling interest rate and low-inflation environment in the same way that they were in a high-interest rate and rising-inflation environment? Should we be looking at traditional P/Es, or instead at forward P/Es or Price/Growth ratios or Economic Value-Added analysis?

- Given the surge in quality earnings in a low-inflation era and given the huge global market potential, should low dividend yields still be a measure of overvaluation? Many companies, not raising dividends to the same degree as in a high-inflation environment, are instead buying back stock to enhance value, and/or rolling dividend dollars into Research & Development (thereby avoiding double taxation and increasing productivity). As more nondividend paying (particularly technology) companies comprise the S&P 500, might traditional dividend valuation measures be skewed and become a less applicable measure of overvaluation?

- Should economic expectations be evaluated differently (given low inflation) as a two-tier economy (rather than melded)? With each tier having different needs and different benefits based on their old-tech, new-tech profiles (and their domestic or global markets), must we adjust our expectations and forecasting of how the more globally-exposed may perform versus the domestically-exposed tier?

- Should trade figures be more carefully defined to account for intrafirm trade, imports, exports, as well as reflecting production in foreign countries?

- Should the U.S. housing market, reflecting a purely domestic focus, still be used as an overall economic measuring stick given the waning domestic demographic profile and a tremendous U.S. growth benefit coming from the forces of global consumption? The ruralization and relocation of America may keep the image of housing growth as an economic barometer but cycles are 30 percent below historic levels (Figure 4–2); and what will become of existing homes as boomers sell ... to whom over the next decade?

- Is the CRB/bond inverse relationship de-linking because of the more domestic focus of the bond market and the more global focus of the components in the CRB index (as discussed in Chapter 14)?

- Like the bond/CRB de-link, could the bond and stock markets further de-link (as they did in 1994 as measured by the DJIA and the S&P 500 and their more globally-exposed growth profile) versus bonds and their domestic, low inflation and demographically affected focus? 1997 may prove to be a mirror image of 1994: Stronger bonds this time while the globally-exposed stocks correct.

- Should indicators like margin debt, whose composition today is radically different and no longer reflective of only equity debt, be used as in the past to measure stock market vulnerability?

- Could telephones slowly be de-linking from their interest-rate sensitivity in light of developing technology, deregulation, and global growth? Could their 1996–1997 underperformance result more from the dislocations of dismantling the old to put the new technology in place? Similarly, could electric utilities, now at an historical RS low, be de-linking slowly from interest rates as they deregulate, reorganize their corporate structures, and expand globally?

Summary

The complex interplay of the trends and forces that influence market and economic behavior and the shifting status of intermarket relationships must be continually re-evaluated if we seek to profitably interpret new market developments. The ongoing question-asking process illustrated in this chapter can be one of our most effective tools in understanding market activity, both present and future. Although we ask more questions than we can answer, in the following two chapters, we will pursue a number of these inquiries to help illustrate evolving market directions in the hope that the process will be thought-provoking.

Chapter

13

New Economic Perceptions

Although I am not an economist, in this chapter I would like to pose a few questions and possibilities employing technical interpretations pertaining to economic-related charts. Over 200 years ago, the economist Adam Smith set forth a classical economic framework based on free-market economic principles: That the key to prosperity lies with the individual, and governments should simply ensure the "right" environment for prosperity, including low taxes, free markets, protection of property rights, and stable currency.[1] He believed, given free trade (of which we have more today than ever before as borders open up), the bigger the consumer market the lower the prices, and that large markets are a powerful incentive for profit motivated producers (of whom there are more than ever before). Success will come to those companies offering the best quality and service at the lowest price. To achieve that end, corporate pressures today to cut costs and increase productivity are enormous,[2] and inflation should remain low.

A portion of the U.S. economic dislocations of our corporate re-engineering was suffered in the 1980s creating a more flexible labor force, freer markets, looser regulation, and more technological advancement. Employees are trading wage/benefits more and more for incentives/profit sharing, improving the work ethic. We know from our studies that U.S. inflation appears to be the most benign it has been in the entire century. In addition to the developing markets of Latin America and Asia, the end of the Cold War and the opening of the Eastern bloc, as well as of China, are further expanding both the number of global consumers and a new source of cheap labor to the global scene. Both of these factors have powerful disinflationary impacts which should be felt in a variety of industries as the decades pass. U.S. exports are continuing at a healthy rate (notwithstanding interim interruptions of over-accelerating cycles in emerging areas). Simultaneously, U.S. companies are taking the lead drastically cutting their cost bases through technology, (this process is still young) and significantly raising productivity.

Measuring Productivity in the Knowledge Economy

Productivity traditionally has been defined as output divided by input. Economic models of growth focused on labor and capital—an increase in both presumably raised output. The increased rate of investment, however, eventually ceased to yield greater returns on economic growth, resulting in the theory of diminishing returns—demand becomes saturated, (this may still apply to the current old-tech sectors). But the old model made no allowance for technology advances. Newer economic growth theory acknowledged that ideas create more efficiency, but still couldn't measure them.

What actually may be developing in the new-tech tier could be considered a major economy of *increasing* returns; high-tech, as we've seen, is light on raw materials and heavy on knowledge; R&D is high, but once a product is developed and sales increase, the cost base falls and prices fall. Success comes from cornering a market, developing an industry standard that others follow. Popularity demands that successful symbiotic industries gear their software and systems to the successful product, furthering the advantage of the innovative companies who then have a lock on the market, thus increasing their returns as long as they can maintain the competitive edge and reinvent themselves with newer products. But they are always challenged by the need for innovation and the fast obsolescence of technology; this threat may keep behavior competitive.

Falling communication costs and the Internet help entry for everyone into many more markets; tiny firms and emerging markets have the same fast and easy access to its benefits. Knowledge-based firms can set up at minimal cost (PC and phone), less overhead with online access to expertise. Again two tiers, one of diminishing returns (for older tech, heavy industrial, and waning domestic industries) and one of increasing returns (of new-tech globally exposed and service industries) that coexist separately and even within the same company (hardware as the former, software as the latter). The *material* base of the economy of diminishing returns is fast being eclipsed by the brain power—*knowledge* base—of the economy of increasing returns.

In addition to the "free" new-tech raw materials (which may be having its own effect on low inflation), the fuel driving the information and communication revolution today could be considered knowledge: The essential without which the new physical capital cannot function. And knowledge "defies the basic economic principle of scarcity."[3] With knowledge, the more you use it and pass it on, the more it proliferates, making it "infinitely expandable."[4] No matter how much of it is used it is never depleted, and it can be replicated inexpensively and recycled over and over without diminishing its value. Unlike any previous fuel, knowledge, has no mass, also contributing to the so called "weightless" economy, while revolutionizing the production and distribution of all industries and offering new products and services[5] throughout the global economy. Further, the only *tool* needed for mining knowledge is education. Those countries/economies that put capital into education just as capital has been poured into drilling for oil, the mining of gold, or any of the other raw material resources of prior technological cycles in order to enrich the economy, will benefit most. Scarcity of knowledge can only occur in the failure of education to communicate the understanding and creative use of increased knowledge. This is a critical investment consideration because of its positive effect on productivity.

Technology Diffusion: Efficiencies Rise and Costs Drop

Recent technological advances are beyond any achieved earlier in the century, moving with lightning speed; crushing time and space; accelerating the pace of change, efficiency, and competition. Internet integration offers simultaneous globalizing of production processes and financial markets: Billions of dollars exchange hands ($1.3T daily) across borders at the touch of a button, and it's still embryonic: only 10 percent to 20 percent of large U.S. companies have adopted high-tech performance techniques.[6] (Only 3 percent of the world's population has access to computers, by 2000, still only 10 percent.) Some sectors are yet barely touched by it, suggesting the diffusion factor, while improving, still has a long way to go even within our borders. Yet it is increasing with the corporate (and private) ruralization effect. The U.S. regional measurement of fiber optic cable is showing a more even diffusion,[7] moving from urban to lower cost rural areas of the nation, for decentralized production nationally, as well as internationally (as more economies open their markets).

Proximity to markets is no longer important; new global partnerships create fewer claims on resources as they are used for production on-site rather than transported. It takes time before technology breakthroughs deliver economywide gains, (consider the dislocations of an established nation dismantling the old to make room for the new). Productivity benefits may not fully show up in the economy yet because computers and communication still are only a small percent of the total U.S. capital stock and global diffusion is minute relative to its potential. Given the biggest participating population ever, there is a much larger base through which diffusion must occur.

At the corporate level, computers, efficiently and beneficially utilized, evidenced an average return boost of more than 50 percent a year;[8] but to learn to use the technology efficiently and to the greatest benefit takes time. The bigger the bank or corporation, the bigger the benefit spread for its fixed cost giving a whole new purpose to mergers today. Bigger beats the competition and offers lower cost products, better service, and an increased customer base. This creates a huge productivity advantage in the economy of increasing returns. Globalization increases the consumer markets, expanding the base for the fixed costs, increasing volume, reducing costs even more, and giving the product an even bigger edge. The more diffused the technology, the more prices drop, dramatically speeding up the global shift to a knowledge-based, low inflation economy.

Many U.S. firms with investment in information technology have shrunk relatively: The average number of employees in many industries has dropped by one-fifth over the decade. Yet technology has created 10 million new U.S. jobs over four years. Computers make many corporate costs (formerly too expensive to outsource) cheaper to outsource, allowing firms to concentrate their focus, increase efficiency in their area of expertise; cost-cutting, specialized outsourcing companies are growing. Outsourcing has both eliminated and created jobs. Falling communication costs favor decentralization,[9] allowing businesses to exploit larger economies of scale, and, as transaction costs plunge, services improve and consumers gain.

Productivity and Intangible Goods: Measuring the Immeasurable

The new technology and the Internet also may be smoothing the path of all U.S. businesses (old- and new-tech), as they streamline and become less vulnerable to the economic cycle. Services are tradable electronically, eliminating the paper work of shipping, clearing, and middlemen. For example, General Electric is converting its entire supply chain to the Internet, saving millions of dollars annually. Chrysler can now increase production without plant expansion. Dell Computer, having created component uniformity compatibility, waits for its orders and then buys the parts and builds—cost-saving inventory management. These methods eliminate inventory overproduction (essential to cost management particularly in low inflation environments) and the consequent layoff phase of the old business cycle.

Electronic transactions eliminate paper and move into an almost friction-free commerce allowing companies to produce more with less.[10] As we have noted, the "data mining" software (that zips through billions of statistics instantly with the search potential in problem solving and defect elimination of the new software programs) allows companies to operate in real time, adjusting inventory, product mix, and cash reserves. In this cyber- and knowledge-based, weightless economy, production/output is shifting its balance from tangible to "intangible goods," making a *literally immeasurable* difference to the shape of the economy. Tangible goods (television, watches, cameras, appliances, and cars) have intangible "smarts" imbedded in them. The intangibles take the form of expansion of ideas (versus materials, raw materials), and speed, services, customization—all less visible. As Fed Chairman Greenspan has noted, today's output in tons is barely heavier than 100 years ago but GDP is 20 times greater. Since 1990, information technology has represented approximately one-third of U.S. economic growth, experiencing a $3 billion trade surplus in knowledge-related services.

World trade is growing five times as fast in knowledge-based goods (new-tech) and services than in resources (old-tech); and more than 50 percent of total GDP in rich economies is already knowledge-based.[11] The intangibles diminish susceptibility to the capital-intensive economic cycle because inventory storage for many industries is now the electronic brain (or hard disk) rather than physical quantities in warehouses, perhaps (Figure 13–1) making the falling inventory statistics (and inventory-to-sales

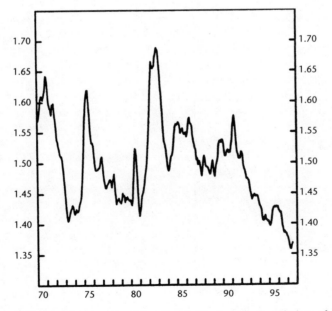

Figure 13–1   Business Inventory-to-Sales Ratio. Used with permission of BCA Publications Ltd., *The Bank Credit Analyst.*

ratios) less pertinent and less accurate in measuring economic health (and perhaps making full employment a more stable economic condition).

The link between knowledge and growth is not yet understood, posing a huge challenge to the measurement of performance, further exacerbated by the failure of government GDP statistics to directly capture corporate application software purchases which have increased from $7.4 billion to $79 billion over 13 years. (This spending increase on technology, with corporations reaping tremendous savings, is characteristic of early long-wave cycle behavior.) High-tech GDP growth (and capital spending, much of which is human capital) has outstripped the old-tech economy and accounted for 40 percent of real growth, (Figure 13–2) yet is not captured.[12]

How do we, for instance, measure rates of return on investment in knowledge? Today's technology has unleashed incredible increased productivity growth, well beyond standard calculations, essentially restructuring

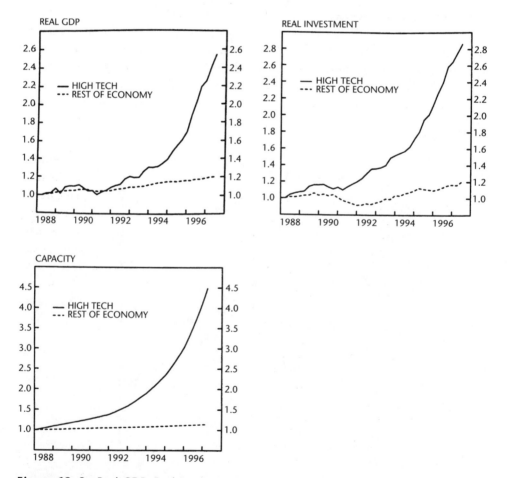

Figure 13–2 Real GDP, Real Investment, and Capacity. Used with permission of BCA Publications, Ltd., *The Bank Credit Analyst*.

the world economy in all areas. As technology shortens product cycles and brings buyer and seller together, productivity and growth benefits may be surging, but the degree of miscalculation and understatement of growth may increase because we aren't capturing it correctly with old economic formulas, standard statistics, and tools which may no longer apply (given the intangibles of a knowledge and technologically driven, speed-and-efficiency productivity of advanced software).

Could technology be impacting overall profit trends in a manner not previously imagined and presently not comprehended? Are old economic formulas inadequate, failing to measure efficiencies and costs in a new electronic age? Should we develop a new economic methodology that is essential to evaluating the profit trends, valuations, and the exponential benefits of productivity in light of the new knowledge-based technological revolution impacting the whole corporate process; therefore also the measures of inflation, wages, prices, and costs?

Productivity Efficiencies Too Swift to Calculate

In theory, output rises with the number of hours worked. Telecommunication traditionally has been measured by the cost of transmission per call, multiplied by the number of minutes (the assumption being *one* call per line). But no more. Today, output can rise with *fewer* hours worked as the intangible exponential benefit of technology transmits information simultaneously through fiber optic wavelength division multiplexing (splits laser light into multiple light streams each carrying data equal to the original signal); but is *not* measured. To obtain the true, much lower costs, it is necessary to accurately represent the multiplicity of transmission. Also hard to define and measure in physical output units is the aspect of quality improvements, customization, and speed—all intangibles. If technology can find a faster, shorter, street delivery route, the mileage covered drops and efficiency rises; but if economic models measure and charge for *distance traveled*, the statistics instead records a *fall* in real output, because the physical distance was shortened. Yet, the "intangible" quality of service improved, and time saved.[13]

As a result, the percent of the economy that can be measured accurately is shrinking: 70 percent of today's economic activity contains the fastest growing sectors benefiting from new-tech, and a larger slice of output takes the form of "intangible" goods and services, yielding greater returns. For example, the cost of writing software programs is in the knowledge (from the brain of the producer) which is recyclable and reusable (versus heavy industry's raw materials). No matter how many software programs are sold, the base cost is the same. In the case of software that writes software, this base cost is even lower and more elusive. Thus, the larger the sales in software, the lower the cost per unit, the higher the profits: heavy on knowledge, light on material resources and less inflationary, actually disinflationary.

We may not be able to define full capacity anymore because the speed of increase is rising exponentially with the speed of technology, and there are no figures for how much computer and telecommunication capacity is used. Therefore, government numbers designed for the heavy industrial era may not be useful to capture and incorporate accurately the intangible benefits of the booming information sector; which may be lost in traditional economic measurements of productivity.

Lost in the measure is the value or quality gains added by technology in services such as medical conferencing (or a better product). Also lost in the measure is the cost of savings from quality improvement due to technology, as faults, defects, malfunctions and errors are discovered in the production line, benefiting in fewer repairs (lost hours) or fewer returns (lost money). Fraud detection that saves money on theft losses; quality improvement of personal customization; wider choice; better customer service, time saving, convenience—all these are lost. ATMs add convenience and lower the paper costs, yet because *fewer* checks are processed, productivity is recorded as falling.

Lost in the measure is the speed and efficiency gained in productivity growth as output rises with fewer more efficient hours worked. Also lost in the measure is the time saved as computers raise productivity of high skilled workers. Remember that Boeing created the 777 with global digital design integration among geographically dispersed engineers simultaneously accessing the design on line. No raw materials were used to construct the laborious and multiple models eliminating trial and error (money not spent, raw materials not used, fuel not wasted, pollution not resulting), saving 30 percent to 40 percent of normal delivery time. That faster delivery to the customer allows him, in turn, to reap profits sooner, provide faster service to his customers (and in turn, to their customers): An exponential technological growth, or *hyper-productivity*, contracting time and increasing efficiency. Lost in the measure also may be the value of knowledge itself. How do we measure the benefit gain of knowledge in the old economic formula of productivity that requires physical tangibles? We never had to before.

An Economy of Physics

Until recently, the economy had been measurable according to standard principles of economics and accounting which sometimes included an arbitrary designation of value added in the form of minimal intangibles (an immeasurable quantity) referred to collectively as good will. But the technological gains and benefits to today's economy, (as it shifts from a heavy industrial natural resource-based era to one of brain power) have developed such a tremendous intangible component, that the measurement task may require something unique to capture it.

Today, economic measurement seems to need a way to capture the benefit of *an absence* of the former properties (what I call the *anti-matter*) that results in a positive economic productivity gain and bigger profit to the bottom line (Figure 7–3). If what economists may be missing is the *anti-matter*, or the absence of what used to be measured, but essential to the whole: how do we measure the hours *not* worked (which can be funneled into brain power, education, and more creativity and invention), the time *not* elapsed, the raw materials/fuel/resources *not* used or spent, the waste *not* occurring in both materials and time (efficiency), the defect repairs *not* required, the money *not* spent, and the disorder (trial and error) *not* created or occurring? These represent the *new intangibles*, which are becoming a larger and larger portion of the economic formula in the electron-age economy. In not being able to correctly measure these intangibles, the output and growth of the economy may be very inaccurately reported.

If we think of the cyber-economy more precisely as what it really is, an electron-economy, then the solution may become more obvious. Technology has taken quantum leaps that may need to utilize the science of physics to capture the invisible and intangible benefits of electron-based economic activity. Could it be that physics theories, formulas, and measurements of speed and mass and volume and work and time, rather than those principles of pure economics, may now be more applicable and may need to be incorporated into the traditional economic formulas and principles to accurately capture (and quantify) the effects of the electron technological age, the increasing efficiency of "work" and its intangible returns, benefits, and contributions, in order to measure productivity accurately today?

I went and dragged out my old college physics books. Several basic principles of physics may be considered essential. Let's visit these very basic physics concepts to see how they elucidate the economic productivity issue, to at least demonstrate why and how productivity today is perhaps not being measured accurately by traditional economics, and further to show the startling implication of the dimension of the gain of the intangibles that is being missed in the economic measurement.

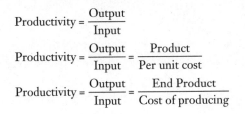

$$\text{Productivity} = \frac{\text{Output}}{\text{Input}}$$

$$\text{Productivity} = \frac{\text{Output}}{\text{Input}} = \frac{\text{Product}}{\text{Per unit cost}}$$

$$\text{Productivity} = \frac{\text{Output}}{\text{Input}} = \frac{\text{End Product}}{\text{Cost of producing}}$$

The first Law of Thermodynamics relates to conservation of energy in a process. But it can easily be converted to an economic concept in the electron economy to demonstrate the incredible growth of the intangibles in the economy today.

For instance:

$$\text{Energy} = \text{Heat} - \text{Work}^{14}$$

If we represent Energy as equivalent to economic Productivity; and we represent Heat as the Intangibles (the knowledge-based, technology advantage), which *are not* measurable (e.g., the faster the chip the more heat); and Work represents the Tangibles, (labor and raw material costs), which *are* measurable; then the formula looks like this:

$$\text{Energy} = \text{Heat} - \text{Work}$$
$$\text{Productivity} = \text{Intangibles} - \text{Tangibles}$$

So, we know, in this new technological era, the Work or Cost component—the Tangibles—is much smaller. (Technologically efficient corporations have fewer employees, need lower cost, fewer and different raw materials as a result of technology.)

Yet the Heat component, the *anti-matter*—or Intangibles—is rising exponentially (as a result of technology), as discussed.

If we subtract something getting smaller (Tangibles or Work) from something getting bigger (Heat or Intangibles) then the Total Energy, or Productivity of the economic system, has, by definition, to rise: If Heat (electron chip speed) rises proportionately (as chip speed factors increase), and Work goes down, then Productivity soars.

Since one ingredient we have not factored in is Time, we have to turn to another simple physics formula:

$$\text{Velocity} = \frac{\text{Distance}}{\text{Time}}$$

The Productivity we have just solved from the last formula becomes the numerator here, or the Distance, (in our economic equivalent).

$$\text{Velocity} = \frac{\text{Distance}}{\text{Time}} \text{ or} = \frac{\text{Heat} - \text{Work}}{\text{Time}} = \frac{\text{Energy}}{\text{Time}} = \frac{\text{Productivity}}{\text{Time}}$$

We know from our first equation that technology's benefits today have increased productivity significantly. We know, too, that technology has *splintered* the Time factor. So the numerator gets dramatically larger (from the result of the prior formula) and the denominator becomes a *fraction* of a whole (which effectively acts as a multiplier). Therefore the Velocity or the Rate of Change of Productivity *soars exponentially* as a result of the *absent* factors.

And none of this is being captured by economic measures!

Today's knowledge-based electron technology *defies* old economic theory. It reduces costs, prices fall, inflation falls, employment rises, real wages rise as a result of low inflation, savings rise, and profits rise because of the intangible rise in productivity; a coexistence unheard of, and claimed to be impossible, in the twentieth century economic realm (Figure 13–3).

The purpose of this process is to try to show how the electron element, reducing work and splintering time, has brought a very large intangible, immeasurable factor to productivity, and how much more significant it becomes as a lost quantity. This exercise is not meant to, and cannot, solve the actual quantification of the intangibles, but it may help to show that a serious economic measurement problem exists; that there is enormous growth in the intangibles of today's productivity quotient in the economy; and how much more significant it becomes as a lost quantity that can no longer be ignored because of its enormous tangible results on the corporate bottom lines; and that new methodologies may be essential to capture them. Measuring the intangibles of productivity also becomes urgent and critical for decisions made

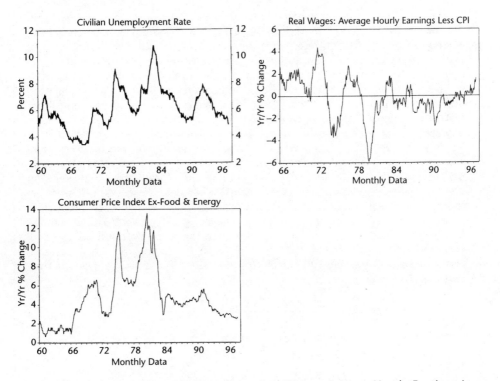

Figure 13–3   Civilian Unemployment Rate, Real Wages: Average Hourly Earnings Less CPI, Consumer Price Index Ex-Food and Energy. Used with permission of Salomon Smith Barney.

to curb a perceived inflationary trend which may not be present in this cycle for a very long time to come.

Output, and revenue per worker may well be growing more swiftly than in any previous technological revolution and may be a better measure of productivity (one large technology company is said to have had $1 million in revenue per employee in 1996). Output per hour is rising at a rate in excess of the official growth rate (for those utilizing new-tech). Workers are producing more with their time, and the added revenues can go to profits and more growth, wages, or both, without inflation. Efficiency of technologically reengineered corporations is rising such that they are taking on cash so fast they can barely spend it efficiently, utilizing stock buybacks, takeovers, consolidating operations, payouts and cushions for bad times. Yet cash gained needs to be accurately translated into productivity and economic strength. Even more advanced physics would be needed to quantify the exact electron benefit of ever faster chips and modems, communications and volumes transmitted. I'll leave that to the quantum physicists and engineers. Freeman Dyson where are you?

FOR MORE ADVANCED PHYSICS LOVERS: THE THIRD FORMULA

The Second Law of Thermodynamics measures the order or disorder of a system: the Entropy (or Efficiency). Implicit in this law is that no system can operate at 100 percent efficiency, friction free: No system can convert into work all the heat it takes in, because some is always lost in the process. No matter how much heat one puts into a system, some will always be lost to the environment; not all of it will be converted to work. This can be demonstrated by Murphy's law: No matter how simple a project will appear, something always goes wrong. In medical research, for example, a pipette can be used to measure out a very precise amount of water, but once you transfer the water to a small tube, there is actually a little less in your tube because some water has been lost during the transfer, because it stuck to the pipette, or due to evaporation, or slight human error. This introduces the topic of Efficiency. In the ideal, theoretical world, Efficiency = 100 percent, or unity. In the *real* world, it is always *less* than 100 percent. (Perfection can never be reached.) The real productivity will always be less than the theoretical productivity because the Efficiency of the system will never be 100 percent. This phenomenon is not limited to the scientific world, but to the whole world in general and economics in particular. But Efficiency can always increase, moving closer and closer to the unachievable 100 percent (or the theoretical textbook ideal of a friction-less economy). So,

$$\text{Efficiency} = \frac{\text{Heat input} - \text{Heat output (Work)}}{\text{Heat input}}$$

$$\text{Efficiency} = \frac{\text{Intangible component} - \text{Tangible component}}{\text{Intangible}}$$

As the Tangible component falls, the Efficiency moves closer to 100 percent. This effect is what is being experienced in the ever-more effficient electron eonomy.

Wage Gains Consistent with Increased Productivity

Wages may be the next, more multifaceted issue. One might ask whether or not the traditional relationship of tighter labor, higher wages, higher inflation, higher interest rates will prove true given today's waning demographics and unique technology?

When the economy is close to full employment, productivity growth traditionally suffers, leading to a rise in unit labor costs as labor supply dries up. While the corporation can shrug off commodity price increases, it is harder to shrug off labor increases which traditionally represent two-thirds of the cost of economic enterprise, so a rise in labor has resulted in rising prices.[15]

Yet unit labor costs are flat to lower as a percent change year to year (Figure 13–4) maintaining low levels for this decade not seen since the early to mid-1960s. It is clear, as a technician looking at the Employee Cost Index (ECI) charts (Figure 13–5) that the wage and salary chart alone does show a potential 4-year base and a broken downtrend. But benefits alone are in a steep downtrend and the total compensation ECI chart, which includes both wages *and* benefits, and is considered a broader more reliable measure of labor costs than average hourly earnings, includes almost all payroll jobs, and is a fixed weight index, and has a more benign trend. A long-term downtrend for total compensation is still intact from highs of 1982. This suggests that worries of

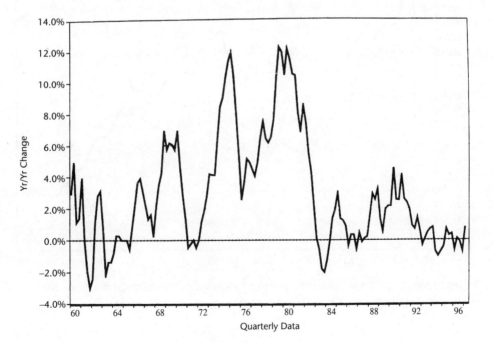

Figure 13–4 Unit Labor Costs—Manufacturing. Used with permission of Salomon Smith Barney.

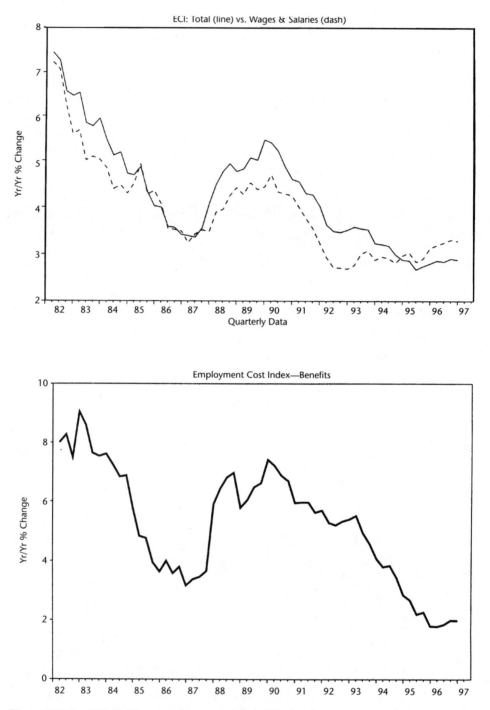

Figure 13–5 ECI: Total versus Wages and Salaries; Employment Cost Index—Benefits. Used with permission of Salomon Smith Barney.

"soaring wages" may be premature. The 15-year downtrend has not yet been breached, and while the trend has entered a neutral phase of stabilization, from which it may ultimately begin to rise, bear in mind that today's levels are way below those even of the 1990 peak. Since trends tend to have relationships to one another, one can presume that if an uptrend takes hold, it may be the next century before even 1990 levels are achieved again. Additionally, with low inflation one could suggest a much slower increase in the ECI, evident in its extended basing and the gradual, still very low, year-to-year growth.

With a low-inflation economy, the declining union power, lower pay raises, slowing rate of health care costs, and the use of contract workers, are all helping to keep compensation costs down. Technological control of inventories, quick supplier turnaround for "immediate ship" basis, appears to be giving the economy more equilibrium and less of the vicious cycles of the past.

Another consideration is how the two-tier phenomenon of old-tech versus new-tech plays out with wages. The higher wage trend is primarily in the new, high-tech areas (Figure 13–6). The wage trend in old-tech areas is much more gradual or rising at a lesser rate. An even less threatening perspective on wage growth, is the hourly wage compensation for private sector workers which is running well below the ECI.

It may be interesting, too, to think of the cost of labor differently in high-tech areas (where the wages have been growing faster), as not solely representative of labor cost in the old-tech sense. The labor cost in the high-tech arena also incorporates the cost of knowledge, thus melding the

Figure 13–6 Wages. Used with permission of BCA Publications Ltd., *The Bank Credit Analyst.*

knowledge-as-fuel-or-raw material factor into the faster rising cost of high-tech, skilled labor; and melding also the education (or mining) cost into the labor figure. If the human capital costs are rising, but are replacing a diminishing physical capital cost (raw material, fuel, heavy industry), couldn't these expense shifts offset one another? And what of its effect on productivity?

Another approach is to look at wage trends relative to the value of worker output (also a measure of productivity (Figure 13–7) to see if wages are moving in line with productivity or whether productivity is keeping pace with wage gains. We showed that output per unit of time (which has splintered), was rising beyond measure; thus unit costs must be falling relative to productivity, particularly in the new-tech sectors (still young in their diffusion). With this in mind, another formula:

$$\text{Unit labor costs} = \frac{\text{Compensation}}{\text{Unit of output}} = \frac{\text{Wages}}{\text{Productivity}}$$

We know the denominator in this case is enormous; we can see in Figure 13–7 that the real wage factor, the numerator, has remained flat. So the result is effectively much lower unit labor costs.

What may be getting lost in the concern over wages going up, is also that ability today of new technology beneficiaries to spread those costs

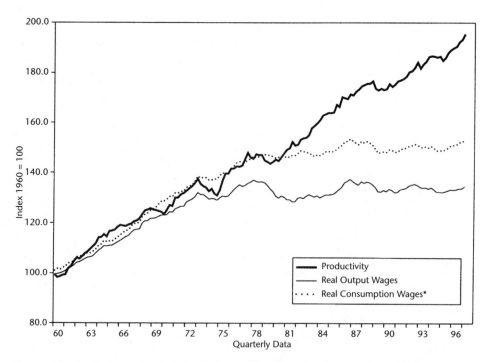

Figure 13–7 Productivity and Real Wages: Nonfinancial Sector. Used with permission of Salomon Smith Barney.

tremendously (the increasing returns) over a larger base than previously possible thus creating a false concern about the traditional effect of rising wages on inflation. That traditional wage/inflation relationship may still exist in the old-tech realm (but even there technology has the potential of increasing efficiency and, to a degree, offsetting the wage factor; for instance, wage costs have increased in housing construction, but new-tech design and materials hold costs down). My concern is that in an effort to prevent an old illness, any prophylactic rise in interest rates may weigh more heavily on the already suffering domestically-oriented and old-tech industries. If the high-tech areas and global-induced growth areas are primarily responsible for higher wages (and employment) while some domestic and low-tech sectors languish, then the statistical rise may not represent the entire economic picture, or rather the economic picture needs to be considered by its separate, specific tiers.

Unemployment: Low, Stable, and Non-Inflationary

There used to be a link between unemployment and inflation. Non-Accelerating Inflation Rate of Unemployment (NAIRU) is a rate of unemployment (in the vicinity of 5 percent) below which it cannot fall without igniting inflation (pushing wages and prices up). Unemployment has been near and below that level for 2 years, but no inflation has surfaced; total compensation is not rising significantly and profits and productivity are good with lower interest rates of past years. The rules of these economic dogmas may have ceased to work. Smaller demographics may suggest fuller employment and this NAIRU indicator may no longer function as it has in the past when the environment consisted of a nearly double upcoming generation of workers.

The populations of developed nations are no longer replacing themselves. The supply of new workers is shrinking just when technology is reducing the need for labor, resulting in low unemployment and low inflation. If there is a smaller upcoming demographic generation, and if, with cost-cutting technology, there are fewer jobs in traditional and domestic industry, might the suggestion be made that things may begin to function like a gear: fewer jobs, fewer people suggests fuller employment, or an equilibrium with a steadier economy, with the NAIRU lower? A perfect fit we've never seen before.

Also, wages are up for some workers (but not necessarily for the job) by upgrading from within,[16] and by taking advantage of rural lower wage areas (versus the big urban centers, see Figure 13–8). Yet wages would be recorded as rising while in both cases still staying below the former wage costs, for the same job. Also, corporations are educating the unemployable for entry level

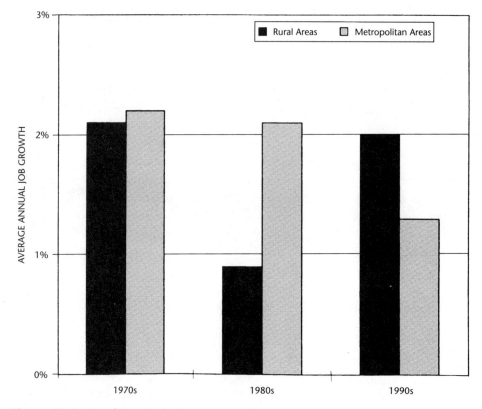

Figure 13–8   Rural America's Employment Revival.

jobs/wages lowering the unemployment rate. The labor shortage is witnessing older people returning to the work force, a large number of women and skilled immigration influx, all contributing to fuller employment. Consider, too, if there are fewer jobs as a result of technological productivity and worker layoffs/early retirement packages, couldn't wages go up somewhat on those fewer jobs that exist (having the same effect as more jobs at a lower wage) without carrying the same negative wage inflation implications as in the past, enabling fewer to make more with a neutral impact on traditional economic expectations? Additionally, if technology is making inventory control more "immediate" and effectively smooths the boom/bust cycles of the past (lessening the cyclical need for layoffs) isn't it possible that full employment may become a feature of that more stable economic condition with the added benefit of increased productivity. NAIRU, as it stands today, may be inapplicable (Figure 13–9, also see Figure 13–6).

   We are not isolated from global factors. Demographics, price, inflation, interest rates all seem inextricably intertwined. Technological diffusion is still young globally and not complete here at home as we dismantle the old, but corporations have the option to pay the wages of a lower cost

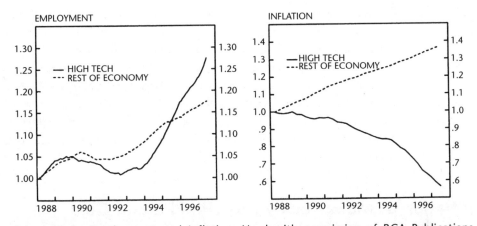

Figure 13–9 Employment and Inflation. Used with permission of BCA Publications Ltd., *The Bank Credit Analyst.*

area or country for jobs such as software programmers, design engineers, data managers. There is always another lower cost area, even for knowledge. Eastern Europe is thriving on jobs for U.S. companies at lower pay than here but higher pay by their own country standards, thus raising local purchasing power for our multinational products. As we develop a global electronic economy there may be no huge surge in worldwide demand for labor that cannot eventually find supply. Therefore as diffusion increases so will wage equalization (and it may be a factor in the slowing rate of ascent of the compensation progressions on the charts), hence no imminent inflationary implication.

Increased global outsourcing of tech-related services and design, global job accessibility through the Internet (with English prevalently spoken), already occurring at all skill levels, takes advantage of cheaper skills of global labor pools and may change assumptions about tight domestic labor markets. Employee leasing is growing 30 percent to 40 percent per year, with longer term assignments, making it less cyclical.[17] Global labor supply and new "labor sharing" Internet links (providing a 24-hour workday: half here, half there) provide the world a better division of labor and 24-hour productivity. Internet outsourcing and software exports advance technological skills and productivity and improve the trade balance. Ultimately wages (and prices) will be set globally not locally, through the global diffusion of technology; it may take years before inflation reappears. Full employment, in face of global disinflationary forces, seems a nonfactor and makes it cost effective to educate and to value human resources. We may not see unemployment problems until we are faced with the next oversize population.

There is an important point for workers to understand regarding the real value of today's wages in a period of low inflation relative to their value in a period of high and rising inflation. When the percentage of wages rises in an inflationary period, the buying power goes down because of that inflation. The buying power of paychecks with inflation low, is larger today, so workers have more in their pockets, enabling them to both spend *and* save. (In the 1970s, inflation was rising rapidly and, as the percentage in pay rose, workers appeared to make more, but because inflation robbed them of *real* spending power (prices rose faster than wages), they actually ended up with less.[18]) With high inflation and big raises people feel richer even though they are not better off. Low inflation makes it harder to see and understand the stealth growth in real income.

Inflation as Measured by the CPI, PPI, and Gold

The technical evidence by many measures certainly has suggested that inflation is not in sight, except as it appears in the potential demographic inflation of financial assets. We have examined the Dow/CPI and have found inflation at the lowest levels of this century. Gold, by any measure, whether based on the London PM price of gold (Figure 1–11), or by the breadth of gold (Figure 13–10) has also collapsed versus the world's major currencies and, as noted, other precious metals are in bear markets.

If productivity is not measured correctly, inflation probably is not either. The CPI has a several year lag in measuring new products, so it never captured the early technology years' higher cost (PCs were not included for 13 years). In spite of this, the core CPI reading was the lowest since 1965,

Figure 13–10   Gold A-D Line. Used with permission of BCA Publications Ltd., *The Bank Credit Analyst.*

even in face of what is thought to be a tightening labor market with a slow wage creep. The core rate of inflation actually is falling[19] (Figure 13–3) and is at its lowest level in three decades. The high-tech portions of the economy have been growing at a rapid, double-digit pace, yet inflation in high-tech has plummeted over 17 years (Figure 13–9). The Producer Price index (PPI), Intermediate Goods core rate and Price to Sales versus the materials sector, are equally benign; while fluctuations are a given, its relative level is not impacting inflation (Figure 1–10 and Figure 13–11).

The bond market and the price of gold may be one intermarket relationship that holds, given the perceived domestic inflation focus of both (Figure 13–12). Gold in the long term is driven by inflation perceptions and concerns—rising with worry, falling without worry—and has been a leading indicator (versus wages) and is not a problem technically. Gold prices in U.S. history have been a harbinger of inflation—a protection against it. Gold has held an interesting trend relationship to the U.S. long-term government bond market. If one examines the trend of the London gold price and overlays it on the yield trend for the U.S. long-term government bond, one can note that peaks in the price of gold have generally preceded peaks in bond yield by about 15 months.[20] By this measure, the recent drop in gold from the 1996 peak, if the analogy holds, implies a bond yield peak around 15 months later; the early 1997 interest rate rise (as the technical work on bonds has suggested since 1981) may in fact be temporary, another contratrend move; and that the

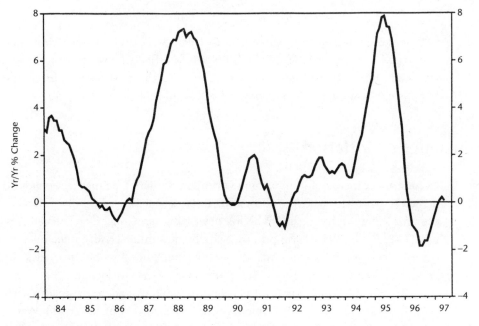

Figure 13–11   Producer Price Index—Intermediate Goods Ex-Food and Energy. Used with permission of Salomon Smith Barney.

Figure 13–12 London Price of Gold Compared to Long-Term Government Bond Yield. Chart created with Supercharts® by Omega Research, Inc.

bull market in bonds may resume later in 1997, (which our analysis confirms) resulting in another peak in yield. This would reflect the realization or perception that inflation demons are not present. (As this book goes to print, the bond is challenging the 6 percent level and gold is dropping below 300.)

Absence of Inflation

In looking at history for an example of Adam Smith's free market economic principles to relate to expectations for today's global market, low inflation economy, one might consider the history of British Consumer Prices (Figure 13–13). The British Empire (on which the sun never set), once encompassed one-fourth of the world's population, and possibly provides an historical free-trade, large-market equivalent to the world today. Fascinatingly, from 1600 to 1914 this measure of inflation was *relatively* steady (with rises for wars, in the 1800s, but leveling off again). But as World War I chipped away at the British Empire's colonies, inflation began to creep in. After World War II, Lord Mountbatten turned India over to Nehru, and

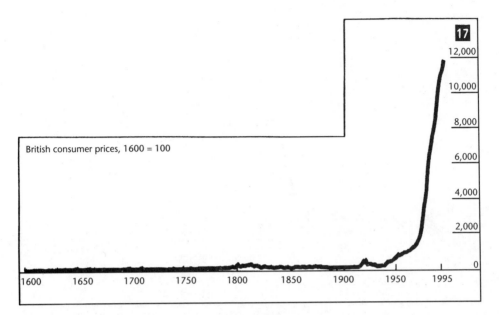

British consumer prices, 1600 = 100

Figure 13-13   The Birth of Inflation. (© 1996 The Economist Newspaper Group, Inc. Reprinted with permission.)

Britain reluctantly shed its empire, covering 450 million people, inclusive of 69 territories in its 340-year span. With dissolution of the trade advantage, inflation soared. At its height, the British Empire had experienced an extraordinary period of time absent *soaring* inflation.

Perhaps we should think of the United States today as similar to yesterday's British Empire (in terms of opening world trade), being the nation primed to take advantage of it in what we might dub the new "global alliance;" being way ahead of our developed trading partners in corporate restructuring, flexible labor markets, utilization of the new technology, and in penetration of the emerging markets—all essentials in developing and maintaining a competitive edge (Figure 13–14). Today's global alliance has the potential of billions (not millions) of people, representing 80 percent (not 25 percent) of the world's population participating as consumers and could continue for years.

We don't really know where we are in this economic cycle because we've never seen one like it before (one in which inflation potential has become harder to explain through traditional relationships). Increasing wage growth may be more than offset by raw material shifts and by the increased (yet unmeasured) gains in productivity. We don't know how far this economy (with all its new demographics and technology implications) can go without seeing the specter of inflation.

The suggestion has been made that inflationary forces are dead. But beware of the "inflation is dead" concept. There is always risk in believing

Figure 13–14   Exports as Percent of GDP. Used with permission of Salomon Smith Barney.

it's dead in the early phase of a new technology. Given the global demographics there appears a seemingly limitless demand potential in the world's population just beginning to consume. But historical technical evidence indicates all new technology eventually suffers, as complete diffusion of its innovations is achieved. Overcapacity and an eventual squeeze on margin did occur as each successive technology ceased to be a growth industry. We must remember the emergence into a free-trade global economy of such a large population may take much longer to saturate this time, and therefore much longer to re-ignite inflation (although there can still be interim shortages, e.g., pharmaceuticals, food, water). The implications of this enormous population may take years (but maybe not 340 years) to see inflation rise. Information technology will increase the speed of saturation, allowing faster diffusion and also faster production and innovation. The enormous number of potential consumers may push our inflation pressures out in time because the markets are bigger; but hopefully not so far out in time that people forget inflation's insidious nature (allowing history to repeat itself when the memory and experience of inflation is not present in the lives of those who must anticipate, identify and curb it). It is also possible, as we will explore in Chapter 15, that the inflation risk is structurally shifting elsewhere in the economy.

The global trade alliance concept appears infinite today but our children's children may see change akin to the decline of the British trade empire.

Individual emerging nations with younger populations and rising quality of life will experience demographic inflationary cycle pressures as well as 1997 Southeast Asia-style debt bubbles, of their interim overcapacity, as inexperience with free trade economic principles, etc., create fits and starts; the global ebb and flow of all the same demographic/economic cycles. The problems may arise in not studying history; not understanding the *changes* in the macro underlying forces; forgetting the role of demographics in creating its shifts and changes. Could economic equilibrium eventually reign if developed nations move toward zero population growth, (and excesses disappear temporarily), until the demographics change again? If we are lucky, we may be able to keep major wars, irresponsible governments, and protectionism at bay, but those social jolts to equanimity can arise and upset the course. We must stay alert for the changes and pitfalls.

Summary

One of the most vexing topics and most demanding pursuits of the new market environment will be the ongoing effort to quantify productivity in the almost diaphanous realm of the electron economy. We have seen in this chapter how the conventional measuring sticks do not capture the frequently weightless, instantaneous, nearly infinite and free-of-raw-materials-cost nature of technology's gifts. Only by constantly asking newly relevant questions can we keep pace with the changes in productivity. Perhaps by incorporating the laws of physics, we can better assess the flow of the economy and understand the anomalies we have seen, such as wage gains coupled with nearly full employment absent inflation.

Chapter

14

Stock Market Implications and Expectations

Identifying the two-tier equity market trend, as we did in Chapter 2, is one step toward grappling with the new market realities. Defining the various intermarket behaviors and how they may vary from the norm, and identifying the key intermarket relationships that may de-link as a result of new macroforces (including how stock market behavior relates to valuations and expectations in differing environments) is another. Continuing the question-asking process of Part Three, in this chapter we will examine a number of specific aspects of the stock market and the financial forces that affect it to see how the market is responding to the macrotrends of globalization, demographics, low inflation, low interest rates, and technology. The results can be surprising, as in the apparent de-linking of the historic inverse relationship between the CRB and bond prices, and in the emergence of growth as a major additional factor in value investing, as well as in the diminution of high levels of margin debt as an unambiguous warning sign of looming market reversals. Stock market valuations also may be viewed in a new light with tradition levels subject to re-evaluation given the productivity gains.

Is the CRB/Bond Intermarket Relationship De-Linking?

Could the inverse relationship between bonds and the CRB de-link based on the global implications of the CRB components today and the more domestic economic bias of U.S. bonds? Might this be another intermarket relationship that needs to be revisited? And further, may we be witnessing a rotation in the economic commodity leadership for the first time in over a century?

If we accept the thesis that the dominant force of the CRB today may be more reflective of the thrust of global factors and pressures, particularly agricultural, as opposed to the domestic and old-tech pressures that it has reflected in past industrial cycles, then the CRB may need to be revisited in its familiar intermarket relationship to the bond market (which is still a reflector of domestic economic influences). A new way of perceiving this intermarket relationship may be required: One might need to ask the question whether the historical inverse relationship between the now more fundamentally global CRB and the domestic bond market is pertinent today. Further, could that relationship de-link (as global stocks and bonds de-linked in 1994 and are appearing to do so again in 1997)? If so, should the CRB continue to be considered a yardstick for *domestic* economic inflation?

Historically, as the CRB rose, implying impending inflationary forces in the domestic economy, bond prices fell (yields rose in response to these same perceived pressures) in an inverse relationship. If we expand the lens to a wide angle and look at these two measures, from an historical perspective, the longer-term, more secular trend of the CRB was rising in a structural inflationary trend from the 1970s to 1980; and in an inverse response, the bond price was in a secular trend of falling prices (rising rates). Both those longer-term trends reversed in 1981 (Figure 14–1) when falling inflationary pressures brought the CRB into a structurally (disinflationary) declining trend, to a low in 1992. Simultaneously, as would be expected, the bond price followed an opposite trend of structurally rising price (taking the bond yield down to 6 percent in 1993). From 1993, however, one can technically postulate that a de-linking phase began for the following reasons: In 1993, the CRB violated the 14-year downtrend from its 1980 high, and the CRB price began to rise. The bond price, on the other hand, which would be expected to fall, in face of and in response to, this CRB action, has *not* violated its corresponding uptrends for higher prices (lower rates) set in place in 1981 (and in 1984). (And the lack of U.S. inflationary pressures in our technical work suggest it should not.) In 1995, the CRB did not retreat in price (it consolidated), yet the bonds experienced a very strong rally in mid-1995 rising *in tandem* with the CRB. The technical rising profile for the bond price continues to suggest the dominant trend for interest rates in this country has been, is and

Figure 14–1 Historical Relationship of the CRB Index to Long-Term Government Bond Perpetual Futures Contract. Chart created with Supercharts® by Omega Research, Inc.

will continue to be down. For the first time in the CRB progression since 1981, a higher peak (versus 1989) was put in place as it moved through resistance at 245, suggesting a major trend reversal. Based on the history of the CRB/bond inverse relationship, this development should have boded ill for bonds, yet in face of this CRB rise, bond price remains, into late 1997, unaffected and is quite positive.

The 1996 pullback in the CRB price is a normal technical expectation, pulling back to the breakout level, or even back toward the broken downtrend, before witnessing a swing to the upside. The bond price in face of this evidence, were its CRB relationship intact, should have corresponded with a break of its uptrend as well as with a series of lower lows. Not so.

Remember from Part One that the rises in interest rates (declines in bond price) since 1981 were projected to represent nothing more than contratrend moves to the major trend toward lower rates (higher bond prices). One can see this contratrend thesis to have been the case. The CRB/bond relationship appeared to hold through these contratrend moves until 1993, when a divergence began to suggest a de-linking of their relationship may be in its infancy; that a change may be underway, however imperceptible. The bond price has failed to either decline proportionately or to break its up-trend. Given the degree of advance in the CRB, one might have expected the bond yield to have suffered, by slipping back to its 1988 level of over 9 percent.

The longer-term progression still shows the bond price establishing and maintaining a series of higher lows (indicative of demand) while the CRB has ceased to portray a downtrend pattern of lower peaks followed by lower lows (supply) and appears poised to continue a series of higher highs and higher lows once the pullback consolidation completes. So a nearly 5-year breach of the historical CRB/bond relationship appears to be evolving. It must be considered that the CRB/bond relationship came into being with an inflationary cycle; but now, in a trend of declining inflation that correlation may no longer be valid. It is of further interest that the 1993 origin of the suspected de-link corresponds to the exact point at which the two-tier domestic versus global U.S. equity market forces came into play. If the separate domestic and global pressures are also now in play for bonds and the CRB respectively, we may be witnessing another intermarket decoupling, reflecting those forces as we enter the twenty-first century.

Macroshift in Commodity Leadership

If we reflect on the discussion in Chapter 7 on the old-tech heavy industrial commodities versus the new-tech (sand, air, and light), we realize that there is no inflation implication inherent in these new raw materials which are both plentiful and easily accessible. In fact, these emerging new raw materials themselves may be contributing to the low inflation/growing economy puzzle. Could we even suggest further that the world is witnessing, for the first time in over a century, the early stages of a major shift in its commodity leadership base? We know that leadership shifts can create some unsettlements. (This may add to the bullish profile of bonds, as a measure of protection.) We know also that shifts of leadership bring about a decline in prices of the old capitulating leadership, as well as a period of initially low prices of the new emerging leadership. Such a macroshift would imply a disinflationary (deflationary) impact of the falling prices of the waning old-tech raw materials of the capitulating old industrial cycle. Low prices are also being reflected in the new commodities (sand, air, and light) of the emerging new-tech leadership cycle. Even more pertinent is the current low (though eventually rising) price of agricultural products and water reflecting growing global consumer demand. Of these new economic forces—only one, agriculture—is yet a component of the CRB. This rarely seen economic macroshifting process is not dissimilar to the cyclical Capital/Consumer shifts of stock market leadership.

The major shift taking place within that C/C ratio, described in Chapter 9 (Figure 9–4), may be another leading piece of evidence in suggesting the new bias toward Consumer Goods cycles (and the relevant raw materials). This proposed major shift in economic commodity leadership focus, in moving toward Consumer (agriculture/water) commodities, reflects the forces of emerging global populations on the consumer scene.

Stock Market Speculation: The Value of Growth

We know we cannot expect the equity market to respond in the same way in an environment of low inflation and interest rates as it did in a period of high/rising inflation and interest rates. In an underlying structure of rising inflation and rising interest rates, market participants have frequently bought the more speculative stock in a group, even a negative earner, and anticipated a profitable inflation-driven rise, as occurred in the late 1960s through the 1970s. But today, in an underlying structure of low inflation and low/falling interest rates, that has not happened and may not happen (though many may look for it). This is an environment not of inflationary rewards, but one of growth and quality rewards, not one of value rewards alone but of value with growth potential. Growth, predominantly (though not exclusively) globally- and technologically-driven now, is the focus and the seed of reward in today's equity market. A lack thereof can and has resulted in dramatic sell-offs in stock price.

Part of the problem in attempting to quantify this equity bull market, and ferret out the expectations of its behavior/direction, has been that many compare today's data to that of the dissimilar 1967–1982 period. For example, stock market peaks are said to occur in a trend of rising smaller stocks in a speculative bubble and market blow-off (as has occurred in inflationary speculations). But since this is not an inflationary period, the driver of a speculative bubble might be different, might need to be growth-driven. It may come in a hyperextension of the large well-established globally-exposed U.S. stocks (as with the nifty 50 of the 1960s), or as a selective growth-oriented speculation in the mid-capitalization or smaller stock tier. Added to this consideration is whether the smaller issues become globalized over time and/or possess dynamic growth potential, and thus also will be driven well beyond perceived valuation, aided also by the financial baby-boomer bubble. The underperformers, big or small, without the growth factor, are unlikely to reward/lead into whatever final frenzy the market may see. Value investing has been disappointing in this decade; unless accompanied by growth, it may not be working because other new forces are at work. Today, those low valuations issues may be there for a very different underlying reason, and may not allow those stocks to outperform. Value may be perceived in the areas (sectors) of our waning domestic demographic profile or, even in areas of old-tech. Value in such companies today may not represent the potential to come strongly to the fore because of the underlying emerging macroshifts. So value picking in some of those relatively declining sectors may prove disappointing this time.

Margin Debt: No Longer a Purely Equity Indicator

Many equity market observers set forth statistics to argue for an imminent end to this bull market. One such statistic, the margin debt number, warrants review. Margin debt represents how much debt (borrowing) stock buyers are incurring to speculate on the equity market (Figure 14–2). Historically, when margin debt became excessively high, the market became vulnerable: In the event of a decline, brokerage customers investing "on margin" (borrowed money) are called by their broker to cover (pay back) their debt to protect the broker (the lender) from loss. Some margin debt investors may not have money available and the broker then sells the underlying stock, which feeds

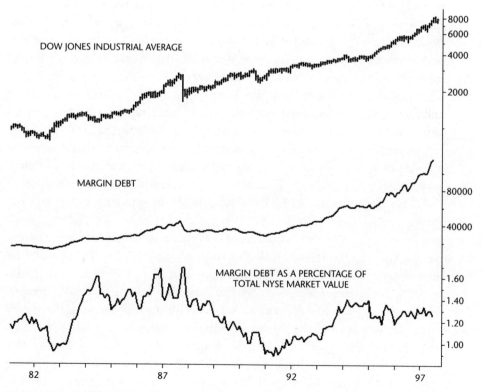

Figure 14–2 NYSE Margin Debt. Chart created with Supercharts® by Omega Research, Inc.

into an already weakened market, aggravating the decline. Margin debt was a good technical indicator of speculation until the 1980s. The seemingly staggering level to which margin debt has now climbed, accompanying the equity market advance, leaves many observers fearful. But we must recognize and unveil the mystery of the new margin debt growth, which no longer exclusively represents debt on equities.

Under the surface of 1991, a year with one of the narrowest equity trading ranges in history for the DJIA, margin debt rose approximately 54 percent from its lows at $27.8 billion in early 1991 to $43 billion by November 1992. It has since more than doubled (along with the equity market itself), rising to over $80 million. Looking at the margin debt chart, one cannot help but make comparisons to the 1987 level of $44 billion just prior to the crash. But margin debt today is a very different statistic than it was in 1987 (or even 1982). Prior to 1983, the margin debt in brokerage accounts only reflected margin debt on NYSE equities. After 1983, margin debt was expanded to include other indices and new derivatives like futures that contributed to the debt run-up into the 1987 highs. Since 1987, derivative products have proliferated, and margin debt has been expanded to include all of them, as well as to debt on mutual equity and bond funds offered by brokerage houses. Additionally, with the continued drop in interest rates over the past decade and a half, a whole new business has developed within brokerage houses as a "prime broker service." This allows large institutional and other clients to consolidate their debts under one account umbrella, that of the brokerage house, often diverting business away from commercial banks that may not be able to offer as low an interest rate on the debt. Today, all of this nonequity-related debt is reported in the total margin-debt figures, and the high level represents much more than just equities or strictly tradable financial assets.

Comparing today's margin debt to the years prior to 1987 is essentially meaningless. With regard to equities and/or derivatives on the financial markets, rising margin-debt levels may no longer represent the speculative bubble they have traditionally, primarily because of all the unrelated credit now included in the margin-debt figures. Perhaps a much higher level of total margin debt might be expected before representing a so-called vulnerable excess for the equity markets, but we don't know what that level is. What might be more appropriate to monitor is the margin debt as a percent of total NYSE market value. From this perspective, the margin-debt impact is more benign. The levels over the past few years have been steady. The solution may be to find a way to segregate the data and modify it to again reflect only the equity and equity related portions. But for now, we can at least understand the changed composition margin-debt number and appreciate that its impact on the equity market, as historically known, may no longer have the same validity. However, margin debt measured as a percent of GDP (Figure 14–3) may be a little unsettling as it rises to post-WW II highs.

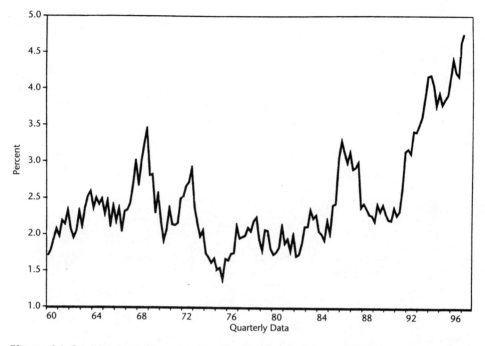

Figure 14–3   Margin Debt as Percent of GDP. Used with permission of Salomon Smith Barney.

(We might also note that short sales have grown to serve arbitrage pur-poses and similarly have been rendered inaccurate in their former measure of investor sentiment. Arbitrage techniques are also affecting odd lot numbers today.)

Savings and Debt Trends

Personal saving rates are frequently described as dangerously low or in de-cline, an obvious negative for domestic money flow availability to sustain a bull market. Yet mutual fund inflow has been setting records, suggesting the possibility of incomplete statistics. In fact, 401(k)s and IRAs are not generally factored into some savings data. The inflows to 401(k)s are tremendous and rising (Figure 14–4), some of the rise clearly due to asset appreciation. This painless, employer-extracted savings vehicle is creating wealth for many who otherwise might not be saving. 401(k) assets have quintupled over 10 years representing over 25 million participants. Real savings may not be accurately captured in the personal saving statistics, and this is without pension fund measures, which have expanded (topping $6 trillion) through the third quar-ter of 1996 (Figure 14–5), due in large part to stock appreciation. Nonethe-less, in this low inflation period, people are not using savings/retirement

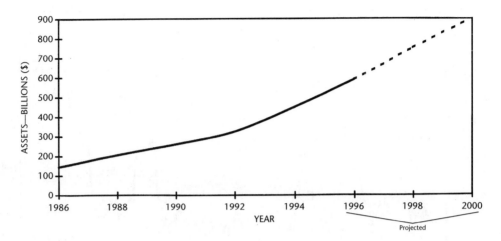

Figure 14–4 Money Invested in 401(k) Plans. (© Access Research, Division of Spectrem Group, Windsor, CT.)

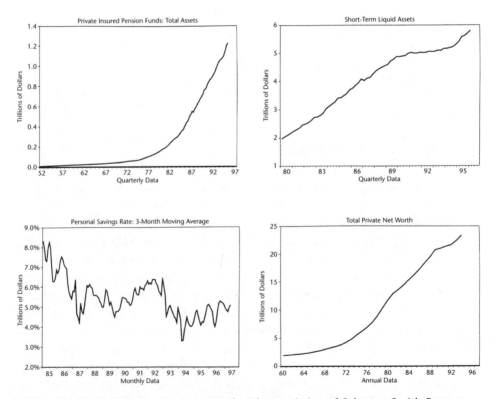

Figure 14–5 Savings Perspectives. Used with permission of Salomon Smith Barney.

caches to fund consumption. Invested assets are growing, which also may off-set the statistic on lower savings. Household net worth has grown to exceed levels of the mid-1960s. What may not be recognized in this is that the baby boom generation is the first since the Depression to become recipients of trillions of dollars of inheritance over the next 25 years.

Other statistics from the Federal Reserve quarterly flow of funds show record savings by Americans, putting 70 cents out of every dollar saved into mutual funds, representing an *increase* in savings, improving since 1994 (Figure 14–6). Through the third quarter of 1996, the Federal Reserve data reported that individuals sold $165 billion in equities, yet mutual funds bought $184 billion, evidence of this transfer of funds.[1]

Federal debt has the potential of achieving the fifth consecutive lower federal budget deficit (Figure 14–7) this fiscal year; currently government spending is at its lowest level relative to that of any expansion in the post-1960 period; military capital goods orders have declined by ⅔ since 1986 (and the 1990's expansion could be considered healthier because the 1960s experienced rising government spending). Even the budget deficit is down from 6 percent of the national income in the 1980s to 1.5 percent and real federal debt has decreased (Figure 14–8).

The other side of the savings coin is the consumer debt level that grows and recedes in cycles and recently appeared concentrated in lower- to

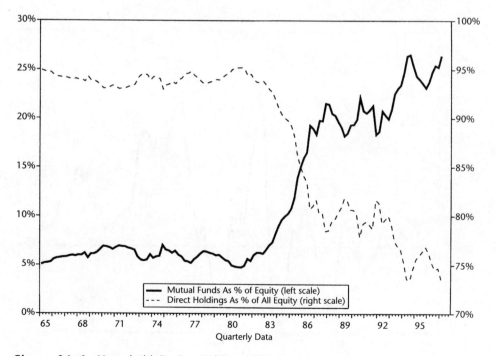

Figure 14–6 Household Equity Holdings. Used with permission of Salomon Smith Barney.

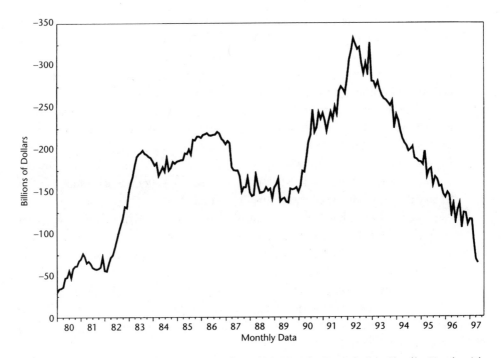

Figure 14–7 Federal Government Deficit (12-Month Cumulative Total). Used with permission of Salomon Smith Barney.

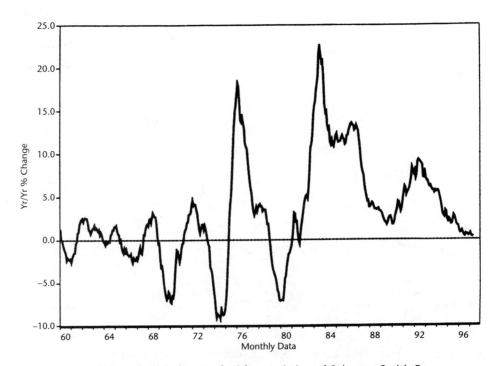

Figure 14–8 Real Federal Debt. Used with permission of Salomon Smith Barney.

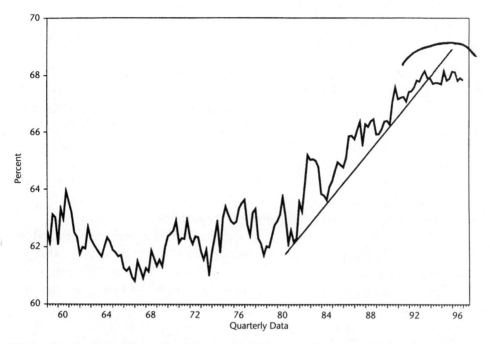

Figure 14–9   Personal Consumption Expenditures as a Percent of GDP. Used with permission of Salomon Smith Barney.

middle-income households, which make up the bulk of U.S. spending. Its level can exacerbate economic swings but historically does not cause them; income growth remains strong in this low inflation environment.[2] Both the consumer credit and the personal expenditures as a percent of GDP progressions depict topping configurations, suggesting debt levels will recede (Figure 14–9).

These implications reinforce the domestic/global thesis by suggesting the globally-exposed U.S. equities should continue to outperform longer term (contratrend corrections such as 1997 not withstanding), and domestically-exposed sectors may struggle as the domestic consumer holds back on spending to pay down debt.

Stock Market Valuations

As the market has risen higher and higher, rising valuation levels are creating unease. Traditionalists use history to show that high valuations relative to earnings and dividends may result in a serious market decline. But with low inflation, nearly infinite global markets, technology and the baby boom adding force to today's financial assets, revisions in corporate dividend policies, and new productivity benefits, it might be possible some valuations may be skewed: the old rules for stock valuations may no longer hold today or may need to be adapted to reflect low inflation and higher productivity. Also, prior to a market top in this cycle, valuations may increase more than we have previously experienced.

Companies are also making different decisions today with their capital, and their choice and method of reported earnings (operating, forward, etc.). (We also may have to make the distinction between domestic and the global companies.) We perhaps should not rely on price-to-dividend valuation measures because many companies are choosing not to pay out increased dividends in favor of redeploying money by buying back shares. High-technology companies, quickly becoming a large share of total companies, traditionally pay no dividends, so the dividend measures may no longer reflect the same overvaluation considerations (Figure 14–10). The argument can again be made that valuation methods working in periods of rising or high inflation and interest rates should not be used for valuation measures in periods with low inflation and low to stable interest rates. Lower yields allow higher valuations, and the impact of higher productivity on stock values can be astounding. Adding 1 percentage point to long-run productivity growth can raise future earnings, possibly boosting stock price by 20 percent. Consider, too, whether financial asset valuations could exceed prior levels (specifically those of the early 1960s in the last great bull market) because of the new-tech productivity gains and the baby-boom demographics and their tremendous savings dollars. As a result, overvaluations could rise beyond historical levels.

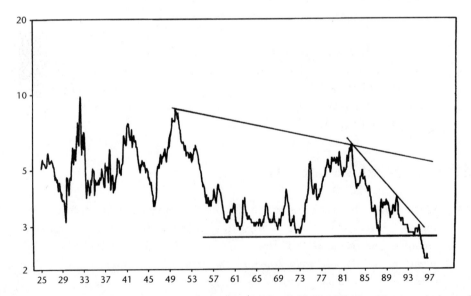

Figure 14–10 S&P Composite—Forward Dividend Yield. Used with permission of Salomon Smith Barney.

Mutual Funds/Stock Supply/Volatility

Other factors making unique impacts on the equity market include the boom in mutual funds. Mutual fund assets now exceed the gold in Fort Knox and the New York Federal Reserve combined, and there are three stock funds today for every two listed NYSE stocks (Figure 14–11). That is a powerful statistic. Let's look at how and when this event progressed to its current imbalance.[3]

In January 1987, there were 1,376 mutual funds and 2,252 NYSE issues trading, for a ratio of .61 funds to NYSE issues. In January 1990, the ratio was one to one, 2,256 funds to 2,250 issues; by January 1993, it was 3,014 funds to 2,677 NYSE issues, a ratio of 1.13. And through December 1996, the number soared to 5,282 funds to 3,530 issues, for the cited ratio of 1.5—another possible effect of the demographic savers seeking investment vehicles.

Nevertheless, this leaves one with the feeling that we may fast be approaching a situation where the tail is wagging the dog. Additionally, available supply of stock is narrowed not only by a lower new issuance of stock but also by cost-cutting mergers and stock buy backs (companies repurchasing their own stock) (Figure 14–12). This is assumed to be managing cash more efficiently for shareholders, and reflects management confidence (investing in the business it knows best and believing the stock price to be reasonable with potential further gains) and eliminates the inefficiency of dividend double

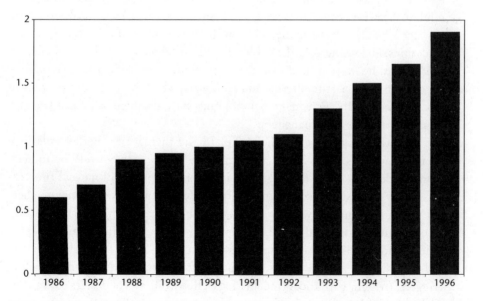

Figure 14–11 Another Day, Another Fund. (© 1997 Access Research, Division of Spectrem Group, Windsor, CT.)

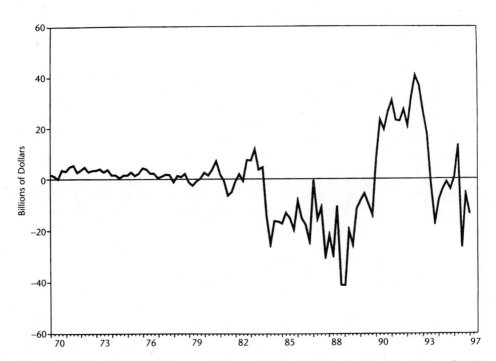

Figure 14–12   Net New Issuance of Domestic Equity. Used with permission of BCA Publications Ltd., *The Bank Credit Analyst.*

taxation. This process, added to the quantity of baby-boomer money looking for a home, results in demand that pushes fewer shares higher and faster than might otherwise occur, particularly in growth tier large-cap global, including new-tech, names. More money chasing fewer stocks results in rising prices, valuations, and rising volatility. The share of total money in the stock market represented by mutual fund investment (including money market) is increasing, due in large part to 401(k)s and IRA plans which represent 35 percent of mutual fund assets. Personal stock holdings have declined as people transfer money to mutual fund managers.

All these factors could help explain the increase in market volatility over recent years: Individuals are less likely to trade as actively or in such large blocks of stock as mutual fund managers. The flows of mutual fund assets are by their sheer size having a larger effect on market movements (abetted by mutual fund newsletters directing their growing readership to buy, sell, or shift funds). Add to this not only the mutual fund mechanisms (particularly for the liquid large capitalization stocks in many funds that buy and sell each day at a certain hour to execute shifts), but also the program trading triggers, (which, with today's technology allows billions of dollars to transfer with the speed of the push of a button) and even intraday volatility becomes more understandable.

The volatility becomes self-reinforcing. The chicken-or-egg debate about which is leading which, mutual funds or stock market, may not be the question. The mutual funds are not separate from the stock market; they provide an alternative to personal stock selection, and their proliferation and ratio to the number of stocks has made them a major component of stock market behavior, and they have a finite number of stocks to choose from, so stock ownership overlaps.

Volume itself has increased from 200 million share days, considered extraordinary in the 1980s, to 600 million share days which we take in stride in the late 1990s as it progresses to the October 27, 1997 Billion Share day. This reflects the tremendous increase in available money: more money chasing fewer stocks, pushing prices up, and having its own effect on volatility.

Another DJIA volatility factor is the effect of component stock splits. The DJIA is not a capitalization-weighted index like the S&P or the NYSE. It is a price-weighted average. Were we to create the average today the prices of the 30 Dow stocks would be added and divided by 30 (known as the divisor). But as stocks in the Dow split, adjustments in the divisor have to be made to keep the Dow level consistent. There have been so many splits over the years that the divisor is no longer even a whole number, but a fraction reflected roughly in thousandths of a point. So the divisor, at 0.251 in November 1997 essentially acts as a multiplier. Each 1-point move in a Dow stock results in a 4-point move in the DJIA. Said another way, if each Dow stock were to move up (or down) one point simultaneously, with this divisor it would represent a move of 120 points up (or down) in the DJIA. When the news gives reports of the second largest point day in history, perspective is needed: A similar number of points at a DJIA height of 8000 represents a much smaller percentage move than the same number of points when the DJIA was at 2000. Another way of putting the larger point moves in perspective is to recognize that a 100-point move in the Dow at 8000 is akin to a 1-point move for an $80 stock. And now there are futures traded on the DJIA which may increase volatility.

Thinning Markets: Perception versus Reality

There also may be a performance effect from the growth of Index funds—funds created to track a particular stock market index (S&P 500, for instance). Since the end of 1994, the assets in the largest S&P 500 index mutual fund rose 276 percent. As funds flow in, the money goes into those same stocks, driving prices higher and making outperformance versus the S&P 500 harder to achieve. The S&P 500 index is capitalization-weighted and equals 69 percent of a now $8+ trillion U.S. equity market. The 10 largest stocks drive 19 percent of the index and the largest 50 stocks nearly half the

Figure 14–13 NASDAQ and AMEX A-D Lines. Chart created with Supercharts® by Omega Research, Inc.

index. These largest companies also include the U.S. globally-exposed stock names. Funds owning smaller-cap stocks, which are generally not as globally-exposed, and not in the somewhat self-propelling large-cap index funds, have not seen the same good relative performance. The appearance of a thinning market (fewer stocks pushing the index up), is evident in the divergence of the price of the NASDAQ to its A-D line (Figure 14–13). But this trend divergence has been in force for 10 years, and now may be aggravated by the nonglobal nature of its many smaller stocks versus the large-cap influence of only the top 25 in NASDAQ. The NYSE A-D, by contrast (Figure 14–14), continues to make new highs, which controverts those who say there is a thinning market there, too. Their argument tries to equate today to the 1970s. But a study of the breadth line (refer to Figure 1–3) shows that breadth in the 1970s was in a definable downtrend (inclusive of small and interest rate-sensitive stocks). Today it portrays a strong uptrend.

Perhaps the understanding is that even as stocks are rising broadly, many are rising by only one-eighth of a point, or fractional increments, while others (the big capitalization, blue chip, globally-exposed, including technology) may be rising by full and multiple point increments, giving the appearance of a

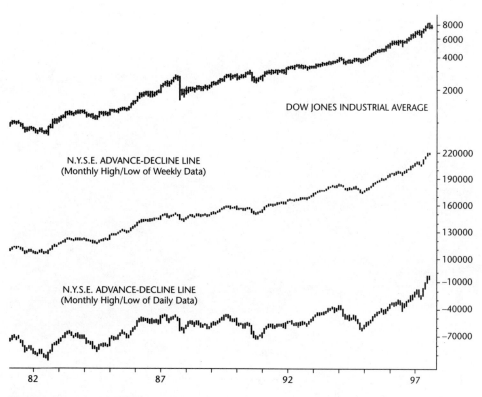

Figure 14–14   NYSE A-D Lines. Chart created with Supercharts® by Omega Research, Inc.

thinning market. These are all factors to keep in mind when wading through the daily noise of trading.

Summary

In this chapter, we took a fresh look at familiar aspects of the stock market and began to question and reassess their relevance in today's changing environment. We saw, for instance, that U.S. savings and debt trends may be less worrisome than many believe. So, too, should high levels of stock valuations be judged against today's trends and possibilities rather than rigid, established formulas. In this chapter, we concluded our question-asking process and we will now proceed to attempt to pull the parts of this book together in our concluding Part Four.

Part Four

CONCLUSION

Chapter

15

What Lies Ahead: Other Emerging Forces at Work

We have laid forth and interpreted technical evidence that suggests a continuation of the bull markets for both stocks and bonds within the framework of a unique global dynamic that is subtly creating groundswell shifts in many long-held beliefs and in traditional technical and economic behavior. More than anything the question-asking process is requisite. We have posed many questions in this book in an effort to provoke a thought process; as the evolution opens new windows completing the view, more answers will emerge. Based on the weight of the evidence at this juncture, we will in this last chapter try to wrap up and share some final thoughts.

Interest Rates

All the technical evidence and the related data indicate a continuation of current trends. The bull market in bonds (lower interest rates) still appears intact.

Evidence suggests the resolution of the already 5-year trading range in bonds (between 6 percent to 8 percent) to break to lower levels is at hand.

Looking at our point-and-figure chart (Figure 15–1) the long-term uptrend remains intact and, since 1994, the bond has been tracing out a bullish demand pattern called an ascending triangular (higher lows) configuration. The breakout through 116 suggests that a resolution through 120–122 is approaching. This would suggest a long bond rate below the 6 percent level to targets at 5½, 5, 4¾, and even 4½ percent over time.

A review of Figure 1–1 and the concept of alternation of cycles might suggest the style of the next move in interest rates. The fall in rates (Cycle 1) from 1984 to 1986 was steep and steady carrying interest rates significantly lower; this was followed by the 1986–1991, 5-year trading range (Cycle 2); Cycle 3 in turn, witnessed another steep and steady fall in rates from 1991–1994; Cycle 4 resulted in a second 5-year trading range which may be on the verge of resolution. The price pattern suggests that Cycle 5 could be another steep and extended cycle, when/if interest rates fall below 6 percent.

A conceptual perspective on the supply/demand for money relates to the macro considerations we have discussed and tends to support the case for a continued trend toward lower to stable rates (barring the dislocations of war or unpredictable monetary policy). If there is a smaller upcoming U.S. generation, its demand for money in the borrowing/spending years of the 20-plus-year-olds would be less than in prior cycles (a trend seen in the declining RS for domestic sectors). In addition, the baby boomers or the country's largest population are moving into their savings years, also implying less demand for money. If we accept the thesis that the new technology is less capital-intensive than prior heavy industrial era technology, there is again less demand for money; and if corporations are as cash rich as their rising productivity profits and corporate compensation suggest, they should be able to provide for capital outlays from their own coffers; plus the federal

Figure 15–1 Treasury Bond Futures.

deficit is declining. Then where is the demand for money that would push interest rates up significantly?

Any preemptive rise in interest rates could be more devastating to the struggling domestic tier (and old-tech) sectors, than it would be restraining to the less affected globally-exposed tier (responsible for U.S. growth) which will be slowed more effectively as pockets of global slowdowns occur and trickle back to slow the pace of our economy.

Interestingly, global industrial demand for capital could also be lower than expected because, even in crises, the Asian countries in particular traditionally have a much higher savings rate; overcapacity is prevalent, and corrective currency devaluations, while making investment both less attractive and unnecessary, also make their labor cheaper.

Inflation, Deflation . . . Shifting Seats?

The technical studies we've seen suggest inflation is not on the U.S. horizon, except as demographically induced pockets as in the area of financial assets. We would expect to see a topping process in the Dow/CPI prior to any major shift of inflationary factors (just as a head-and-shoulders bottom formed in the early 1980s suggesting the end of rising inflation, see Figure 1–8). The benefits of technology not only decrease the volatility of the business cycle but also contribute to falling costs; there does not appear to be any specter of U.S. inflation now or in the near future. But as we will see below, inflation may just be shifting seats.

A word must be directed to the new worry over deflation. Simply stated, overinvestment leads to excess capacity, producing excess supply, which creates a competitive cycle of falling prices to correct the excess. A weaker currency (devaluation) speeds the process, dropping prices further to make exports more attractive. Interest rates rise to stabilize the currency. A survival of the fittest puts the weak out of business in a cleansing process that shuts down borrowing for investment and capacity until the excess is absorbed and equilibrium established for growth to begin again.

Deflation is the downwave of each country's Kondratieff (capitalist) economic cycle (Chapter 6). Emerging nations may suffer many smaller economic cycles as they experiment and grow. The concern is that deflation (of lower price, lower currency) can be contagious—threatening prices and profit margins for trade competitors, particularly those dependent on sales to the deflating pocket. This can result in a domino effect; but we have also seen pockets of excess/deflation cycles contained.

Asia has a paradoxical problem—it saves too much and consumes too little relatively (just the reverse of our habits): interest rates remain low, investment pours in, creating overcapacity. Some of this problem may lie in the unfamiliarity of emerging nations (nationalistic, protectionist, and often corrupt) with essentials of free market supply/demand behavior. Their growth needs planning so that savings are deployed efficiently. Education and spending control is necessary—whether from private or world trade establishments. Nevertheless, in spite of these boom/bust cycles and their repair, emerging markets have consistently grown faster than developed economies. (The high savings pattern is unlikely to change and will rebuild the process of growth. Asia, once on track again, could provide double digit growth for over a decade.)

Deflationary Growth—A Concept Never Envisioned

But aspects of deflation are not all bad. There are always pockets of it within economies while other parts remain unaffected. That may be no different, though on a larger scale, than we are witnessing today. The technological trend of deflation today is improving profit margins and bringing value added services/products. We've covered the low interest rate benefits on real wages, savings and spending abilities—all bullish for financial assets, and corporations with foreign operations in place see benefits from local devaluations. (A mild deflation of the late 1800s yielded the U.S. bull cycle of that Kondratieff wave, Chapter 6). Granted, for comparison, there is no period in history with falling interest rates and a regulated equity market, but deflation need not be a negative.

The silver lining may lie in the new technology and the shifts it is creating, which prompts a few questions: How could today's technology alter the potential deflationary spiral to the *good?* The new technology itself is inherently deflationary in its cost-cutting and ill-measured productivity gains. It's just not sufficiently diffused.

Might we consider this a *deflationary growth cycle*, a concept never envisioned before, of increasing returns (versus the former, old inflationary growth cycle of diminishing returns)? Couldn't this seemingly deflationary price trend (in whatever pockets it occurs) in the long run become an "enabler," bringing more of the poorer sectors of the populations into the arms of economic growth—by virtue of providing cheaper goods, raising quality of life even slightly (through technological advances and falling cost), and drawing billions of new consumers into the cycle (eventually even Africa)?

Deflation in prices will hurt the high cost producers but the offsetting benefit is that the new technology is available today to ameliorate that. Price pressure could speed the "tech diffusion" cure; resulting cost savings should help corporations survive an external deflation risk. (It is the old-tech sectors of basic industry that would have greater difficulty, but even they would be helped by technology to stay afloat.) The faster the tech diffusion, the faster the efficiency, the faster the threat of deflation may diminish. Could today's population and technology, if properly managed, be changing what feels like deflation, in reality, to an *equalization* process or a new global equilibrium (similar to that which we discussed relative to wages and jobs)?

In consideration of the possible macroshift of economic commodity leadership (as discussed in Chapter 13), as with any market shift of leadership (to Capital or Consumer Goods, Chapters 1 and 9), the new commodity will always start off low in price, when the demand is just beginning (sand, air, light, food, and water certainly are). And the waning commodity leadership will, by virtue of its loss of prominence (or excess), experience a fall in price. So there is a period of unsettlement and disbelief in the early stage, of both the respective rise and decline: Disbelief that the decline of the old is for real, and disbelief that a new cycle is underway. In equities such shifts create unsettled markets; the commodity shift may now, similarly, be creating unsettled economies. It is at these times of shift that there is tremendous opportunity (in the new) and risk (in the old).

Inflation: Not Dead—Another Shift

The raw material commodities of the old industrial economic Capital Goods cycle were cheap over a century ago. Growing demand came to be experienced in inflationary bouts as demand rose with scarcity; but the demand for the new technological raw materials for the coming Capital Goods cycle may not carry the same element of scarcity, thus giving us real growth in a new Capital Goods cycle without inflation. The commodities of the future Consumer Goods cycle (agriculture and water) while cheap now, may become the inflationary commodities of the next century (as a result of population and industrial demand). That's what the grain charts seem to be indicating.

Could we be seeing a century-long shift from a Capital Goods economy of inflationary growth to a Capital Goods economy of *deflationary* (or just absence of inflation) *growth?* While it will be the new basic (grain, water) Consumer Goods sector of the economy that becomes the one with future inflationary characteristics. This may be what the macroshift in the bias of the Capital/Consumer ratio (discussed in Chapter 9) may be trying to tell us.

What I'm trying to suggest is that we may be seeing *two* shifts simultaneously. One is the shift *within* the Capital Goods area from inflationary old-tech heavy industrial raw materials to the *non*-inflationary new-tech raw materials. The second shift is that the inflationary potential (inflation pressures) for the next century may now be shifting *from* Capital Goods *to* the Consumer Goods (of agriculture and water): A shift of inflation focus from producer (hence lows in PPI and so on) to consumer goods. But because it is still young in the shift, prices (of food and water) in the new inflationary domain (consumer) are still cheap (just as industrial raw materials, in their early phase, over a century ago, were cheap). So the cycle shift may not be openly apparent and may *look* like deflation, but may only be a transition phase from one inflationary base (Capital Goods) to the other (Consumer Goods).

That's this technician's perspective. The general concern is the price decline risk, which will slow the pace of growth. But with no inflation (to take an additional toll) the world should be able to *absorb* the technology-induced global equalization of prices and wages, given the technological efficiency quotient available to all businesses. So, given wise counseling, a slowdown need not be a meltdown in the transition of these altogether new forces.

Stocks

This book goes to press as 1997 is experiencing what will only later be defined as a consolidation, correction, or cyclical bear market within what we continue to believe will be an ongoing stock market advance. Emerging from a summer in which the technical indicators were so strong they couldn't get much better, the need for an unwinding, a period of at least consolidation, was essential. The October turmoil in Southeast Asia provided a catalyst for such. As should be expected given their complexion, it is the globally-exposed tier of U.S. stocks that are primarily (initially) being affected. They are the ones most sensitive to global fundamental issues. This event, as with Mexico and China before, will undoubtedly slow the growth of select globally-exposed stocks proportionate to their involvement in the regions. This should spill over proportionately to slower overall U.S. growth (boosting U.S. government bond prices). The stock market's profile as of November 1997, not surprisingly, looks very much like the mirror image of 1994 (to be discussed). This time it is the globally-exposed tier, including technology, that is correcting after 4 years of outperformance.

Select domestic, old-tech, and small-cap issues are at least temporarily profiling an outperformance trend (not unexpected after 4 years underperforming). Yet their extended multiyear underperformance trends (Figures 2–4, 2–6, 2–7) suggests these rallies may prove to be only contratrends (temporary trends in the direction opposite to the dominant trend), enduring for a time before capitulating again to the dominant global leadership. Their structural RS multiyear breakdowns and declines that have been in place show such depressed performance levels that a rally, even an extended RS rally, could take hold. But even a strong RS advance may still be contained below the downtrend lines. It would take more than one rally and the evolution of much more time to suggest that these relative advances are becoming structural.

A further argument in favor of an eventual resumption of leadership on the part of the larger-cap, more globally-exposed issues, can be made looking again (Figure 2–14) at the DJIA/S&P 500. The DJIA relative to the S&P 500 broke a 35-year trend of underperformance, emerged from a 15-year base, and initiated a trend of outperformance, which began in 1985. Since the DJIA is a pure global proxy the suggestion that a structural trend of outperformance (for globally-exposed stocks) is implicit in the DJIA's RS progression. Once again, there is room for a period of underperformance (for the RS line to come down) without disturbing the major uptrend. This market unsettlement should be part of the expected ebb and flow reflecting the fits and starts of trial and error development of the emerging nations which will affect the globally-exposed tier. But the macrodemographic forces are so strong that it would be difficult to argue against the globally-exposed tier, including technology, returning to the fore as the dominant trend.

The stock market has traditionally moved in 4-year cycles (some greatly extended, some curtailed) interrupted by cyclical bear markets (as in 1962, 1966, 1970, 1974, 1978, 1982). The last great bull of 1942–1966 experienced several as has our bull market. From the 1982 decline, the 4-year cycle extended 5 years to 1987; then contracted to 3 years to the bear market interruption of 1990; then a 4-year cycle to the stealth bear of 1994. The cyclical argument would cite 1998 as due next. Perhaps this cycle is shortened so that 1997 will experience that cycle early.

Given continued low/stable inflation and low/stable interest rates, the new technology benefits, the expansive horizon of global-free trade zones for the world's population and low cost production potential, the stock market should continue to register growth in the globally-exposed U.S. equities (including technology) over the long term. As more U.S. companies penetrate the global markets, the equity market breadth should continue to expand to include globally participating smaller issues. Considering that corporate implementation of technology is still minimal, the diffusion factor is still young, and can spread widely to all size businesses.

Considering the U.S. baby-boom forces pushing stock valuations to unseemly levels we must remain even more vigilant for signs of an evaporation of that monetary inflow. Demographic history suggests 2004–2010 would be cautionary years. But in Chapter 5, we addressed future demographic differences. As technical analysts we would expect to see more specific evidence in the form of structural deterioration in those market indicators that have historically given long-term warning signals.

If we return to Part One and reflect on the two distinct segments of 1942–1966, it might give us an expectation of technical evidence that should manifest itself in preparation of a market downturn (Figure 1–3).

The emergence of a structural top in the 1942–1966 bull market took 9 years to form as the equity market ascended to new highs, nearly doubling. Throughout the 1957–1966 second bull segment, interest rates rose modestly (but rose nevertheless) from around 3 percent to 5 percent. This negatively affected the financially oriented stocks in the NYSE, which in turn was reflected in the negative divergence of the cumulative A-D line as the market continued higher, giving ample warning (as in 1927–1929) of the end of the last secular bull market in 1966.

We would expect no less today, although the period of warning may vary given current volatility. As long as the A-D continues to establish new highs with the DJIA and other major market indices, we can remain constructive on the long term and can suggest months to years before evidence of structural deterioration evolves. Recalling that interest-rate-sensitive issues make up 40 percent of the NYSE, the A-D line may hold up relatively well (given falling interest rates), even in the face of corrective progressions on the part of the globally-exposed stocks. In fact, it may have been the Financials' consolidation in 1994 that was the swing factor in preserving the A-D line uptrend at that time (even in the face of a slight contratrend rise in interest rates). The Financials, aligned with the more globally-exposed issues, would have kept the A-D line buoyant. Today, if the Financials remain stable (in face of stable to lower rates), aligned this time with the more domestically-exposed and some smaller-weighted issues of the NYSE, they may again be the swing factor in the A-D line buoyancy. The market may correct differently under the surface in 1997. Thus our technical determinant of short to intermediate term market health may need to come from the weight of other indicators; and the identification of individual stock breakdowns becomes an important part of that.

Indeed, the subtle difference between the 1960s' segment is that interest rates *were* creeping up (rising interest rates have always made bull markets falter), ultimately ending the advance. Today interest rates are actually falling throughout the entire market advance (similar but not exactly to the 1920s). The underlying global forces and technological implications today do *not* compare to the 1920s (particularly if the deflationary growth and shift of inflationary leadership are in play), suggesting potential for extending this advance well beyond the last. But as the evidence stands now, the 1982–present bull market remains in force. The dynamics that would bring it to an end are not yet in place.

Once again, we are afloat with tried and true, but old, instruments of analysis which may not direct us as effectively in these uncharted waters. But the technology is in place so that we may observe the changing currents and develop a newer, more accurate compass. Necessity is the mother of invention and is what started the evolution of discovery you have shared with me here.

Investment Focus

If Adam Smith's classic economic principles remain intact, countries with low taxes, free markets, and rational unobstructive governments should enjoy the greatest prosperity. Rapid globalization of trade and investment is resulting in 60 percent of world trade being conducted by multinationals. Corporate success is defined more and more by their ability to adjust and compete beyond the economies of their national borders.[1] The new technology will aid their survival.

As the benefits of global markets continue to be recognized, more companies will take advantage of the growth potential. These may be the small and mid-caps (on their way to becoming larger-caps) we could see come to the fore at the end of this market move. For the time being, the global population is large enough for multiple entrants with the United States the competitive leader. Other developed nations have not yet completed their process of corporate and government reengineering. But the competition will heat up.

If the observations set forth in this book continue to be verified and validated by market action, it becomes clear there are certain investment areas that would be preferable to others. The growth potential for each industry and stock must be strong. In the case of mutual funds, many families of funds offer specifically focused sector funds.

Beneficiaries of the U.S. aging demographic profile and developed nations would include focus on financial areas, Banks and Insurance sectors; as well as Health Care-Drugs and Diversified. We would simultaneously shy away from the purely domestically oriented sectors and stocks that may be negatively impacted by a smaller upcoming younger generation of this cycle affecting Home Building, Building Materials, Household Furnishings, Housewares, and select Retailers.

The largest emphasis would be directed toward the sectors and stocks benefiting from the tremendous global populations emerging into consumerist-style economies. Health Care will benefit again from this source, as would Beverages-Soft Drinks, Foods, Household Products, Electrical Equipment, Aerospace, Machinery-Diversified and Manufacturing-Diversified. Technology, driving this cycle, and technology-related areas of communications, computers, electronics and software will also be a major part of the global consumption thrust both for corporate and personal use. The growth component in one's choices is essential.

By the same token, we may wish to step aside from the older industrial era sectors which we have seen are underperforming: Steel, Papers, Printing, Trucks and Parts, Truckers, Waste Management, and even Autos (where global competition is already a factor). Add to these the old industrial raw material areas of Basic Materials, Metals and Mining, Gold and Precious Metals all of which are experiencing ever weaker trends.

Picking up the macrotheme of agriculture would lead one to specific Chemical companies participating in genetic engineering and crop improvement; agricultural machinery and related technology; eventually, railroad considerations also relate to an agricultural growth focus though they have not been outperforming to date. Many Regional Banks may benefit from both consolidations in the financial services industry, the U.S. agricultural renaissance and the ruralization (de-urbanization) trend taking place.

Water filtration, desalinization and pollution technology will be important in the next century to conserve the next precious commodity. And companies offering educational advancement should be best positioned to take advantage of the complex opportunities in services and the new global, technological marketplace. It must be kept in mind, of course, that global exposure does not guarantee outperformance—fundamental and competitive factors will also play a role. In all cases, the growth aspect of each company is critical and must be carefully chosen for that potential.

Other Forces at Work: Competition

Technology spreading productivity and increasing returns is not limited to U.S. industry. Global economies are moving at different paces in the same direction (deregulation, privatization, reorganization and deficit cutting). The result is there's an expanding trend with larger implications: That of domestic and international mergers, or intra- or cross-country production facilitating corporate profitability. Mergers and joint ventures among groups of companies (even mutual funds) for their common fiscal good are adding a new complexity to the shape of competition. The U.S. corporate tendrils for expanding the cost basis are linking with foreign companies, and foreign companies cross-allying with U.S. companies in myriad joint ventures and mergers which defray costs even more; both utilizing and challenging deflationary effects.

Tougher economic realities force survival through mergers, which are different from the 1970s and 1980s when conglomerates bought diverse businesses. Now they are downsizing and merging with businesses within their own expertise to gain a bigger edge, become stronger, and even obtain market control; such control can eventually lead to dangers of monopoly and abuse— major firms paying high school coaches so their teams use a product, for example—which is very different from the natural result of increasing returns.

Free trade and the size of the emerging consumer population suggest there is still a long time for growth to continue. The only deterrent is that there are fewer rivals as a result of the merger mania: From oil companies to telecommunication and electronics; to utilities, retailers, banks and pharmaceutical companies, to name a few. Domestic mergers and acquisitions totaled a record $659 billion value in 1996, according to Securities Data Co. Bigger is better in efficiency gains, and performance has outstripped many smaller companies.

The U.S. economy has created 30 million jobs since 1979 and has lowered unemployment to extraordinary levels. Europe has not fared as well due to their less flexible wage structures and labor markets, policies for high minimum wages and payroll taxes, firing restrictions and high social benefits, and slow technology diffusion.[2] The United States has a wage/cost advantage over Japan and Germany and has made a greater investment in training. Foreign countries are under pressure to make similar cost-cutting benefits to better participate in this global golden age. Foreign competitors are getting stronger as they emulate U.S. reorganizations, downsizing, mergers and shareholder orientation.

Autos and motorcycles are already vulnerable to worldwide competitive forces. In China, local software companies are trying to beat the U.S. competition with the local firms expecting to hold 50 percent of the Chinese market by 2002; the same with Chinese beer. Capital expense in U.S. technology and growth is rising to the faster pace necessary to keep our hard-won competitive global edge.[3] Our economy is being lifted by the technological edge, through exports and productivity growth,[4] both still in their early stages.

Perhaps because export trade is a major qualifier of the long-wave economic expansion cycle, its degree may help shape (propel) the extent and duration of the bull market. Today world trade is the largest ever experienced due to both political and demographic change. This, combined with the important technological innovations, argues not just for an extension of this secular bull market cycle, but also for a new record in its magnitude and duration. The caveat is that as more countries develop our skills, it will be the competitive edge that determine success and survival. This competitive factor may be what determines the eventual slowing of our bull market. A thinning of the A-D line, warning of a top may not come from interest rate sensitivity, but may come this time as competition slows growth, and the affected globally-exposed stocks eventually wane in their market performance as supply (selling) increases over demand. The charts will show the pattern of that selling pressure trend.

Other Forces at Work: Sovereignty

But there may be other forces at work and more questions to ask in anticipation of the international changes and this global meld. Corporations involved in cross-border mergers and ventures are no longer maintaining the same kind of national identity as they have in the past. The need to globalize for survival (and do so with speed) has become of the essence. We are not just seeing cross-border transactions, but cross-border ownership as a result of increasingly severe competitive forces. It is a much more cost-effective solution than starting operations from scratch on foreign soil and dealing with their bureaucracies; buy a local company and operations are instantly in place, and today's technology productivity benefits are immediately incorporated into the new entity, spreading the cost base further, faster.

With this loss of corporate national identities comes the possible evolution of less national sovereignty, as borders melt into nations' commingled corporate and economic interests (the EU will be an important first step). Dr. Peter Watson, former chairman of the U.S. International Trade Commission, has suggested that national sovereignties are being brought into question and may be losing potency. We've seen the beginnings of this in free-trade agreements that infringe on our own stricter environmental, health, safety and quality standards, placing them instead before multinational arbitration to be held in abeyance for years and/or ultimately watered down. Every day untold billions of dollars cross national boundaries in electronic international currency transactions with existing governments unable to control or even monitor the flow. Legal questions that arise include corporate jurisdiction and the SEC's ability to uphold reporting standards for companies with ownership or affiliations in countries with less stringent requirements. These and other issues may come to be settled in global legal/government arenas. But the trend toward border-blind global corporations is in place, making companies even larger and more controlling than the most formidable we've known. Business is a major power in today's world, with its own generals—General Electric, General Motors, General Mills.[5] They will wield enormous power, direction, and force on global society, indeed are already usurping the role of government funding of the arts—seen as a new marketing tool. Could we become a world even more governed by intercorporate interests? Could one even imagine governmental national sovereignty erased, acceding to a global corporate organizational framework? (It has often been observed that corporations operate with more fiscal efficiency than governments; even our defense department outsources for this exact reason.) Could we be looking at the emergence of an entirely new world politic—as a "corpocracy"?

Summary

As market technicians, we know that it is in times of extreme change that the long-term historical perspective may be essential to our understanding of the daily fluctuations. The charts continue to pose major questions just as they did several years ago, which led to the two-tier global/domestic U.S. equity market thesis. It may be the daily "noise" of trading still blurs the bigger picture, but the charts may be indicating the powerful, structural, new-millennium shift, with the changing demographic and economic (technological, agricultural, and inflationary) focus of our country into the twenty-first century.

Could the dynamic new macroforces discussed meld to give impetus to an extraordinary cycle already underway of a totally new complexion? As a technologically and globally positioned leader, the United States is poised to benefit from these new forces/trends, which support the validity of the powerful two-tier equity market advance we have been experiencing and may continue to experience well into the twenty-first century, interim corrections not withstanding.

All the observations in this book are offered to be thought provoking and to suggest there may be other questions, that each of us, in our areas of expertise, may need to continue to ask to better understand this great bull market and the changing forces on the world stage, and to determine how history may unfold into the millennium.

Notes

CHAPTER 2

1. Alan R. Shaw, *Market Interpretations*, Smith Barney, May 1996.
2. John Tsui, *Buy Side* "Mid Cap," November 1996.

CHAPTER 3

1. Lowry's Reports, Inc., 631 U.S. Highway One, Suite 305, North Palm Beach, FL, 33408: Gives a proprietary measure of Buying Power and Selling Pressure in the stock market.

2. Simultaneously, in the summer of 1995, I was interested in a reference in another bullish technical camp's report that likened the market to the 1962–1966 period and, based on this, projected 7000 for the Dow. I believe that there are some structural problems with the reasoning of that thesis. First, 1962–1966 was a period that represented the last four years of the 1957–1966 Consumer Goods cycle, and the end of the 1942–1966 bull market. I believe that we have been in the beginning years of a cycle, akin to the 1946–1957 period. The 1962–1966 period was also a time that witnessed a rise in interest rates to 5.5 percent, prior to much higher levels and ultimately the end of the bull cycle, not at all similar to current conditions. Additionally, from a structural perspective, the cumulative A-D line was in a multi-year topping process from 1957–1966, prior to its plunge into its 1974 low (Figure 3–2). Today, the A-D is still in a long-term advance, as detailed herein, which indicates strength and is not at all comparable to the underpinnings of the 1962–1966 time frame.

3. Alan R. Shaw, *Market Interpretations*, February 26, 1996, Smith Barney.

CHAPTER 4

1. The developed nations, which in the 1990s are experiencing a growing middle-age (40s–50s) population, the baby boomers, include Northern and Western Europe, Canada, Japan (with the most rapidly aging population), Australia, and New Zealand.

2. Richard Hokenson, "Incorporating Consumer Demographics in Industry Analysis," ICFA Continuing Education: The Consumer Staples Industry, 1995.

3. Harold L. Hodgkinson, "Bringing Tomorrow into Focus," Center for Demographic Study, The Institute for Educational Leadership, January 1996.

4. David K. Foot with Daniel Stoffman, "Boom, Bust and Echo," Macfarlane Walter & Ross, Toronto, Canada, 1996.

5. Harold L. Hodgkinson, "Bringing Tomorrow into Focus."

6. Richard Hokenson, "Incorporating Consumer Demographics in Industry Analysis."

7. *Buy Side*, July 1996.

8. Richard Hokenson, "Incorporating Consumer Demographics in Industry Analysis."

CHAPTER 5

1. David Cork, *Boom Time, Vol. IV,* Spring 1996.

2. "Bringing Tomorrow into Focus," Harold L. Hodgkinson, Center for Demographic Policy, The Institute for Educational Leadership, January 1996.

3. David Cork with Susan Lightstone, *The Pig and the Python*, Stoddard Publishing Co., Limited, Toronto, Canada, 1996.

4. David K. Foot, with Daniel Stoffman, *Boom, Bust and Echo*, Macfarlane Walter & Ross, Toronto, Canada, 1996.

5. Cork, *The Pig and the Python.*

6. Foot, *Boom, Bust and Echo.*

7. *Trends* "Special Feature: The Financials . . . In the Midst of a Major Bull Market?" Winter 1996, Smith Barney.

8. Richard Hokenson, "Incorporating Consumer Demographics in Industry Analysis," ICFA Continuing Education: The Consumer Staples Industry, 1995.

9. Nicholas D. Kristof, *The New York Times*, September 22, 1996.

10. Foot, *Boom, Bust and Echo.*

CHAPTER 6

1. Ralph Cato, "Kondratieff in Perspective," *Futures*, 1996.

2. Joseph Schumpeter, "A Theoretical, Historical & Statistical Analysis of the Capital Process," *Business Cycles*, Volume I, 1939.

3. Ralph Cato, "Kondratieff in Perspective."

4. *Bank Credit Analyst*, "A Long-Wave Perspective on the Economy in the 1990s," based on a speech by John D. Sterman, May 1990.

5. *The Bank Credit Analyst*, "Prospects for the U.S. Long-Wave Expansion," June 1995.

6. *The Bank Credit Analyst*, "A Long-Wave Perspective on the Economy in the 1990s."

7. Richard Coghlan, *Barron's*, June 7, 1993.

8. Ralph Cato, "Kondratieff in Perspective."

9. Richard Coghlan, *Barron's*.

10. Nomi Ghez, "Understanding the Basics of the Consumer Staples Industries," Goldman Sachs & Co., February 1995.

CHAPTER 7

1. *Business Week*, April 15, 1996.

2. Steve Lohr, *The New York Times*, April 15, 1996. Additionally, the computer-based new media industry in New York City generated revenues of 5.7 billion dollars in 1996 and now employs over 100,000 full-time, part-time, and freelance workers, making it the second largest media industry in New York after advertising. "Second Annual New Media Survey," Coopers & Lybrand and the New York New Media Association, New York, NY, 1997.

3. *The Economist*, September 28, 1996.

4. Jeanne Dugan, *Business Week*, October 30, 1996.

5. *Business Week*, June 17, 1996.

6. Kathleen Madigan, *Business Week*, December 30, 1996.

7. *The Economist*, September 28, 1996.

8. Don Tapscott, *The Digital Economy*, New York: McGraw-Hill, 1996.

9. *Business Week*, October 28, 1996.

10. *Business Week*, July 1996.

11. John Varity, *Business Week*, October 21, 1996.

12. Laurence Zuckerman, *The New York Times*, January 2, 1997.

13. *Business Week*, January 13, 1997.

14. *Business Week*, July 1996.

15. *Business Week*, October 28, 1996.

16. *The Bank Credit Analyst*, December 1996.

17. *The New York Times*, June 5, 1996.

18. *The Wall Street Journal*, week of April 10, 1996.

19. *Institutional Investor*, December 1996.

20. *The Economist*, September 28, 1996.

21. Claudia H. Deutsch, *The New York Times*, December 2, 1996.

22. Kris Goodfellow, *The New York Times*, December 1996.

23. Larry Armstrong, *Business Week*, December 2, 1996.

24. *Business Week*, September 16, 1996.

25. Stephen Wildstrom, *Business Week*, November 25, 1996.

26. Steven Brull, *Business Week*, November 25, 1996.

27. Peter Cox, *Business Week*, October 28, 1996.

28. *Business Week*, September 30, 1996.

29. Donna R. Fitzpatrick, *Industry Week*, December 18, 1995.

30. The *Financial Times*, September 24, 1996.

CHAPTER 8

1. *Financial Times*, September 24, 1996.

2. Kate Murphy, *The New York Times*, January 6, 1997.

3. *Business Week*, June 10, 1996.

4. Seanna Browder, *Business Week*, December 2, 1996.

5. *Business Week*, November 4, 1996.

6. Michael Mandel, *Business Week*, November 18, 1996.

7. *Business Week*, October 7, 1996.

CHAPTER 10

1. The CRB was created in 1957 by the Jiler brothers, the original owners of the Commodities Research Bureau (later acquired by Knight-Ridder in the 1980s and by Bridge Information Systems in the 1990s). The goal was to come up with one number that would provide dynamic representation of broad trends in overall commodity prices to gauge price movements in the commodity futures markets. The base period was 1947–1949, the same as the Bureau of Labor Statistics Spot Market Index, to facilitate easy comparison between both spot and futures indices. It has periodically been adjusted to reflect market changes and activity, and although it was originally not intended as an inflation measure, it has evolved into such because of its availability and instant information access.

2. Paul Lewis, *The New York Times*, January 20, 1997.

3. Information compiled from the following: Tim Traff, Director, United States Filter Corp.; Sandra Postel, Worldwatch Institute; *National Geographic, Vol. 183*, No. 5, May 1993; *National Geographic, Vol. 183*, No. 3, March 1993; International Rice Institute of the Philippines; Kenneth Whiting, Associated Press; James Sterngold, *The New York Times*, August 11, 1996; Cleary Bull, Filtration Separation, Summer 1996; Clear Solutions, The McIlvane Co., *Vol. 46*, April 1995; and the United Nations Commission on Sustainable Development, Fifth Session, April 1997: Comprehensive Assessment of the Freshwater Resources of the World, Report of the Secretary General.

4. Roger Engelman and Pamel Roy, "Sustaining Water, Population, and the Future of Renewable Water Supplies," Population in Action.

5. Nicholas Kristoff, *The New York Times*, January 9, 1997.

6. Mark Reisner, "The Cadillac Desert," Penguin Books, 1986, updated 1993.

7. An acre-foot is the amount of water it takes to cover an acre of land to a depth of one foot, or about 326,000 gallons.

8. Otis Port, Andy Reinhardt, Gary McWilliams, Steven Brull, *Business Week*, December 9, 1996.

9. Reuters, *The New York Times*, December 22, 1996.

10. Jacob Goldberg, President, Middle East Research International, from a speech at the TransChem Finance & Trade Corp. Roundtable, October 21–23, 1996.

11. Jim Wilbur, *Transcending the Cycle*, Smith Barney, August, 1996.

12. *Environmental Business Journal, Vol. IX*, No. 23, February/March 1996.

13. Jenny Luesby, Leyla Boulton, Carol Jones, and Daniel Green, *Financial Times*, September 26, 1996.

14. Lisa Sanders, *Business Week*, 1996.

15. Gary McWilliams, *Business Week*, September 23, 1996.

CHAPTER 11

1. Hugh Ulrich, *The Amber Waves of History*, Commodity Research Bureau; 1996; Robert W. Hafer, Publisher.

2. *Ibid.*

3. John McCamant, *Buy Side*, May 1996.

4. *Business Week*, May 20, 1996. Globally there is not an abundance of idle land (and returning the 14 million acres in the U.S. Dept. of Agriculture's "set aside" program adds less than 1 percent to global grain acreage).

5. Laura Johannes, *The Wall Street Journal*, week of April 12, 1996.

6. Warren E. Leary, *The New York Times*, April 26, 1996.

7. Mark Bittman, *The New York Times*, September 18, 1996.

CHAPTER 13

1. Robert J. Genetski, Director of Research and Asset Management, Chicago Capital, Inc.; "The Relationship Between Economic Schools of Thought and Economic Analysis," AIMR Economic Analysis for Investment Professionals.

2. Dr. Edward Yardeni, Chief Economist, Deutsche Morgan Grenfell, C. J. Lawrence, "10,000 in 2,000," November 6, 1995.

3. *Ibid.*

4. *Ibid.*

5. *Ibid.*

6. *Business Week*, September 30, 1996.

7. John Markoff, *The New York Times*, February 24, 1997.

8. Erik Brynjolfsson and Lorin Hitt, "Information Technology as a Factor of Production: The Role of Differences among Firms," *Economic Innovation and New Technology*, Vol. 3, 1995.

9. Erik Brynjolfsson and Thomas Malone, "Does Information Technology Lead to Smaller Firms?" cited by Vijay Gurbaxani & Ajit Kamgil in *Management Science, Vol 40*, No. 12, December 1994.

10. Laurence Zukerman, *The New York Times*, January 2, 1997.

11. Andrew Wyckorr, "The Growing Strength of Services," *OECD Observer*, No. 200, June 1996.

12. *The Bank Credit Analyst*, May 1997.

13. *The Economist*, September 29, 1996.

14. Energy = Energy transferred to the system – Energy done by the system
    = What goes in minus what goes out

Heat (stays the same or goes up) – Work (goes down) = Productive energy (has to go up)

Work done *by* the system is positive, it comes into the system; work done *on* the system is negative, it goes out. The energy of a system can be increased by doing work on it, or adding heat to it. (The more productive the company the more gets accomplished.)

15. Mitchell Held, Chief Fixed Income Economist, Smith Barney, *Portfolio Strategist*, July 11, 1996.

16. Robert Kuttner, *Business Week*, November 4, 1996.

17. *Buy Side*, January 1997.

18. Louis Uchitelle, *The New York Times*, August 30, 1996.

19. Cooper and Madigan, *Business Week*, December 2, 1996.

20. Alan R. Shaw, *Market Interpretations*, Smith Barney, March 3, 1989.

CHAPTER 14

1. Geoffrey Smith, *Business Week*, March 3, 1997.

2. Mitchell Held, Chief Fixed Income Economist, Smith Barney, *Portfolio Strategist*, December 20, 1996 and February 7, 1997.

3. Mutual fund data courtesy Investment Co. Institute.

CHAPTER 15

1. Center for Strategic and International Studies, Executive Summary: "Corporate governance: A perspective on the U.S. system," February 10, 1997.

2. Gene Koretz, *Business Week*, March 17, 1997.

3. Gene Koretz, *Business Week*, February 17, 1997.

4. *Business Week*, August 12, 1996.

5. Murray Weidenbaum, Mallinchroot Distinguished University Professor, Washington University, St. Louis, TransChem International Roundtable, November 1997.

Index